ANCIENT WAYS

About the Author

Pauline Campanelli and her husband Dan are author and illustrator of *Wheel of the Year: Living the Magical Life*, Llewellyn, 1989, and also have contributed to the *1991 Magickal Almanac*, edited by Ray Buckland. Pauline has also written for *Witchcraft Today*, edited by Chas Clifton, Llewellyn Publications.

Pauline and Dan have been practicing Wiccans for twenty three years. Because of their deep religious beliefs they have evolved a lifestyle based on Natural Magick. In their 18th century home in western New Jersey, magick is a part of their everyday life.

Pauline has contributed articles in Pagan symbolism and traditions to *Circle Network News*, and *Fate* magazine has published her articles on Witchcraft as well as her personal experiences with the Spirit World. Other paranormal experiences shared by Pauline and Dan have been included in Alan Vaughan's *Incredible Coincidence*, Lippencott 1979, and are on file at the University of Virginia. *Haunted Houses: U.S.A.* by Joan Bingham and Dolores Riccio, Simon & Schuster 1989, include more experiences by the Campanelli. *Multiple Realities* by D. Scott Rogo, to be published in Great Britain, will contain more mystical experiences.

Both Dan and Pauline are professional fine artists. Dan works in watercolor, Pauline in oils. They are each listed in thirteen reference books including *Who's Who in American Art* and *The International Dictionary of Biographies*. Their home and artwork were featured in *Colonial Homes* March/April 1981 and *Country Living Magazine*, April 1985. New Jersey Network produced a program on their art work and lifestyle for P.B.S. in 1985. Their paintings have been published as fine art prints that are available throughout the United States and Europe.

To Write to the Author

We cannot guarantee that every letter written to the author can be answered, but all will be forwarded. Both the author and the publisher appreciate hearing from readers, learning of your enjoyment and benefit from this book. Llewellyn also publishes a bimonthly news magazine with news and reviews of practical esoteric studies and articles helpful to the student, and some readers' questions and comments to the author may be answered through this magazine's columns if permission to do so is included in the original letter. The author sometimes participates in seminars and workshops, and dates and places are announced in *The Llewellyn New Times*. To write to the author, or to ask a question, write to:

Pauline and Dan Campanelli
c/o THE LLEWELLYN NEW TIMES
P.O. Box 64383-090, St. Paul, MN 55164-0383, U.S.A.
Please enclose a self-addressed, stamped envelope for reply, or $1.00 to cover costs.

Llewellyn's Practical Magick Series

ANCIENT WAYS
Reclaiming Pagan Traditions

written by Pauline Campanelli

illustrated by Dan Campanelli

1991
Llewellyn Publications
St. Paul, Minnesota, 55164-0383, U.S.A.

FIRST EDITION

Cover art and interior illustrations by Dan Campanelli

Library of Congress Cataloging-in-Publication Data:
 Campanelli, Pauline, 1943-
   Ancient ways : reclaiming Pagan traditions / Pauline Campanelli : illustrated by
 Dan Campanelli. — 1st ed.
     p.   cm. — (Llewellyn practical magick series)
     ISBN 0-87542-090-7 : $12.95
     1. Magic. 2. Paganism—Rituals. 3. Religious calendars—Paganism.
 I. Title.   II. Series.
 BF1623.R6C35 1991   91-26543
 133.4's—dc20   CIP

Llewellyn Publications
A Division of Llewellyn Worldwide, Ltd.
P.O. Box 64383, St. Paul, MN 55164-0383

About Llewellyn's Practical Magick Series

To some people, the idea that "Magick" is *practical* comes as a surprise.

It shouldn't. The entire basis for Magick is to exercise influence over one's environment. While Magick is also, and properly so, concerned with spiritual growth and psychological transformation, even the spiritual life must rest firmly on material foundations.

Magick can, and should, be used in one's daily life for better living! Each of us has been given Mind and Body, and surely we are under Spiritual obligation to make full usage of these wonderful gifts. Mind and Body work together, and Magick is simply the extension of this interaction into dimensions beyond the limits normally conceived. That's why we commonly talk of the "super-normal" in connection with domain of Magick.

The Body is alive, and all Life is an expression of the Divine. There is god-power in the Body and in the Earth, just as there is in Mind and Spirit. With Love and Will, we use Mind to link these aspects of Divinity together to bring about change.

With Magick we increase the flow of Divinity in our lives and in the world around us. We add to the beauty of it all—for to work Magick we must work in harmony with the Laws of Nature and of the Psyche. *Magick is the flowering of the Human Potential.*

Practical Magick is concerned with the Craft of Living well and in harmony with Nature, and with the Magick of the Earth, in the things of the Earth, in the seasons and cycles and in the things we make with hand and Mind.

Other books by the author:

Wheel of the Year

Forthcoming:

Circles, Groves and Sanctuaries

**Dedicated
to
The Old Gods**

Contents

Ritual for Making Masks. The Rutting Season. The Witch's Hat. The Witch's Nose. Warts. Some Wart Cures. The Waning Moon. The Witch's Cauldron. The Besom. The World Tree. Offerings to the Spirits. A Ritual of Offering.

A Time to Look to the Future. A Bull's Hide Ritual. Another Method of Yuletide Divination. Signs and Omens. Weather and Seasons. Animals. Animals in Folklore. The Coyote as an Omen. Herons and Cranes. Messengers of the Gods. Signs in Stone. Runes. Death Omens. Fetch Lights. Birds. Feathers. Crows. Signs in the Sky. Sun Dogs. People as Omens. The Bride on the Bride. Affirmations. Yule and New Years Eve. Methods of Reviewing Past Lives. A Ritual for Past Life Recall. Fossils as Amulets: "Thunderbolts," "Snake Stones," Faery Loaves," "Toadstones." The Moment of Death. Recalling a Previous Life. Yuletide Music: "O Tannenbaum," "Deck the Halls," "The Holly and the Ivy." Wassailing. The Fir Tree. The Ornaments: Fruits and Vegetables, the Pinecone Elf, Pine Cones and Acorns, Berries, Birds and Animals, Musical Instruments, Bells, Witch Balls, A Witch Ball Amulet, Tinsel, Candy Canes. Tree Decorating as a Ritual. Gift Giving. The Yule Log. The Magick of Loud Noise. Greeting the New Year.

Illustrations

Photographs

Tables and Diagrams

Introduction

The Wheel of the Year has turned four times since I wrote a book by that title, and for Dan and me the quest for the Old Ways continued.

As Pagans we believe that:

All of Nature is a manifestation of Divinity or the Creative Forces, and that everything in Nature has a spirit.

These Divine Creative Forces can be perceived as a pantheon of Gods and Goddesses.

As everything in Nature has its complement, so must it be with the Gods, a polarity of male and female, spirit and matter, God and Goddess.

As Nature proceeds in the cycles of the season, so must we be born to die and be born again.

And that by actively participating in these natural cycles through ritual, we can attune ourselves to the Creative Forces that flow through us, to live happy, creative and productive lives, for our own benefit, and that of the planet.

The simplest way to do this is to celebrate the seasons of the year according to the ancient Pagan traditions of our ancestors, and we have all of the traditions of all of the nations of the Old World to examine for Pagan origins. Some of the places these traditions have been found are in the seasonal celebrations of the new religion, in legends and Faery tales, and in the objects and ornaments used to celebrate the seasons.

This book is arranged according to the Great Sabbats, and it tells of ways of preparing for, enhancing, and celebrating the Sabbats of the Old Religion. The magical charms, spells and rituals given here are drawn from ancient sources, but are easily applied to contemporary practices. Many of the activities are planned to use to fullest advantage the currents of magical energy that ebb and flow prior to and following each Great Sabbat.

The time has come for all of us on the Pagan path to examine these ancient ways and to reclaim them as our own.

Flying Witch Farm
Oak Moon, 1991

Chapter One
IMBOLC

Imbolc

Intricate and lacy designs etched in frost on the window panes frame a scene rendered in shades of gray, of horses in a snow storm, as the winter sun rises just a bright spot in a lead colored sky. In the sheep's pen the sweet smell of hay and grain scent the warmer air of the cozy straw-filled shelter, and on the roost in the chicken coop the hens take turns being in the middle and warmed on both sides by the other hens.

Inside, the fire is kindled early and every minute of daylight is used to advantage. With the gardens resting in the frozen ground beneath the snow, daily activity is turned inward. Creativity flows in the silent snowy days of winter, and ideas for projects to be carried out in times of greater light and warmth begin to take form.

As the sun climbs higher in the sky and begins to break through the clouds, the snow tapers to flurries, and droplets of it, melted, flash like beads of crystal hung from every branch and twig. On the downspout above the rain barrel, a brilliant drop hovers for a moment, flashing colors of the rainbow as an icicle begins to form.

The dark curtain of the winter night descends early, and we gather by the fire's glow after dinner to discuss the events of the day and to plan tomorrow's. The pungent smell of simmering herbs and warm, wet wool, wafts through the house as another skein of handspun yarn is dyed, and the results are admired and hung to dry.

When the fire has died down and the embers have been banked, we climb the stairs to the warmth of camphor scented quilts; while outside on this frosty winter night, beneath Her quilt of purest white, the Earth Mother has been visited by the Spirit Father as She slept, and even now new life begins to stir in Her.

Late in January, as the Wolf Moon wanes or the Chaste Moon waxes to full, we begin to prepare for the Imbolc Sabbat. Since Lammas, the Corn Mother which presided over the Lammas Feast has rested in silence and darkness in a cedar chest in the attic. The Corn Mother is a physical representation of the Goddess, and while it rested the Goddess Herself went to the Land of Spirit (or Avalon, or Anwyn) where she rested and regained her youth. Now she is the Maiden again, so the same figure made of wheat or oats or corn that represented the Corn Mother at

Dressing the Corn Dolly

A Corn Husk Doll

Lammas now represents the Corn Maiden. Lammas and Imbolc stand opposite one another across the Wheel of the Year like two sides of the same coin: one the Maiden who, from Imbolc to Lammas will wax to full; the other, the Crone, who from Lammas till Imbolc will wane like the Moon, until She is renewed.

Every Sabbat has its opposite on the other side of the Wheel of the Year. Just as Lammas and Imbolc express the waxing and waning aspects of the Goddess, so do Midsummer and Yule oppose one another as the waxing and waning aspects of the God. At Midsummer, He is seen as the sun at its zenith in all its radiant splendor, just as it is about to begin to wane; while at Yule, He is seen as the Divine Child reborn on the darkest night of the year. This same quality is expressed in the myth of the Oak King and the Holly King who take turns defeating one another at Midsummer and at Yule.

The Vernal and Autumnal Equinoxes also stand opposite one another and both represent a time of perfect balance between the light half of the Wheel of the Year and the dark half; but the Vernal Equinox is that moment when the balance is about to shift and the time of light, growth and physical life is about to become greater than the dark. The Autumnal Equinox is that moment of perfect balance just before the Wheel turns into the dark, the time of physical death and spiritual life.

THE SABBATS
AND THEIR OPPOSITES

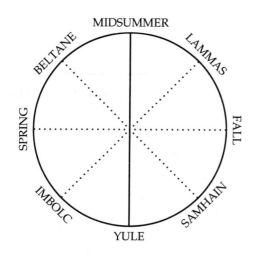

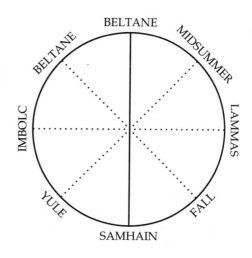

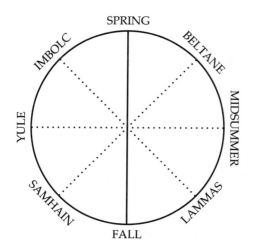

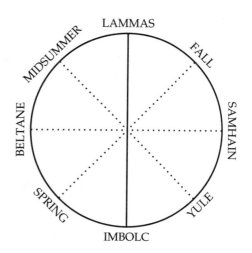

Just as the Vernal Equinox and Autumnal Equinox oppose one another, and Lammas and Midsummer oppose Imbolc and Yule, so do Beltane and Samhain stand across the Wheel from one another. Beltane is the time of the Sacred Marriage when the Goddess, as Earth Mother, is united with the Spirit or Sky Father, who descends upon her in order to renew life and replenish the Earth. Samhain is the Sabbat of communion with Spirits, when the Goddess as the Crone leaves the earth's realm and ascends to the realm of the Horned One in order to rest and renew herself there. The symbol of Beltane, the Maypole planted upright in the earth (or sometimes in a sacred well), is the venerated phallus or the World Tree through which Spirit descends into the material world and impregnates it with new life. While its opposite, the Crone's broomstick at Samhain, represents the same World Tree upon which we can ascend into the world of Spirit.

Each Sabbat has its opposite on the other side of the Wheel of the Year, one always on the dark half, the other always on the light half. This polarity is as much a part of the balance of things as the God and Goddess themselves.

A similar polarity occurs once a month on the "fifteenth night." That is, the fifteenth night of the Moon, or the night after the Full Moon, when, as the Sun is about to set in the West and stands just above the horizon, the Full Moon rises over the horizon in the East, and the two, the Sun and Moon, the God and Goddess, stand opposite one another for a brief moment in perfect balance and perfect harmony. Then, the Sun slips below the horizon relinquishing the night sky to the Moon alone.

This is a powerful time for any magick that involves balance, power, a uniting of opposites, or the charging of a charm or an amulet with the energies of both the Sun and the Moon.

Here is a typical example of such a charm: prior to the fifteenth night obtain a twig of oak (about 2 inches in length) and a length of willow of similar proportions, two herbs sacred to the Sun such as bay laurel and angelica, and two herbs sacred to the Moon such as lily and orpine, a length of red thread, a piece of white cloth (about 2-1/2 inches by 3-1/2 inches) and a piece of black cloth the same size, and a sewing needle and thread. Sew the black and white cloth together to form a pouch.

To make a lined pouch, simple make a slightly smaller pouch of silk or satin and stitch it in place with the running stitch that forms the drawstring of the outer bag. These pouches can be embellished with powerful magickal signs and symbols in textile paints or embroidery stitches before they are assembled.

When the pouch is ready, just before sunset of the fifteenth night, assemble the ingredients of the charm, preferably in a place where both the Sun and the Moon will be visible (but if that is not possible, then in a place where the Moon will shine). Tie the oak and willow twigs together

TO MAKE A SIMPLE POUCH

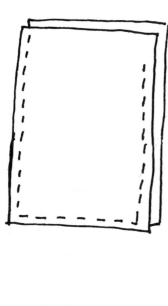

1. PLACE TWO PIECES OF MATERIAL FACE TO FACE AND STITCH AROUND THREE SIDES.

2. TURN RIGHT SIDE OUT. TURN TOP OVER ONCE— THEN ONCE AGAIN.

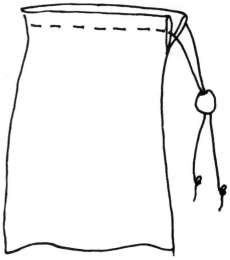

3. KNOT A THREAD AND PUT A BEAD ON IT. STITCH THROUGH TOP HEM. SLIP THE THREAD THROUGH THE BEAD AND KNOT IT AGAIN.

to form an equal armed cross with the red thread. Place the cross on a flat surface and arrange the herbs so that the two Moon herbs are at either end of the willow twig and the Sun herbs are at the end of the oak twig. Then at the moment when the Sun and Moon face each other, enchant the objects with words like:

> *By life giving Sun and mystical Moon,*
> *I conjur this charm to grant a boone.*
> *By the power of this night,*
> *By sunshine and moonlight,*
> *A charm of magickal power (or protection, or healing) this will be,*
> *By Artemis and Apollo, so mote it be!*

This charm can then be worn whenever magick charms are being performed to enhance their power.

As the Sun and the Moon represent opposite polarities, the God and the Goddess, so do the Corn Mother at Lammas and the Corn Maiden at Imbolc represent the two aspects of the Goddess Herself.

At Imbolc, the Maiden aspect of the Goddess might be represented in a great variety of ways. She might be symbolized by a simple bunch of corn or the same figure made of grain that was used at Lammas may now be dressed as a bride, or straws of wheat or grain braided into an intricate or abstract form often called a Corn Dolly may be made for this occasion.

In many cases, the straws used to weave the Corn Dollies were plucked from the Lammas Corn Mother, or the last bundle of grain cut at the harvest. This handful of wheat straws (with grain still attached) is sometimes called "the neck."

Regardless of the style of Corn Dolly being woven, certain preliminary steps must be taken first. To begin with, a number of the finest straws of grain are chosen. These are soaked in a tub of cool water for about half an hour, and then kept wrapped in a towel for another fifteen minutes. Now the grain is ready to be woven or braided.

One of the earliest forms of the Corn Dolly is the tall spiral. To begin making this type, select five straws of wheat and tie them together using a clove hitch knot, just under the grains of wheat. Then turn the wheat upside down so that the wheat hangs down like a tassle. Lay the straws out flat in the form of a solar cross with one of the arms being made of two straws. Begin weaving by taking one of the two straws and folding it over the straw next to it, so that it is now parallel to the next arm of the cross. Bend that straw around the new one and fold it over so that now it is parallel to the third arm of the cross. When the first round is complete, a square will have been formed. Continue weaving in the same manner, laying each new round of straw outside the square, thereby increasing the width of the Corn Dolly's spiral until the desired width is reached.

The spiral can then be decreased by folding the straws to the inside of the square formed by the previous round. If the straw should run out, replace it with a plain headless weaver. When the neck of the Dolly has been reached, braid the remaining straws together and tie them into a loop.

Bride's Cross (St. Bridget's Cross), is somewhat simpler. Select four short straws of wheat with heads. Tie them together in pairs, end to end, so that each pair has a head of grain at each end. Then begin weaving an "Eye of God" by holding the end of a length of straw across the center of the cross and winding it across, behind and over each arm. If the straw runs out add more by inserting a new straw into the hollow center of the last one. To finish, tie the end of the last weaver to an arm of the cross with cotton thread.

Simpler versions of the Corn Dolly at the Love Token or the Lover's Knot. These are made by braiding the straws of wheat together rather than weaving. Some of the most complex are the Welsch Fans, which are sometimes further complicated by combining several of the fans to form a circle.

Corn Dollies are kept as amulets of protection and fertility, and according to Rhiannon Ryall in *West Country Wicca*, a pair of them were hung up on the gable ends of houses as protective charms, by the men who thatched the roofs, one Dolly representing the God, the other the Goddess. It is easy to see how the Welsch Fan might represent the Horned God while others might symbolize the apron or pubic area of the Goddess.

Whichever form of the Corn Maiden is chosen, whether simple ears of corn, or an intricately woven Corn Dolly, or the Corn Mother from the Lammas Sabbat, the ritual of Bride's Bed is becoming a popular Imbolc tradition. The Corn Maiden is dressed as a bride during the Imbolc sabbat. This might be done with cleverly folded white lace handkerchiefs or lengths of white lace, ribbons and linen. A necklace or beads or other symbols of the Goddess might be added to the figure to add power to the rite. When she is ready the figure is lain in a basket, which might be adorned with ribbons and flowers befitting the Goddess' bridal bed. Finally, an acorn tipped and ribbon-entwined wand, representing the God, is placed across the Corn Maiden. Candles are lit on either side of the basket, while symbolic figures of the God and the Goddess are enchanted with words like:

Welcome Bride,
To your bed and cover.
Blessed be the Maiden,
Blessed be the Mother.

Bride's Bed

Bride is typical of the universal Goddess of Fertility. Her counterpart in Celtic traditions is the Cailliach, or Crone. In some traditions the Maiden is held captive by the Cailliach during the winter months; in others, she is the Cailliach, beautiful on one side, dark and ugly on the other, bringing life and fertility on one hand, death and destruction on the other. In these details the two Goddesses who are one, are very similar to the Roman Goddesses Ceres and Proserpina, and their Greek predecessors Demeter and Persephone. In the myth of these Goddesses, the Mother blasts the crops in anger while her daughter, the Maiden, is held captive in the Underworld. Both Ceres and Proserpina, and Demeter and Persephone are considered two Goddesses that are one, and probably had their origins in the ancient goddesses of Old Europe who presided over the coming of Spring, the harvesting of sacred grain and the ritual baking of bread.

In many Pagan traditions, the mythology of the Goddess tells of her descent into the Underworld. Probably the oldest such myth is that of Ishtar. But in other traditions the Goddess is said to be sleeping or resting while her consort, the Horned God as Spirit Father presides. In cultures that believe in reincarnation, death is looked upon as a rest between lives. Even in our present culture "eternal sleep" and "rest in peace" are euphemisms for death. The tale of Snow White is in a sense a version of this myth of the Goddess's descent into the Underworld, where she rests until she is united with her consort. At which point, of course, she becomes the Mother, and the tale begins again, and repeats itself "happily ever after."

Thus one of the earliest descriptions of the Goddess most of us ever heard began with this tale of a lonely queen sitting in a tower, working on an embroidery. As the queen stitched she pricked her finger and a drop of her blood fell on the pure white linen. The queen gazed at the drop of blood and made a wish. "O, for a child with skin as white as snow, lips as red as blood, and hair as black as ebony." The queen's wish was granted, but she lost her life giving birth to Snow White. Her place was taken by another queen, older and sometimes cruel, but still quite beautiful. This stepmother raised Snow White in her castle until she was warned by her magick mirror that Snow White was becoming a beautiful woman, and as such was a threat to her reign. The stepmother ordered that Snow White be killed, but the plot failed and Snow White escaped and found shelter and protection with seven dwarfs who spent their days digging and tunneling in the earth. When the queen discovered Snow White's whereabouts, she took upon herself the appearance of the Crone and presented Snow White with a magick apple. When the Maiden took a bite of the apple, it caught in her throat and she fell into a death-like sleep. So beautiful was the Maiden, even in death, that the dwarfs could not bring themselves to bury her. Instead they placed her in a coffin of glass where they could admire her beauty.

Then one day a handsome young prince happened to be riding in the forest when he came upon the Maiden in the coffin. Her beauty stirred something in him and he bent and kissed her. His kiss stirred something in her which dislodged the bit of apple, and brought the Maiden back to life, and as we all know, they lived happily ever after.

This story contains a description of the Triple Goddess, Maiden, Mother and Crone. The description is given symbolically in the first few sentences of the tale, when the Goddess in her aspect as the Mother describes the child she desires "with skin as white as snow, lips as red as blood and hair as black as ebony." White, red and black—Maiden, Mother and Crone—represent the three Goddesses who are one. That Snow White is the Triple Goddess is shown by the fact that she has the three colors, in her skin, lips and hair. That in this tale she is the Maiden aspect of the Goddess is shown by her name, Snow White.

That our ancient Pagan ancestors took the trouble to disguise the truths of the Old Religion so cleverly as to make them go unnoticed in order that the tales be told and retold, even by the enemies of the Old Religion, so that they would be preserved for future generations, is a tribute not only to their wisdom but also to their undying faith.

Another such tale is that of Rapunsel. In this story a mortal woman who is pregnant had a craving for a certain kind of radish that grew only in the garden of the Witch who lived next door. Her husband climbed the garden wall one night to pick the radishes she craved, only to be caught by the Witch. Instead of punishing the man for stealing her radishes, the Witch made a bargain with him. She gave him his freedom in exchange for the daughter about to be born.

When the child was born, the Witch took her and raised her, and locked her in a high tower where no man could reach her.

Then one day a handsome young prince was wandering in the forest when he heard Rapunsel singing a sad and lonely song. He found his way to the tower and when he saw Rapunsel, he fell in love with her. But there was no way into the tower so Rapunsel let down her long braid of hair which had never been cut, and the prince climbed up to her chamber. Each day after that he would come to the tower where she was imprisoned, and utter the most memorable line of the tale: "Rapunsel, Rapunsel, let down your golden hair"; and each day he visited her and loved her.

But then one day they were caught by her stepmother the Witch, or Crone, who then cut Rapunsel's hair off and banished her from the land,

Butter Churn

and blinded the prince. The prince, however, still loved Rapunsel, and vowed to spend the rest of his life in quest of her. At last one day he found her in a far distant land, and when her tears of joy fell upon his eyes, his sight was restored.

This tale tells us of the version of the myth in which the Crone aspect of the Goddess, or the Cailliach, keeps the Maiden locked in a tower during the winter months. The famous line from the tale, "Rapunsel, Rapunsel, let down your golden hair," is reminiscent of one of the titles of Demeter, the Grain Goddess of the ancient Greeks, "She of the Corn Ripe Yellow Hair." It is also a description of a golden head of bearded wheat at the top of its stalk. In any case, the Maiden imprisoned in her high tower, between Heaven and Earth, in that place between the worlds, is united with her consort, the Lord of the Spirit Worlds. His blinding is a symbolic death and his reunion with Rapunsel and the restoration of his sight is his resurrection. There are many tales in Celtic myth that tell of a princess in a tower. In some the tower is suspended between heaven and earth by golden chains, and the hero must perform tasks, often in multiples of three, before he can be united with her. This theme is sometimes interpreted simply as man's striving toward his own higher self by those who do not recognize the symbolism of the Lord and Lady of the Old Religion; but then, what really is the difference?

Another way of portraying the union of Spirit and Matter or the descent of Spirit into Matter at Imbolc, is the tradition of a wreath of candles worn as a crown by the priestess or other member of a coven. In some Scandinavian countries this crown of candles was a part of the Yule traditions, and the candles were worn on a wreath of holly; and in some countries of Eastern Europe, a young girl wearing this crown is drawn into the celebration area in a sleigh.

In Latin countries, this same image of a maiden wearing a crown of burning candles is called Santa Lucia. Lucia is obviously a feminine form of the name Lucifer, the Light Bearer, who in Italian traditions is the brother/consort of Diana Maiden Goddess of the Moon. To the ancient Greeks, he is the son of the Goddess Eos, Goddess of the sunrise and is identified with the morning star.

Another old tradition appropriate for the season was to leave a slice of buttered bread on the butter churn on the evening of February first, as an offering to the Goddess who presides over the production of milk, cream and butter. It is probably because of this aspect of the Witch's Goddess that Witches were accused of working magick so that the "butter would not come." Here at Flying Witch Farm, we do not churn our own butter (we use margarine); but we do have an old butter churn decorating the front porch. Its old red paint has faded and flaked, and the dasher within has been still for decades. But on the night of Imbolc we leave the traditional offering; and as the sun rises on the morning of February second, and the greens of the Yuletide season are replaced by the three ears of corn (symbolizing the Goddess) that will adorn the front of our house until Yule returns, we remove the buttered bread knowing that its essence has been accepted.

As the sun rises on this date, it is a tradition in America to note whether or not the ground hog will see his shadow. On a cloudy day, of course, he will not see his shadow and this foretells an early Spring. An analogous belief is held in a number of European countries, that fair weather at this time foretells six more weeks of Winter, and clouds promise an early Spring.

As days grow longer, there are flowers everywhere in the Witch's garden. Winter aconite opens its buttery yellow cups to the sun while snow drops bow to kiss the earth. The huge waxy flowers of white helebore that have been in bloom almost since Yule, now fade to pink as the new shoots and purple flowers of black helebore begin to emerge. The strange orchid-like flowers of witch hazel burst open on branches without benefit of stems. It is interesting to note that among the first flowers to appear are aconite, helebore and witch hazel. All these have associations with magick.

Magickal Potions

As the psychic currents that flow through January and February are still turned inward onto the spiritual planes, and thus potions, charms and oils prepared now can be particularly effective. This is a good time to check the magickal cupboard to be sure that it is not bare in spots. The magickal cupboard is itself a great source of power and should be chosen for its ability to stimulate your imagination and psychic impulses. Once the proper piece of furniture has been selected, or more likely it has found its way to you, it will begin to be filled with all of the herbs and oils and magickal objects that will be needed for magick in the months and years to come.

For most of us this means the joy of combing antique shops and yard sales for just the right containers, not just during the winter months, but all year around. Whenever this is being done, one's psychic abilities should be in use. A bottle that once contained a poisonous substance would not make a very fit container for a healing herb. Let intuition be your guide. Although you will probably never be able to prove if your feelings are correct, they probably will be. Eventually the shelves of your cupboard will be filled with an assortment of glass jars and bottles in palest shades of amber, amethyst, or aquamarine, all opalized with age. Containers with wider necks are more suitable for dried herbs, while those with long narrow necks are best used for fluids. Antique medicine bottles usually are without their stoppers, but these can be replaced by shaving down corks from wine bottles to fit. Bottles and jars are not the only sort of containers that are necessary. A well-equipped cupboard will hold not only herbs and oils, but stones, feathers, candles, amulets, Tarot cards, and probably ritual tools when not in use. Many of these will be self-contained, but some will need to be kept in boxes. Keeping magickal objects and substances in separate containers is important because it keeps them from canceling out one another's properties. It is especially magickal to find a box that is decorated with just the right designs to contain a particular stone or root or amulet.

Before going out on a day's antiquing, here is a little ritual that can be performed to help you to locate what you are looking for, or to help you to recognize what you need.

Place one drop of magnet oil (the recipe is given later in this chapter) on the point between the eyebrows, usually referred to as the "third eye," saying,

> *That I may recognize,*

place a drop on your purse or wallet,

> *That I may afford,*

place a drop between your palms,

That I may possess
O gracious Goddess
That which I seek.
Aid me in my quest as I go forth
That ere I return I find
That which I desire.

If you have something specific in mind state it at the end of the charm and then go out with perfect faith in the knowledge that what you are seeking is on its way to you.

The well-equipped Witch's cupboard will contain, aside from herbs and oils, a good assortment of colored candles. A pair of each color is preferable. As long as the candles have not been anointed and consecrated to any specific purpose, they may all be kept together in the same box. Once they have been dressed and consecrated, it is advised to keep them wrapped separately in white linen which is then tied (loosely) with a cord or thread. This helps to contain the magick. Candles consecrated to a specific purpose might also be marked with Runes appropriate to that purpose. The magick of the Runes enhances the power of the candle when burned, and they also help to identify the purpose of the candles, should they get mixed up. For instance, green candles to be burned for prosperity might be marked with the Rune ᚠ which is the Rune of material or moveable possessions, while a candle dressed with a healing oil might be inscribed with the Rune ᛉ which means a change for better.

Magickal stones; lodestone or magnetite, selenite, smokey quartz crystal
and a faery cross or staurolite crystal.

Since the dawning of the "New Age," a tremendous amount of credit has been given to the mystical, magickal and/or healing properties of certain stones, especially quartz crystals. But there is also an ancient tradition of certain stones having magickal properties, and there is ample evidence that early man sought out and collected unusual stones, probably as much for their magickal properties as for their beauty.

The well-equipped Witch's cupboard will have a small assortment of stones for a variety of magickal purposes. I will mention a few of the more easily obtainable ones, and their properties and associations, but the following list is by no means a complete one.

Amber is the fossilized resin or sap of ancient trees and is sacred to the Goddess. For this reason many Witches wear a necklace of amber beads or amber beads combined with beads of jet. Amber ranges in color from pale yellow through orange to a rather deep brown. The lighter colors, when combined with jet, produce a necklace in the traditional colors of Halloween. Fine clear beads of amber can be costly, but small unpolished chips, just as sacred to the Goddess, are less expensive. These are excellent to include in charms for healing, or for protection, especially against inflammatory diseases.

The beautiful banded colors of polished agate are believed to give the wearers of it the gift of eloquence and to gain for them the favors of their listeners. It is also said to cause a person to be truthful, which is probably the reason for the speaker's eloquence and favor in the first place. Like other semi-precious stones that can be polished to a high gloss, agate is said to be able to soothe or prevent skin irritations. Agate is sacred to Mercury, both the messenger of the Gods and the planet named in his honor, and is therefore especially lucky for Gemini natives. Moss agate, which is chemically related, and which bears tiny greenish branch-like patterns, has the reputation of being a fortunate stone for gardeners.

Apatite is a mineral who's name means "to deceive," so named because it can take on such a variety of shapes and colors. For this reason it is a valuable ingredient in charms and rituals performed for the purpose of "shape shifting," that is, to change one's appearance. And, apatite crystals occur in such variety that a color or shape to suit your specific purpose will probably be available.

Crystals of beryl in palest blue-green are called aquamarine. They have the property of causing harmony between people and can attract love, so they might be added to love charms or used in rituals created to attract love.

A dark green stone splashed with spots of blood red is called bloodstone. It gives courage to the wearer and insures victory in battle. It also grants fame and long life and protection from drowning. Include bloodstone in charms for power and protection to be used in times of conflict. It can also be worn as an amulet of protection and especially if you are a

Pisces, since it is sacred to the Sea God Neptune, for whom Pisces' ruling planet was named.

Although not a stone in the truest sense, coral has long been considered a gem of protection, especially the red and pink varieties. Coral is produced by colonies of tiny marine animals which secrete calcium carbonate obtained from sea water. Since Roman times, and probably before, it has been used as an amulet of protection against the Evil Eye. Still today, Italians carve it into the tiny charms known as "Mano in Fica," and "Mano in Cornuta," or "the hand in the sign of the fig," and "the hand in the sign of Horns," respectively. The former is a human hand in a fist with the thumb showing between the first and second fingers; and which is also a symbol of the Goddess; and "the hand in the sign of the Horns" is a fist with the index and smallest fingers extended in the sign of the Horned God. It is also polished and set in a simple horn shape that is both an amulet of protection and of male virility. Coral is considered especially protective for children, and has been hung on cribs and on the infants themselves by Italian grandmothers for untold generations. It also has the power to banish nightmares and should be included in any charms of protection.

Crystals, especially those of quartz, have become as popular today as little plastic pyramids were in the early 70s, due mostly to the belief of the "New Agers." This is attributed to the memories of many now incarnate, of previous lives on the lost continent of Atlantis. It is my opinion that Atlantis never existed on the material plane, but certainly now exists on the more ethereal planes, having been created there by those who do believe in it. Still, crystals have been considered to be the highest form of consciousness in the mineral kingdom by some Eastern mystics since ancient times, and crystal has always had a special place in occultism. The crystal ball is one example, and many of the magickal jewels of the ceremonial magicians were precious gems; rubies, emeralds, sapphires and diamonds, are all the crystal forms of certain minerals.

But of all the crystals, quartz has definite electromagnetic properties, and there is an apparent link between electromagnetism and psi. For this reason, quartz can help to form a link between the physical plane and the astral and spiritual planes. It can also be charged telepathically, or enchanted with magick for healing or protection. Quartz crystals might be included in any charm or ritual done for the purpose of contacting higher planes or for spirit communication.

Amethyst is a purple or lavender form of quartz, and because of its color, which is usually associated with the higher spiritual planes, it is often used when meditating. When warmed by the sun, wrapped in silk and held against the forehead, amethyst is said to have the ability to cure headaches. It bestows on the wearer the high ideals and virtues of the sign of Aquarius.

Rose quartz is a beautiful pale pink form of quartz, and because its color is associated with love; it is an excellent addition to charms and spells to attract love.

The deep brown or black crystals of smokey quartz may be used as aids in scrying, or in rituals performed at the Dark of the Moon; or they may be worn as amulets in rituals dealing with the Crone aspect of the Goddess or Hecate.

Quartz crystals come in a variety of colors, and in general, the color will suggest the type of magick it is best suited for. Citrine is another form of quartz, bright amber in color. This would suggest that it be used in magick dealing with mental abilities, knowledge (as opposed to wisdom), memory and clear thinking. It would also have associations with the sun and its qualities, as well as the sign of Leo. Not all of the citrine crystals sold are natural. Amethyst crystals exposed to extreme heat will turn the same bright golden color, but then natural citrine is formed in a similar way, so let intuition be your guide.

I have also seen clusters of quartz crystals with the most extraordinary aquamarine irridescent sheen that is the result of being treated in a solution of gold, and lovely translucent slices of banded agate dyed a most unnatural blue, as well as feldspar (moonstone) dyed a brilliant and equally unnatural yellow. I am usually offended by objects that are the result of man's improving upon Nature, especially where beauty is concerned, but if you find yourself mystically attracted to such an object, or your intuition tells you that you must have it, then by all means buy it.

Some of the single quartz crystals sold today have been polished and cleaned up in order to appear more perfect, but this does not necessarily add to their magickal properties. Also, the perfect "double pyramid" flourite sometimes sold as flourite crystals, are not crystals at all but cleavage fragments, that is, when flourite is shattered, it always breaks up into these perfect "double pyramid" shapes. But that alone should suggest all sorts of possibilities for magickal uses.

The doubly terminated quartz crystals known as Herkimer diamonds that come from Herkimer County, New York, are not only unusual in that they are doubly terminated (pointed at both ends), but they are often extremely clear and flawless. These are the perfect tips for the Witch's magick wand. This might sound more New Age than Old Religion, but in fact, illustrations of old Faery tales often show the Faery-godmother's wand as being tipped with something that shines like a star, and this would certainly suggest a crystal. Furthermore, the wand is just another version of the magician's staff or the shaman's walking stick, which is usually believed to be the off-shoot of the World Tree. All of these magickal staffs of power are undoubtedly the forerunners of the kingly scepter, jewel-tipped emblem of his station for which he was chosen by the Gods.

The wand is a sort of antenna. When pointed upward, and with ritual and magick and concentration, a Witch can draw into herself magickal energy. Then, by pointing the wand at a chosen object, she can release the power down her arm, through the wand where it is intensified by the crystal and directed into the object. It is easy to see why the doubly terminated crystal works best here.

Flint has close associations with the element of Fire, and has been used by ancient man for thousands of years because of its sharp cutting edge. For this reason it is sometimes made into ceremonial knives by those on the shamanic path, and it is an ideal material for a blade for the ritual harvesting of herbs and sacred grain, a more Wiccan variety of the "white handled knife." Flint is sometimes worn as a protective amulet, and a small flint arrowhead makes an excellent pendulum for dowsing.

Garnet, the birthstone of both Capricorn and Aquarius, confers upon the wearer loyalty and faithfulness. If worn as an amulet it is believed to protect the health, grant cheerfulness, and warn of danger by changing color.

Hematite, magnetite, and meteorite are all forms of iron. Hematite, a blackish mineral, is non-metallic in appearance, but when rubbed on an unglazed tile or other surface it leaves the unmistakable blood-red color of iron oxide. This makes the mineral sacred to Mars. It is iron oxide that was placed on the corpses and bones of ancient man, and upon the bones of sacred animals in order to give them life. Blood gets its red color from iron oxide. For this reason, iron oxide can be used to color Runes or other magickal alphabets; that is, to give them life after they have been inscribed.

Magnetite is also called lodestone. As its name implies, it is magnetic and attracts to itself iron and other metallic substances. It is associated with water and should be placed in water periodically to renew its powers. It can be worn as an amulet to attract good fortune, or placed in oil for a period of time to produce magnetic oil which can then be used to anoint candles or charms or one's self to attract good fortune. To make Magnet Oil, place a magnet (a magnetite crystal is especially powerful) in olive oil on the night of the Moon's first quarter and swirl the container three times deosil. The following night swirl it widdershins, the next night deosil again, and so forth, until the night of the Full Moon, the seventh night, when it will be swirled again doesil and the crystal (or magnet) can be removed from the oil which will possess the magickal power to attract.

Meteorites, or shooting stars, are one of the few metallic forms of iron that occur in nature, and they have the added magick of having fallen from the sky. For this reason they were considered sacred by ancient man, and still can be looked upon as a sign of favor from the Gods, as well as being worn as an amulet that can connect us with the higher realms.

Metal from heaven, or "ba-en-pet," was what the ancient Egyptians called iron: beads made from iron, strung together with beads of gold, agate and carnelian, were found on a corpse in a tomb that dates to four thousand years before the current era (B.C.E.). In ancient Rome the wedding ring, one of the most important articles of jewelry, was made of iron, and iron is sacred to the Celtic Goddess Bride, who is also a Goddess of the hearth and forge.

Although jade can occur in just about every color of the rainbow, it is the bright glossy translucent green of oriental jade, or the softer more opaque green of "jadite," that most of us are familiar with. In the Far East, where jade is very highly prized, it is said to grant all desires both in this lifetime and in the next. For those of us who are more involved in Western traditions, its green color is reminiscent of the colors of the sea, and is therefore sacred to all sea deities, including Neptune, Llyr or Aphrodite. Thus it is considered fortunate for those born under the sign of Pisces, which is ruled by the planet named for the Roman Pagan God of the Sea, Neptune.

As the green of jade reminds us of the sea, so the gold-flecked blue of lapis lazuli reminds us of the star studded sky of night. The ancient Babylonians carved cylindrical seals of this stone. These seals often depicted scenes of offerings to the ancient Gods. The Egyptians carved scarab amulets of lapis and shaped it into beads for the finest funerary jewelry. When worn as an amulet, lapis lazuli has the power to increase psychic ability and to enhance magickal energy.

The beautiful green banded stone called malachite is an ore of copper. When worn as an amulet, it gives protection from falling. It is also sometimes used as an ingredient in love charms because of its association with the metal copper and the color green, both sacred to the Goddess in her aspect as Venus, Goddess of Love.

Feldspar, when found by itself and not in combination with other minerals, is popularly known as moonstone. When polished, its silvery white color shifts and shimmers with the light like satin. Like malachite, it is sacred to the Goddess in her aspect as Goddess of Love and Fertility. But moonstone is also sacred to the Goddess in her aspect as Queen of the Faeries, and it is worn or carried when one wishes to see Faeries. It also makes a fine amulet to be worn when the rite known as "Drawing Down the Moon" is performed.

Turquoise is a stone that the Native Americans considered sacred to the Sky or Spirit Father because of its sky-blue color. It is said to protect both horse and rider.

Opal is a gem sometimes associated with the element of Fire because of the blue, green or red fire that seems to flash from its depths. It is sometimes called the gem of hope, but some consider it an unlucky stone. It is believed to be especially unlucky for those born under the signs of Capricorn or Cancer, but it is fortunate for natives of Libra. It is sometimes worn as an amulet to improve memory.

Large pieces of black volcanic glass called obsidian have been used in the past as magickal mirrors in which one could see the future. Because it can be chipped and shaped like flint, it is an excellent material for making into ritual knives and ceremonial blades. Small nuggets of obsidian called Apache tears are sometimes made into magickal jewelry. Because of their color they are worn to enhance psychic ability or when doing psychic readings or working with the Goddess in her aspect as Hecate.

Selenite, named for Selene the Goddess of the Moon, is one of the very few minerals that forms curved and sometimes twinned crystals which most often grow in caves. For this reason it is sacred to the Moon Goddess who is also Queen of the Faeries; and is therefore favored by the Faery-folk.

Many of the stones and gems mentioned here are from exotic places, and were brought into Europe by crusaders and explorers, only later to be brought into the craft by way of ceremonial magick. While Witches and Pagans have indeed adopted much of their beliefs in the magickal properties of gemstones from the tradition of ceremonial magick, it should be kept in mind that the origin of the idea is Pagan, and that even before the Crusades it was believed by Witches and Pagans that stones had magickal properties. The fact that thousands of years before the current era certain types of stones weighing many tons were dragged great distances to sacred sites is proof enough of that. Small stones or pebbles with enigmatic markings painted on them in red or yellow ochre have been found in ancient sites. Their purpose is unknown, but it is very likely that they are the ancient ancestors of Runestones or some other sort of divinatory system of casting lots. Many stones are sacred because of their shapes. Round stones and holey stones are favorite amulets among Witches, especially Italian Witches, and both are treated with special ritual.

Some say that the pearl is the gem of tears, while others say that it brings tears of joy. It certainly didn't bring tears of joy to the oyster from whose living flesh it was cut. For this reason, Wiccans who believe "to harm none" applies to all forms of life do not consider the pearl as a gem of good fortune. Still, others believe that because of its round white shape, luminous luster, and association with the sea, it is another gem sacred to the Moon Goddess.

Finding a holey stone is considered a special sign of favor by the Gods and it is an amulet of good fortune. Asperge it with salted water and hold the stone high with the fingers of both hands while reciting words like:

O Gracious Goddess
You have placed this Holey Stone
On my pathway for me to find.
Grant it now become a vessel
Of your divine power
To aid me in my magickal work.
In your name Gracious Goddess
Do I consecrate this Holey Stone.

Stones that are perfectly round are considered to be containers of good luck and prosperity, and if given away or lost the luck goes with them. If a round stone is found, toss it in the air three times, catching it each time. Then hold it high saying words like:

Spirit of this Stone so Round,
Not stone, but fortune have I found.
Spirit of fortune abide with me,
As I will, so mote it be!

Then make for this stone a special pouch, that you can wear or carry in your pocket.

One of the most intriguing of all crystal formations must certainly be the twinned crystals of staurolite, known as Faery Crosses. These pairs of long flat-sided crystals intersect one another at 45 or 90 degree angles, and those that are at 90 degrees to one another form perfect Solar Crosses. What they possess in shape, however, they lack in color, being earthy brown to black; but this too, along with their mysterious shape, identifies them with the Faery-folk, and especially gnomes, dwarfs and brownies. If you obtain a Faery Cross, or are so fortunate as the find one, you might wish to perform this ritual.

On the night of the Full Moon, anoint the stone with Faery Oil (the formula is given in chapter 3) and place it in a Faery Ring (also described in chapter 3). If you cannot find a Faery Ring place the stone on the ground (or some earth) and inscribe a circle around it. Sprinkle it with spring water, intoning:

Cross of Stone
By Moonlight bright,
Give to me the special sight
That when I wear thee
I may see
The folk that dwell
In the Land of Fee.

Allow the stone to remain in the moonlight as long as you like, but be sure to put it away at the first rooster's crow, or before the rising of the sun, in a green pouch, or one bound with a green cord, along with herbs attractive to Faeries.

Many stones and gems are associated with the different elements, but it is important to remember that all stones have a primary association with Earth, just as all candles are primarily associated with Fire.

The well-equipped Witch's cupboard will also contain an assortment of incense primarily associated with the element of Air. It should also be remembered that before the Old Religion came into contact with ceremonial magick and the exotic gums and resins of the so-called Holy Land, such as frankincense and myrrh, or the frangipangi and sandalwood of the Far East, the Witches and Pagans of Europe burned the native fragrant woods and herbs (that is, if they burned any incense at all). Cedar and pine give a scented smoke, as do sage and lavender.

By mid-month, the fertility rites of Imbolc are recalled once again in the last vestiges of the Roman festival of Lupercalia, Valentine's Day. Quick to replace the Pagan celebration with one of the new religion, Christians named the holiday St. Valentine's Day after a saint who was allegedly martyred by Emperor Claudius for insulting the Old Gods. But neither the most contemporary of Valentine's cards nor even antique ones of the most delicate paper lace show pictures of a martyred saint. Rather they show pictures of Cupid, son of Venus, Goddess of Love, identified by his bow and quiver of arrows. His Greek counterpart is Eros, son of Aphrodite. In his myth, Eros falls in love with the beautiful mortal Psyche. Jealous of Psyche's beauty, Aphrodite tricks her into inhaling the poisonous fumes contained in a mysterious box, causing her to fall into a deathlike sleep. Eros finds her and his love for her is so great that he brings her back to life again.

Cupid, son of the Goddess Venus.

Here once again is a story of Snow White, of Sleeping Beauty and of Bride's Bed. It is a story of love and of the union of the Goddess and the God, but not of the union that takes place on the physical plane. That still lies ahead at Beltane. It is a story of the union of the Goddess and the God, but not of a union that takes place on the spiritual planes, prior to manifestation on the material plane, because this is still the dark time of the year, long before the Vernal Equinox when the balance shifts from the darkness to the light. It is still the time when activity is turned inward.

As February warms into March, on the backyard feeder one huge black shape stands out among the small pale winter birds, the kinglets and juncos, the nuthatches and chickadees. It is a sleek black grackle that we call Odin. He came to us two winters ago—injured and unable to feed. Dan fed and watered him along with our chickens every morning and evening, until he was able to fly. He returned last spring and again this year, to feed very un-grackle-like on the bird feeder while his mate calls to him from a safe distance.

On the back porch, most of the firewood stacked there before winter set in has been burned, and in the cellar jars that last summer were filled with fresh-picked fruits and vegetables, now one by one are being emptied. But the snow melts away, lingering only in the hollows and shady places not yet warmed by the Sun. The buds of oaks and maples swell in response to the lengthening days, and catkins hang from birch and hazel twigs, all signs that the season of growth and renewal is about to begin.

Chapter Two
VERNAL EQUINOX

VERNAL EQUINOX

The warming, waxing sun of March melts the Onion Snow and coaxes daffodils to bud. Sheep in shaggy winter wool are ready to be shorn, and lambs, black Suffolks and white Dorsets, explore their fresh new world. Hecate, the Flying Witch weathervane, squeaks a rusty squeak as she turns in shifting breezes. The buds of maple blossoms swell and burst, inviting bees that have just awakened from their winter sleep. And silence is to be broken by a sound that has not been heard since autumn—the song of birds.

To Christians around the world, the first Sunday after the first Full Moon after the Vernal Equinox is Easter Sunday, the celebration of the resurrection of Jesus. But for thousands of years before the Christian Era, the Vernal Equinox signaled the beginning of the season of rebirth, the resurrection of nature and of many an ancient Pagan God.

Webster's Dictionary defines resurrection as a return from the dead. One of the first stories ever recorded of death and resurrection is the Egyptian myth of Isis and Osiris. In this story of eternal love, the Goddess Isis and the God Osiris ruled an ancient land in peace and bliss, until Set, brother of Osiris, murdered him in a fit of jealousy. Set cut the body of Osiris up into fourteen pieces and scattered them around the world. Heartbroken, Isis wandered throughout the world, mourning her beloved and gathering the pieces of his body. When the pieces had all been collected, Isis, with the help of Anubis, Lord of the Underworld, brought Osiris back to life. Through the union of Isis and Osiris, Horus the Sun God was born.

Far from the Valley of the Nile, in the ancient land of Sumer between the Tigris and Euphrates Rivers, a similar tale was being told. Tammuz, the God of Grain, was the beloved of Ishtar, the Goddess of Love and Beauty. When Tammuz was killed, Ishtar, driven by despair, pounded the gates of the Underworld demanding to be let in. Allatu, Queen of the Underworld and sister to Ishtar, allowed her to enter. At the first gate, she was told to remove the crown from her head, "as that is the custom of Allatu." At the second gate, she was told to remove the pendants from her ears; at the third, the chains from her neck; at the fourth, the ornament from her breasts; at the fifth, the girdle of birthstones from her hips; at the sixth, her bracelets and anklets; and at the

Making Hot Cross Buns

seventh, the garment from her body. Allatu held Ishtar captive in the Underworld. Because of her absence from the world of the living, all fertility ceased among plants, animals and people. When the great God Ea saw this, he sent a message to Allatu to release Ishtar. She was sprinkled with the Waters of Life, and as she passed through each of the gates, her garments and her jewels were returned to her. The fate of her lover Tammuz is not known because the last tablets of the text are missing. However, a Babylonian version of the same myth suggests that because of Ishtar's intervention, not only is Tammuz resurrected, but also that all the men and women who had ever died, "may rise and smell the incense."

Once again, as with Isis and Osiris, it was the love of a Goddess that brought a God back from the dead.

Ishtar was known as Astarte to the Phoenicians, and by the Greeks she was equated to Aphrodite, the Greek Goddess of Love and Beauty. Ishtar's consort, Tammuz, the resurrected Grain God, was called Adonis by the Greeks after the Semitic word "adoni," meaning Lord. There was a temple to Adonis in the city of Bethlehem, but the center of his worship was on the island of Cyprus.

Aphrodite was the daughter of Zeus and Dione. She fell in love with the beautiful youth Adonis, and hid him in a box so that no one else could see him.

She gave the box to Persephone to hide for her, but Persephone opened the box. When she beheld the beautiful youth Adonis, she too fell in love with him. Persephone, Queen of the Underworld, refused to return Adonis to Aphrodite, who could not be consoled. As the Goddess of Love and Fertility mourned the loss of her beloved, the land became a barren waste. When Zeus saw this, he tried to intervene, but Persephone loved Adonis as much as Aphrodite. At last Zeus decreed that Adonis would spend a third of the year with each Goddess, and spend a third of the year alone. Each spring, Adonis returns to Aphrodite, and each winter he dwells with Persephone in the Underworld.

From the ancient land of Phrygia, not far from the fair islands of Cyprus and Cythera, comes the myth of Cybele and Attis. Attis was conceived when his mother placed an almond in her lap to admire its beauty and was impregnated by its magickal power of fertility. The Mother Goddess, Cybele, fell in love with the beautiful youth, but he was caused to marry another. Upon discovering the couple, Cybele flew into a rage and destroyed the entire town. Attis then castrated himself under a pine tree and died from the self-inflicted wound. Where drops of his blood fell, violets sprang up. Cybele gathered the violets and adorned the pine tree with them in remembrance of her beloved Attis. Cybele implored Zeus to bring back Attis, but Zeus agreed only to preserve the body from corruption.

Dionysus, Greek God of Resurrection

It was in Rome that the cult of Cybele flourished; there, at the time of the Vernal Equinox, the eunuch priests of Cybele performed spring rites that lasted almost a week. On the first day of the festival, a pine tree whose trunk had been wrapped with white cloth (like a shroud) and adorned with violets was carried into the temple. (This sounds remarkably like a description of the May Pole, traditionally a pine tree with all but its uppermost branches removed, entwined with red and white ribbons and bedecked with flowers.) On the second day of the festival, trumpets were sounded. On the third day, the high priest slashed his arm, allowing the blood to fall on the pine tree. In a ritual of mourning for the dead Attis, there was frenzied music and dancing. On the last day of the festival, mourning turned to joy because the god had risen, promising his followers their own triumph over death.

In all of these myths, the element that is the cause of the resurrection is love—in each case, the love of a Goddess for her consort. But in the myth of Demeter and Persephone, it is the love of a mother for her daughter that brings about the return from the dead. Persephone was the beautiful daughter of Demeter, the Goddess of Grain and Vegetation. (To the Romans they were known as Proserpina and Ceres.) Persephone was gathering flowers one day when she was beheld by Hades, Lord of the Underworld. He loved her instantly, and carried her off in his chariot to rule beside him as Queen of the realm of the Dead.

When Demeter realized that Persephone was missing, her grief was so great that she would not eat or drink the nectar of the Gods. After nine days she learned from the Sun where her daughter had been taken. Demeter left Mount Olympus to roam the earth in search of her daughter, disguised so that no one could recognize her. Because Demeter had left the realm of the Gods, all vegetation ceased to grow and the earth became a cold and barren waste. Zeus, who was particularly concerned for the welfare of human life, sent a messenger to Hades, telling him that he must allow Persephone to return to her mother. He promised that he would free her, but nevertheless Hades ensured her return by tricking her into eating a magick pomegranate seed before she left the Underworld. Demeter and Persephone were joyfully reunited, and Demeter of the Corn-Ripe Yellow Hair allowed the Earth to blossom forth once more, and taught them to plant corn. Each year thereafter, Persephone decends into the Underworld with the coming of winter, and returns each year in the spring.

Demeter established the center of her worship at Elusis, where during her quest for Persephone she had been shown kindness by a stranger. The mysteries of her religion taught men to live joyfully and to die with hope, because "Blessed is he who has seen them, his lot will be good in the world to come."

Often associated with Demeter, the Goddess of Grain, is Dionysus, the God of Wine. The most recent of the Greek Gods, Dionysus was born at Thebes. His father was Zeus, King of Heaven, but his mother was Semele, a mortal princess. Zeus loved Semele and he promised to do anything she asked of him. But Semele, who was pregnant with Zeus's child, asked only to see him in all his radiant splendor as the God of Gods. Zeus knew that no mortal could witness this sight and live—and yet, despite his warning Semele of the consequences, she insisted. Upon Semele's death, Zeus took the child from her body and hid it within his own, until the time came for Dionysus to be born. Dionysus was raised by nymphs, but when he grew to manhood he travelled to distant lands, performing feats that proved his godhood. Yet this young God of Joy and Wine, known to the Romans as Bacchus, longed for the mother he never knew; and so he descended into the Underworld to find her. When he had found Semele, he defied Death itself and escaped the realm of the dead with her. At last he brought her to Mount Olympus, where she was allowed to dwell among the Gods.

Once again it is love, in this instance the love of a son for his mother, that is the force behind the resurrection.

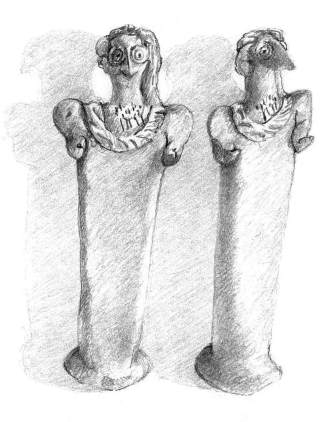

Two Views of an ancient Bird-Headed Goddess.

Although the worship of Dionysus is relatively recent (circa 800 B.C.E.), it has an air of a far more primitive religion about it. His mythological followers, the Meanads, worshiped not in temples, but in wild forests and hidden valleys. The "blood feast" that was part of the Meanads' rites seems to have its roots in the very early shamanistic religion of the hunter-gatherers of pre-history. The actual worship of Dionysus took place not in the temples nor in the wild places, but in the theaters; and the plays that were the acts of worship were the forerunners of today's "Passion plays."

Dionysus was killed, hacked to pieces—some say at Hera's command. But, because he had overcome death when he had previously descended to the Underworld, he rose again. As the God of the Vine, he dies each year, and each year he returns from the dead. Like other gods of resurrection, his rites were held in spring, when the vines put forth new shoots. His worshippers believed that death is not an end—the soul lives on forever.

Far to the wintery north, another tale was being told of another God who would be resurrected. He was Balder the Sun God, the Shining One, son of Odin and Frig. He was loved by everyone because he was as kind as he was beautiful. As a youth, he was warned by a prophetic dream that he would be killed, so his mother made every creature in nature— every animal and every plant, every stone and every element—promise not to hurt him. Every creature in nature, that is, but one: the mistletoe, which was too young. So invincible did Balder appear because of these promises that it became a sport for the other Gods to throw their weapons at him. Then one day, Loki the mischief-maker—who not unlike the Egyptian Set in that he, too, was driven by jealousy—disguised himself as an old crone to learn from Frig the secret of Balder's protection. Frig told Loki that the one creature that could do Balder harm was the mistletoe. Loki then cut a shaft of mistletoe and tricked Hoder, the blind God of Winter, into throwing it at Balder. Balder was struck, and he died of his wounds. The Gods were horrified! Balder's body was given a magnificent boat funeral, while his spirit went to the ancient Norse Underworld "Hel." Odin sent a messenger to Hel to ask what could be done to bring Balder back from the dead. The messenger was told that Balder would be resurrected if every creature in nature and every God wept for him. All of the Gods and all of the creatures loved Balder so that they wept bitterly—all except Loki. And so, Balder was doomed to stay in the Underworld until Ragnarok.

Ragnarok, often equated with the Christian's Judgement Day, is the end of the world, the Twilight of the Gods. It is a time when Fenris, the monster child of Loki's, will devour the world. But for the meantime, Fenris is kept in check, bound by magickal chains forged by the Gods themselves. In the Ukraine and other countries of Eastern Europe, it was also believed that there was a monster that would devour the world, and that it is bound by magickal chains. The monster is not the embodiment of evil, but the natural processes of death and decay. It is also believed that the magickal chains that bind the monster are strengthened in direct proportion to the number of the Pysanky, the famous Ukrainian Easter eggs, made each year. These ancient rites to strengthen the magickal chains maintain a balance between the forces of nature: the forces of death and decay, on the one hand, and the forces of birth and resurrection on the other. Without death there can be no resurrection.

Ragnarok, then, is not the end, but a new beginning. In the final words of the myth of Balder:

"Surely the earth will rise up green and fair out of the sea, and plants will grow there where none were sown. . . There, too, shall come the sons of Thor, Moody and Magne bringing with them Thor's hammer. After these shall come Balder and Hoder from Hel."

Like the Celtic Gods, the Oak King of the waxing year and the Holly King of the waning year, Balder and Hoder are the Gods of Winter and Summer, locked in an eternal cycle of Birth, Death, and Resurrection.

ELEMENT	DIRECTION	SEASON	TIME OF DAY
AIR	EAST	SPRING	SUNRISE
FIRE	SOUTH	SUMMER	NOON
WATER	WEST	AUTUMN	SUNSET
EARTH	NORTH	WINTER	MIDNIGHT

And so, at the Vernal Equinox, Christians are joined in celebration by Pagans throughout the world. Having rediscovered the mythologies of our own ancestors, modern Pagans also celebrate the universal principle of Resurrection at the Equinox—which is, after all, named for Eostre, a Pagan Goddess.

Eostre or Ostre is the Anglo-Saxon Goddess of Spring to whom offerings of cakes and colored eggs were made at the Vernal Equinox. Rabbits were sacred to her, especially white rabbits, and she was believed to take the form of a rabbit. The Christian scholar Bede also claims that she is the Goddess of the East, and this fits with the Pagan tradition of the East being the direction of rebirth. Eostre, then, is the Goddess of Spring, of Rebirth and the East. She is almost certainly the same as the Greek

Goddess Eos, Goddess of the Dawn or Sunrise, since the sun rises in the east, and most directly in the east at the Vernal Equinox. This belief is preserved for us in the Christian practice of celebrating Easter at sunrise services.

Traditionally the four Elements—Earth, Air, Fire and Water—are associated with the four directions—North, South, East, West—and with the Seasons—Spring, Summer, Fall, and Winter.

There is a legend in the Anglo-Saxon and Norse traditions that the Goddess obtained her necklace—Brisingamen—only after spending one night with each of the four dwarfs. Their names are not given, but they are probable similar to, if not the same as, the names of the Norse guardians of the four directions: Austri, Sudhri, Vestri and Nordhri. The magickal necklace Brisingamen is the Magick Circle and the Wheel of the Year. It gives the Goddess power over the cycles of the seasons, or Life, Death, and Rebirth.

The Goddess Eostre, Anglo-Saxon Goddess of Spring and of the East, as the Greek Eos, Goddess of the Sunrise, is also the Maiden aspect of the Three-formed Goddess, the other two in Greek Mythology being Hemera, the Goddess of Day (the Mother), and Nix, Goddess of Night (the Crone). And, this is in keeping with the Goddess of Spring aspect, especially since the Solstices and the Equinoxes also have associations with the specific times of the day: Vernal Equinox—Dawn; Midsummer—Noon; Autumn Equinox—Dusk; and Yule (Winter Solstice)—Midnight (see table). The greater Sabbats, which mark the turning point from waxing to waning of each season, should be celebrated at the Witching Hour of Midnight, that time that is not a time. All of the major Sabbats are actually "eves" or the "night before" a festival: e.g., May Eve—Beltain, or August Eve—Lammas, etc.

Eostre's Hindu counterpart, according to Janet Farrar in *The Witch's Goddess*, is Ushas, whose lover, or opposite, is Fire. The opposite of a Goddess of Dawn would be a God or Goddess of Dusk, or Sunset, which in Latin is "Vesper." This corresponds to the Norse Guardian of the West, "Vestri." It also corresponds to the Roman Goddess Vestra, Goddess of Fire (to the Greeks, Hestra), to whom the Vestal Virgins dedicated themselves; they kept her living symbol, the eternal flame, burning in her sanctuary. If this were so, it would make Fire the element of the West.

West is the direction of Death, and is traditionally associated with the element of Water. The transition called Death was often compared with crossing a body of water. In ancient Egypt, the Necropolis, or "City of the Dead," was on the west bank of the Nile, while the land of the living was on the east bank. To the ancient Greeks, Hades, the realm of the Dead, was entirely surrounded by the River Styx. Later, Greeks had divided Hades into several sections, including prototypes for heaven

An Ancient House Blessing

and hell of the new religion, and each of these sections had an associated river. Among these was the River Acheron, or River of Woe, which the ferryman Charon helped all of the dead across. Later, the Anglo-Saxons and the Norse sent their dead into the next world by "burial at sea," with their famous ship funerals, or ship burials. Or did they? The funerary ships of the Norse were certainly put out to sea, but they were set ablaze first. And, ship burials often contained urns of the cremated remains of the deceased. So it is possible that at some point in history, the direction of the West, with its fiery sunsets, was associated with death and also the transforming element of Fire. Be that as it may—as a traditionalist, I shall continue to place water at the West. But now let us continue the subject of the Vernal Equinox and Eostre, Goddess of the East, of Spring and of Rebirth and Resurrection.

The Pagan Anglo-Saxons made offerings of colored eggs to the Goddess Eostre. They also placed them among the grave goods in burials, probably as a charm of rebirth. The Egyptians, too, placed eggs in tombs—and the Pagan Greeks placed eggs on the fresh graves of their deceased loved ones—all, no doubt, to ensure the resurrection of the deceased by the potent magick of the egg.

Among the earliest examples of the association between eggs and graves are the decorated ostrich eggs found in the neolithic graves of pre-dynastic Egypt. It is very unlikely that these eggs, decorated with incised lines depicting zigzags and highly stylized animals (including the great horned ibex and the ostrich) were placed in the graves as food for the deceased, because apparently they were emptied prior to being placed in the graves, as the neat holes in the eggshell suggest. Also, some graves contain models of eggs rather than actual ones.

The Druids dyed eggs scarlet in honor of the Sun, using furze (gorse) blossoms or possibly madder root. But there can be little doubt that the practice of dying and decorating eggs came—like the Goddess herself—from Eastern Europe. Here, in countries like Rumania, Czechoslovakia, and most notably the Ukraine, the art of coloring and decorating eggs in Spring is unsurpassed. It is also in these countries, including northern Greece, that ancient cultures (ca. 7000-5000 B.C.E.) worshiped a Bird Goddess. She was sometimes portrayed with the head of a bird, and at other times with the long legs of a marsh bird. As a Mother Goddess, the milk of her breasts was associated with life-giving rain. As a Grain Goddess, she was associated with the baking of sacred bread. And she was also portrayed as holding a snake, centuries before the Minoan Goddess. The numerous figures of this most ancient Goddess, and the miniature temples and shrines dedicated to her, are frequently decorated with lines, V shapes, and chevrons, that are still today inscribed on eggs in Eastern or Old Europe. In Hungary, designs were scratched onto eggs that had been dyed red; designs with names like the White Horse, Goat's Claw, the Snake, and the Horseshoe. In Hungary, too, a 1300 year old burial of a woman was discovered in which the woman was buried with an inscribed egg in her hand.

Pysanky were and still are considered to be magickal amulets of fertility, protection, and prosperity. Magickal designs of very ancient origin are inscribed on pure white eggs in beeswax, using a tool called a "kitska" which is heated in a candle flame. The process itself is a magickal ritual. (For further details on designs and process, see *Wheel Of The Year*, and my article in the Summer 1987 *Circle Network News*.)

Pysanky are not the only magickal eggs in the Ukraine. There is another type called "Krashanka." These are the eggs that were hard-boiled, dyed in a color and ritually eaten at sunrise on Easter Sunday. Krashanka comes from the word "krasha," meaning "to color," while Pysanky comes from the word "pysaty," meaning "to write" (referring to the designs inscribed on Pysanky). Krashanka are hard-boiled and intended to be eaten, while Pysanky are kept raw, to preserve their fertility magick.

Krashanka are dyed a single color, usually red, while Pysanky are inscribed and dyed in designs of several colors.

SOME TRADITIONAL UKRAINIAN EGG DESIGNS

	RAM'S HORNS	FERTILITY GOD
	TRIANGLE	THE GODDESS
	8-POINTED STAR	THE SUN GOD
	SOLAR CROSS	UNITY
	DEER	PROSPERITY & FERTILITY
	MEANDER	FIRE OR WATER
	MEANDER	WATER
	SUN WHEEL	THE SUN GOD
	RAKE	AGRICULTURE
	WOLVES' TEETH	STRENGTH & WISDOM
	PUSSY WILLOW	SPRING

BIRD
THE BIRD GODDESS

OAK TREE
THE GOD

ROOSTER
THE SUN GOD

ENCIRCLING BANDS
THE ETERNAL CYCLE OF BIRTH, DEATH & REBIRTH

These Krashanka are closely associated with a race of Spirits called "Blazhenni," or "Kindly Ones," who dwell in darkness in a distant land on the banks of a river that is fed by the rivers of the world. On Eostre's Day, the red shells of the Krashanka were thrown into the rivers so that they would eventually arrive on the banks of this distant island, bringing with them the message that the Sun and the Season of Rebirth have returned. In later Christian times, these Blazhenni became confused with the spirits of children who died before they were baptized.

Another tradition is to place a a single Krashanka on the fresh graves after the burial of a loved one. The original Pagan meaning of this simple ritual is obvious—the egg as a symbol of rebirth insured the return of the loved one to the tribe. Today, if the egg is undisturbed it means that the spirit of the loved one is at peace, but if it is disturbed or missing, it means that the person is in need of prayer—or in the case of a Pagan, in need of a ritual of release.

Pysanky are magickal amulets of protection and fertility. For a barren woman, one with a hen design would be made. For an abundant harvest, eggs with wheat and agricultural design were buried in the first and last furrow of the field. As protection against fire, Pysanky with blue or green meander designs were kept in the home. These were carried around a fire, if one happened to break out, in order to keep the fire from spreading.

Krashanky, too, have magickal uses. Their main purpose was healing by transference. A sick person would wear the egg suspended by a string around the neck, and in this way the egg would absorb evil. Touching a person with a consecrated Krashanka would prevent blood poisoning. An egg under a beehive kept bees from leaving and increased honey production. An egg rolled in green oats was a fertility charm when buried in a field about to be planted. When a new house was built, to appease any spirits that may have been disturbed, and in fact to invoke their protection, amulets of red-dyed Krashanka adorned with tassels of wheat were hung above doorways.

There can be little doubt that the first colored eggs were the speckled pastel masterpieces laid by wild birds. The wide variety of colors, sizes and patterns must have been an inspiration to the earliest people, as well as a welcome food source after long winter months. They also had a variety of natural materials from which to extract natural dyes. Today there are the same materials available. Eggs can be dyed in natural dyes of symbolic colors and decorated with magickal Runes.

Reds can be obtained from madder root or from cochineal (if you don't mind boiling your eggs with insects). Madder root, just 5 or 6 thin sticks of it simmered in a pint of water with 2 or 3 eggs, will yield a soft, flesh-colored pink. The same amount, boiled first and then with eggs added, will yield a deep red purple. Just 5 or 6 pieces of cochineal with a

Pysanky Ritual Tools

pint of water and 2 or 3 eggs will yield a beautiful rose pink. More cochineal will produce a very deep pink. The addition of a small piece of onion skin—about one quarter of the skin of a large onion—to either of the dye-baths will bring the color of the egg as close to a "sacred" red as possible (unless you have furze blossoms).

Yellow is easily gotten from ground turmeric root (available in the spice aisle of almost any supermarket). The smallest amount, perhaps an eighth of a teaspoon, will produce a light bright yellow. More will become an orange color.

A soft orange through apricot and right on to deep rust brown can be obtained from onion skins, depending on the amount used. A handful is more than enough for the deepest color.

Coltsfoot and bracken both yield a soft green. Braken may be a bit brighter. Eggs dyed with these herbs look like pheasant eggs. Again, a tiny bit of onion skin or turmeric will "yellow up" the color for an interesting variation. Carrot tops will produce a beautiful, pale yellow green without the onion skin. Use a handful of the dried coltsfoot, bracken or carrot tops to a pint or so of water, with 2 or 3 eggs.

Crushed blueberries (these will need to be frozen ones from last year) with a splash of vinegar will give a grey-blue color to the egg shells. If left in the dye-bath to cool, the color can become a dark grey-violet.

The outer leaves of red cabbage will color eggs an unbelievable robin's egg blue, if boiled with eggs and a tablespoon of vinegar. Allow the pot to cool for an hour after boiling, then drain the liquid and allow the eggs to stand in it overnight. The incredible color is worth the extra effort, but handle these eggs carefully because the dye is easily scratched off.

The magick of naturally dyed eggs can be greatly enhanced by inscribing them with magickally potent Runes and symbols. This can be accomplished in several ways. The simplest, of course, is to write signs and symbols on the egg with pen and ink, or even a magic marker (pardon the pun). A more natural way that works well on dark eggs—those dyed a deep rust with onion skin—is to inscribe them with a pen dipped in lemon juice or bleach, blotting as you go. This removes the color, leaving the Runes and the symbols white. Some natural inks are the juice of black walnut hulls, the juice of pokeberries, or the yellow-orange juice of celandine stems. The stems can be used as marking pens.

NATURAL DYES

COLOR	HERB	TYPE OF MAGIC	RUNE
GREEN	COLTS-FOOT BRACKEN	GROWTH PROSPERITY	ᚠ
YELLOW GREEN	CARROT TOPS	FERTILITY NEW BEGINNING	ᛒ OR ᛝ
YELLOW	TURMERIC	SUN, ENERGY VITALITY	ᛊ
ORANGE	ONION SKIN	SUN, ENERGY, VITALITY	ᛊ
RUST	ONION SKIN	STRENGTH	ᚢ
RED	MADDER ROOT COCHINEAL	SACRED EGGS	⊕ OR ᛊ OR ✶
PINK	MADDER ROOT COCHINEAL	LOVE AFFECTION	ᚷ
BLUE	BLUEBERRIES	PROTECTION	ᚦ OR ᛉ
BRIGHT BLUE	RED CABBAGE LEAVES	SPIRIT SKY FATHER	ᛏ OR ᛗ OR ᚨ

Once the eggs have been colored and (if desired) marked with the magickal signs and symbols, they are ready to be consecrated. This can be done as part of the Spring Rites, or in a separate ritual, earlier (for instance, if you wanted to bring the magickally charged eggs to a coven meeting to be eaten or exchanged after the Sabbat Rites have been performed). To consecrate the eggs, place them on the altar and surround them with the symbols of the four elements. Hold the athame high, and intone such words as:

> *In the names of the Goddess of Spring (name),*
> *And the ever returning God of the Sun (name),*
> *By the power of the four elements—*
>   *Earth, Air, Fire, and Water,*
> *I do consecrate these eggs.*

Then point the athame at each egg, and make a sign of the pentagram as you visualize the energy flowing from you through the blade into each egg.

> *Now do they contain new life.*
> *In accordance with their signs,*
> *And with my will,*
> *So Mote it Be!*

Now the eggs are ready to be ritually eaten as part of the Spring feast, or exchanged with other coveners to be eaten at a later date.

The Goddess of Fertility was also Goddess of Grain, and so offerings of bread and cakes, as well as those of colored eggs, were made to her. Most European countries have a traditional Eostre bread. In the countries of Eastern Europe, it is a sweet yeast bread made with white raisins, called "babka." It is traditionally served with a sweetened cheese cake adorned with candied violets, called "pashka." In Italy, it is called "pan de Pasque," a sweet bread that has the colored eggs baked into the braided loaf. (While the name "Easter" in the Germanic languages comes from the name of the Goddess Eostre, the word for Easter in Latin languages comes from the Hebrew word for Passover—hence, the word "Pasque" for Easter in Italian.) Italy has several traditional Easter cakes and breads.

Here is a rare recipe for an Italian Easter cookie that features ground almonds. Almonds are sacred to the God Attis, whose resurrection was celebrated annually at the Vernal Equinox. It is made in the shape of an Eostre basket and also contains hard colored boiled eggs.

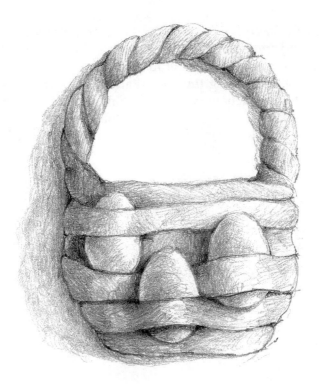

Italian Eostre Basket Cookies

Preheat oven to 375°; combine:
    2 lb. 4 oz pastry flour
    1 1/4 lb. ground almonds
    1 1/4 lb. sugar
    7 1/2 oz. vegetable shortening
    1/4 tsp. ammonia powder (available at bakeries)
    1 tsp. cinnamon
    8 eggs

Mix all ingredients to a medium soft dough. Add water if the dough is too stiff. Spread a 3 oz. piece of dough by hand to form the lower part of the basket (about 6-8 inches in diameter) on a cookie sheet. Place 2 or 3 colored hard boiled eggs on the basket. Add strips of dough to form the basket weave and to hold the eggs in place. Make 2 rolls, 1/2 in. by 12 in., and twist together to form the handle. Bake to a light golden-brown, about 15-20 minutes. When cookies are cool, decorate them with icing and colored sprinkles.

    Icing:
        4 egg whites
        1 lb. powdered sugar
        5 drops vanilla
        1 tsp. lemon juice

Hot Cross Buns

Among people of Western Europe, it is traditional to eat hot cross buns on Easter Sunday morning. These small, sweet buns are usually decorated with equal armed, or solar crosses made of white icing; but the Pagan Greeks also made offerings of cakes inscribed with the solar cross to several Goddesses. Eos, the Goddess of the Sunrise, was probably among these. Anglo-Saxons too made offerings of cakes incised with solar crosses, and they were worn as amulets and hung in the homes for protection and prosperity. Here is a recipe for hot cross buns:

Hot Cross Buns

    7 or 8 cups of flour
    1/2 cup sugar
    1 tsp. salt
    2 packages of dry granular yeast
    2 cups milk
    1 stick sweet butter
    3 eggs

Combine yeast and sugar in 1/4 cup of warm water, and set aside until doubled in volume. Heat milk to a scald 150°, then let it cool to luke-warm. Add the yeast mixture to the lukewarm milk. In a large bowl, combine yeast-sugar-milk mixture, butter, salt, eggs, and 3 cups of flour.

Beat this with a wooden spoon or mixer until frothy, then blend in remaining flour, a little at a time. For an extra special cross bun, add 1 cup seedless raisins and/or 1 cup chopped candied orange peel. Turn the dough out onto a lightly floured board and knead until elastic and smooth, about 10 minutes. Shape the dough into a ball and place in a large greased bowl. Cover with a clean towel and keep in a warm place until doubled in size (about one hour). Punch down the dough and divide into 18-24 ball-shaped pieces, and place on a greased baking tray, lightly covering them; again, put in a warm place until doubled in size (about 1 hour more). Using the white handled knife, slash two lines on the rounded cakes to form the solar cross, saying words like:

> *By North and South,*
> *By East and West,*
> *By the Goddess (name),*
> *These cakes are blessed!*

Bake these cross buns in a preheated oven at 350° for 30 minutes or until they sound hollow when tapped with a finger. One minute before removing them from the oven, brush white icing on them (a mixture of 1/2 cup of confectioner's sugar and 1 1/2 tbsp. of milk).

The fact that the holiday named for the Goddess Eostre is traditionally celebrated at sunrise services suggests that in ancient times, the Vernal Equinox was a sunrise celebration. This is entirely in keeping with the nature of the Sabbat. In fact, it tells us something about all the Equinoxes and Solstices, and that is that each is, or should be, celebrated at a specific time of day. The Vernal Equinox at sunrise, because it is a celebration of new beginnings, the re-awakening of nature from its death-like sleep of winter, and the very moment when the time of light becomes greater than the time of dark. For this reason too, the rooster, whose crow announces the dawn, was sacred to the Sun God Apollo.

The Summer Solstice is best celebrated at high noon, the moment when the sun is at its peak of strength and power. High noon, of course, the moment midway between sunrise and sunset.

It would be most appropriate to celebrate the Autumn Equinox at the setting of the sun, in honor of the beginning of the dark time of the year. And, the darkest night of the year, Yule, should be celebrated at midnight, the darkest hour. As mentioned before, the major Sabbats are celebrated at midnight.

The Wheel of the Year is in time what the Magick Circle is in space, and both represent the Goddess and the eternal cycle of Birth, Death, and Rebirth. And the little cakes inscribed with the equal-armed cross symbolize all of these and the most potent magickal amulet of all—the necklace of the Goddess.

The necklace in some ways corresponds to the jewels of Ishtar, the Sumerian/Babylonian Goddess of Fertility and Resurrection, who had to remove her jewels as she descended into the Underworld, but had them returned to her upon her ascent. The Anglo-Saxon Goddess, too, had to spend time in the Underworld to obtain her necklace—since that is the realm of the Dwarfs in Anglo-Saxon and Norse myth. Among the jewels of the Goddess Ishtar is the "girdle of birthstones" that she wore about her hips. This is the probable origin of the practice of wearing birthstones, and it predates any Biblical reference to birthstones by almost 1,000 years. Considering, too, that the girdle was worn about the hips, there can be little doubt that the girdle of birthstones was an amulet of Birth and Rebirth. Its association, then, with Women's Mysteries would likewise associate it with the Moon, another symbol of the Goddess Ishtar, rather than the Sun and its relationship to the signs of the zodiac, and so the stones would be thirteen in number rather than twelve.

As every ending is a new beginning, so is the reverse true. As we move with the turning of the Wheel into the time of Light and Life, so do we move away from the time of Darkness and of Spirit, and from those in Summerland who had come to join us from time to time, to share the warmth and companionship of our winter evenings by the fire during the long, dark months that are now coming to an end.

One night before the Vernal Equinox, light violet or purple candles and place them in the window, in the place where at Samhain you lit Jack-o-lanterns to invite the Spirits. Burn patchouli incense and carry it slowly through all the rooms of your home. If you feel that it is warranted, have an Ouija board or wine glass ready to receive any last messages. Then when you feel that the time is right, extinguish the candles in the windows, and as you do so whisper, "Merry meet again." Then prepare to greet the Spring.

This is the time for the blessing of seeds that are to be planted in the earth, and which have lain dormant through the dark half of the year since the Autumn Equinox. As you prepare for the rites of Spring, gather together the seeds which have been stored, some in the cool darkness of the cellar, some in the airy dryness of the attic, and place them in a basket or other container. This can be kept beneath the altar during the ritual where the seeds will be charged with the magickal energy of the celebration, or where they can be easily reached to be placed on the altar for a specific blessing such as the one given in *Wheel Of The Year*.

After the ritual—whether the seeds have been blessed, or have just absorbed energy by their presence in the Circle—put them aside in a suitable place until the New Moon, and all danger of frost is passed.

As the Circle is being prepared for the ritual of Spring, let each object and ornament be of magickal significance appropriate to the season. Pussy willow, being a willow, is a plant that has long had associations with Witchcraft, as well as with Spring. It is ideal for adorning the altar at the Vernal Equinox. The Circle itself may be adorned with bowls and baskets of colored eggs, some dyed with plant materials in soft shades of natural hues and intended to be eaten; others inscribed with Runes or the intricate and powerful patterns of the Pysanky, intended to be kept as charms or amulets. On the altar a plate of round cakes bearing the solar cross, or cakes formed in the shape of a basket containing eggs might await the blessing, and become part of a feast following the ritual. The Lady might be represented on the altar at this rite by a figure of a rabbit. It might even be made of white chocolate.

In other times, Sabbat rituals were followed by feasting. Today, some covens have potluck suppers following their rites. In any case, there are some foods that are traditionally associated with certain Sabbats. The traditional Easter ham, whether fresh or smoked, is probably just as Pagan in its origins as colored eggs, hot cross buns and Eostre bunnies. Among the ancient Celts, warriors after a battle celebrated by feasting on roast boar, competing among themselves to see who earned the "hero's portion." Archaeologists are uncertain as to what exactly the hero's portion was. Obviously, it was something a pig had only one of—the head or the tail. As there is nothing to eat on the tail, and considering that right down to the seventeenth century, large pewter plates called chargers were produced to hold the hog's head during holiday feasts, the head is probably the hero's portion. Especially since the Celts also believed that the head was the seat of the spirit, and that the boar or sow was sacred to the Goddess.

Among Germanic people, it was believed that those who died in battle were taken to Valhalla by the Valkeries to feast each night on a magickal sow that was reborn each morning. The resurrection of the pig at sunrise certainly suggests a connection to the Vernal Equinox, one that is confirmed by the tradition of the Easter ham.

When the feasting is finished, and the ham and the hard boiled eggs, the babka and the kielbasa, the pane de Pasque, hot cross buns, pizza rustica and jelly beans have all been eaten, gather up the fragments of the colored eggshells and take them to a place where the river flows. Then toss the colored fragments into the flowing water, chanting words like:

> *Rivers flow and grasses grow,*
> *The Goddess has returned!*

Reflect for a few moments on the eggshells on their journey down stream to a river, the river to the ocean, to a misty Land of Faery far beyond.

Wild Bird Eggs

There is a wonderful Gypsy folktale from Eastern Europe that tells of a young girl who was very curious. One day she was eating an egg on the bank of a river. She left the eggshell on the river bank and watched to see what would happen. Eventually, a Witch came along. Finding the eggshell, the Witch intoned a magick word and the eggshell turned into a boat and the Witch sailed away. The young girl remembered the word and obtained another eggshell. She spoke the magick word, and instantly it too turned into a boat and the young girl sailed away. She returned with exotic flowers and rare fruits which she sold to her neighbors. Each night she sailed away and returned with some treasure, and she became quite wealthy. But, there was a jealous woman in the village who followed her one night. When the young girl returned, she left the boat on the river bank. As soon as she was out of sight, the jealous woman got into the boat. But she did not know the magick word so the boat would not budge. The woman cried out in anger, "In God's name— MOVE!" and the boat immediately turned back into an eggshell and sunk, with the woman inside.

On a remote island in the South Pacific a strange annual ritual had been performed for hundreds of years. Here, among rocks carved with strange figures, half bird, half human, the migratory frigate bird lays its eggs of the season. Each man competed in place of his shaven-headed master. The master of the man who found the first egg ruled the island for one year. Little is known about the Bird-Man Cult. Its rituals were abolished by Christian missionaries at the end of the eighteenth century. The island was discovered (by Europeans) on Easter Sunday morning of 1722, and named Easter Island. In her mysterious way, the Goddess of Spring made this sacred island a monument to her ancient and almost forgotten name. The mariners who discovered it had sailed around the world—and the circle was complete.

The frosty nights of March warm into April mornings, the misty mornings that promise sunny afternoons, and the gray mornings that promise rainy days. But the gentle rain of April forces the herb garden into luxurious growth, and brings the promise of flowers in May.

Chapter Three
BELTANE

BELTANE

In the orchard, the pink and white blossoms of the apple trees buzz with insect activity, and the green grass is a polka-dot pattern of dandelion flowers. The downy buds of the rowan tree open into leaves that will shade the woodland wildflower garden during the hot summer months that lie ahead. Here, delicate blossoms of bloodroot have faded, and Virginia bluebells, red columbine and white trillium now bloom in their turn. April rains have forced the growth of many of the herbs and each is greeted like a dear old friend after a long winter's absence. Sitting on the hillside, with our sheep grazing contentedly nearby, looking down at the rooftops of our home and the neighbors' pastures beyond, I seem to recall another time—when the mighty Gods participated more directly in the affairs of mortals than they seem to do today.

May is the time when all of nature comes alive and the Spirits of Nature are most active, and for this reason I believe it is the time when Faeries are most likely to be seen. It was in the month of May that as a child I saw Faeries. I remember that it was when the Canada May flowers were in bloom. But who are these creatures of the other world that we call the Faery? They seem to be many things to many people.

One definition or explanation is that the Faery-folk are, or were, an ancient race of people who lived in the British Isles long before the Anglo-Saxons or the Celts arrived. These people, somewhat smaller in stature than the Anglos, Saxons, Celts, and Romans, lived in round, sod-covered huts that were partially underground. They hunted, and probably practised a shamanistic form of religion, and stained their bodies blue with juices extracted from wild woad. But surely it was not the Picts that I saw in the last vestiges of a virgin oak forest, in suburban New Jersey, in the late 1950's (although, if there were a lost tribe of Picts lurking in New Jersey at that time it certainly would have been among those ancient oaks). Still, there seems to be a connection between those ancient tribes of mortals and the Faery-folk.

In some of the early testimonies given during the persecution known as the Witch Trials, there is occasionally found a reference to "Witches of the Air." These seem to be regarded as being distinctly different from "Earth Witches," or living human beings. These Witches of the Air are also described in the same terms as Faeries.

The crowning of the May King and Queen.

Another class of entities that are also often grouped together with Faeries are ghosts and spirits. For the purposes of this chapter, and for that matter throughout my writing, I will use the term "ghost" when referring to the spirit of a deceased person, one who is temporarily between incarnations. One of the reasons for the confusion, I think, is the association of the Wiccan term Summerland, or dwelling place of the spirits of the dead, with the Land of Faery, or the dwelling place of Spirits (as opposed to spirits). It is very likely that this is the same place, but these entities are different. The Faeries referred to in Faery-lore are not the ghosts of the recently deceased, but a different class of entities altogether.

Most Wiccans seem to agree that everything in nature has a spirit. The group of entities to whom I am referring when I use the term "Faeries" is any one of an infinite number of Nature Spirits, including the consciousness or spirits of plants, animals, trees, springs, wells, stones, storms, etc. In other words, the astral bodies both of physical, living entities, and also the non-incarnating forces of nature, somewhere between the physical plane and the Gods themselves. What we call Faeries are often the "astral bodies" of living entities that dwell on the Earth Plane, and so their realm of activity is the Astral plane (to use a term popular in many branches of occultism). But the Astral plane is most likely Summerland.

The connecting thread between all of these different concepts of definitions of Faeries is the shamanic religion. In ancient times, when shamanism was the prevalent religion, it was the shaman or priest who worked for the benefit of the tribe or village by traveling to the spiritual or Astral planes in order to gain magickal information, or to make the necessary arrangements with the spirits of hunted animals. (This last function, I believe, degenerated with the advent of civilization and agriculture into the practice of human and animal sacrifice.) The shaman was able to leave his body through trance and ritual, and travel either to the world of Nature Spirits or to the Underworld of the Dead.

So, the Land of Faery is inhabited by Nature Spirits which are the astral bodies of plants, animals and even minerals, by the spirits of non-incarnating entities; by the spirit bodies of people who are traveling on the Astral plane through the practice of meditation, ritual, or other shamanic devices; and in all likelihood, by the spirits of the members of ancient races such as the Picts, who have gone beyond the need to reincarnate. The Astral world or Land of Faery occupies the same space as the physical world and is every bit as real. Unfortunately, modern civilization recognizes only one side of reality and denies the other, and since we are all part of this modern civilization, whether we like it or not, we have all learned to focus primarily on the material side of life. This focus on the material is evident in many subtle ways. For example, most of us

SOME OF THE DIFFERENT KINDS OF FAERIES
~ WHERE THEY DWELL & WHAT THEY DO ~

FAERIES ELVES	FORESTS FAERY HILL & RINGS FIELDS & WILD PLACES FLOWER GARDENS	DANCE & PLAY. KNOW THE MAGICKAL SECRETS OF HERBS, STONES & ANIMALS. SEE THE FUTURE.
GNOMES TROLLS DWARFS	IN CAVES & MINES UNDER BRIDGES HOLLOW HILLS	KNOW THE LOCATION OF PRECIOUS GEMS AND METALS AND HOW TO FORGE AND FORM THEM.
BROWNIES KOBOLDS	HOMES AND COTTAGES	HELP & PROTECT THE FAMILY. DO CHORES BY NIGHT.

~ AND WHAT THEY ARE CALLED IN DIFFERENT COUNTRIES ~

ENGLISH	FAERIES
IRISH	SIDH
SCOTTISH	SITHS
CORNISH	PIXIES
FRENCH	FEE
GERMANIC	ELVES, TROLLS
ARABIC	DJINN
HAWAIIAN	MENEHUNE
ITALIAN	IMPS, FAUNS
GREEK	NYMPHS, SYLPHS
UKRAINIAN	BLAZHENNI

are right-handed, and thus the left hemisphere of the brain is dominant. It is the left hemisphere that deals with logic, math, language, etc. while the right deals with emotion and intuition, and therefore the spiritual side of life. In a left-handed person, the reverse is true. This imbalance is also reflected in our politics—right or left; conservative or liberal. Science focuses on the physical while modern religion preaches that the material world, or nature, is what we are here to rise above. Science and religion are at constant odds with one another and neither has the wisdom to see that they are each dealing with a different side of reality.

The only way to begin to accomplish this is for each of us on the Pagan path to come to know the world of the Faery. This will take a lot of magick. Happily, there are several charms and methods still preserved for us.

A Tyrolian charm to see Faeries is to gather together a sprig of rue, a broom straw (this might be a straw from a besom, or a bit of the plant called broom), agrimony, maidenhair fern, and a sprig of ground ivy. Bind them together with a green yarn, or tie them into a pouch with green yarn and wear this next to your heart.

To make an oil that, when applied to the eyelids, enables one to see Faeries, place in a small glass jar three buds of hollyhock, three flowers of marigold, three sprigs of thyme, three buds of witch hazel and grass from a Faery Ring, or "throne." Cover these herbs with olive oil and allow them to stand in the sun for three days before pouring off the oil into a clean bottle for storage or until it is needed.

When the charm has been made and the oils has been prepared, it is still necessary to go to a place that Faeries have been known to frequent in order to see them.

The first place that comes to mind, of course, is a Faery Mound.

These exist all over the British Isles and much of Northern Europe. They are of two types, the burial Mound and the sod-covered dwelling. The tales of Manawydan, Son of Llyr, in the *Mabinogion* (a collection of Welsch myths and tales which were written down in the 13th century, but which came from a much older oral tradition), begins with Manawydan and Pryderi going to a Mound because they were told that if they sat there they would see a beautiful lady on horseback. They did so and a thick mist descended upon them. When the mist cleared, everything seemed to be the same as it had been before, but there was no one to be seen. Everyone had vanished. "Where they had once seen flocks and herds and dwellings, they now saw nothing . . . only the houses of the court, empty, deserted, uninhabited." Manawydan and Pryderi wandered about until they came to Ireland, where they had several adventures before returning home.

In 1690, during the height of the Witch Trials, the Reverend Robert Kirk of Aberfoyle, Scotland, began to visit a Faery Mound called Doon

Hill, just beyond the graveyard of his little church. After many nightly visits to the Mound, this conservative and well educated man wrote a detailed account of his visits to Faery Land, entitled *The Secret Commonwealth of Elves, Fauns and Fairies*. One night a few years later, Kirk, clad in his nightgown, walked out to the Faery Mound and fell down, apparently dead. Legend tells us that although he was buried, the coffin was empty because his body vanished into Faery Land.

It is said that if one falls asleep on a Faery Mound, one will sleep for one hundred years. Before giving up the hope of finding Faery Mounds in North America, remember that the ancient ancestors of modern Native Americans also built mounds. Both the Hopewell and the Mississippian people were mound builders, and the mounds they built were either ceremonial platforms or burial mounds like those of Europe.

But these are not the only mounds in North America. When I was nineteen years old and a student in art school, two friends took me to see some structures that they had discovered in the woods behind their home. Both structures, as I recall, were of very old, low-fired brick with entrances made from native red sandstone cut into wedge-shaped blocks to form a perfect arch. But most importantly, both of these structures were entirely covered by a circular mound or hill of soil that had obviously been placed over them after they had been built. The mounds were approximately eighteen feet in diameter and ten to twelve feet in height. The second, larger mound, a short distance from the first, had a huge oak tree growing on top of it, so it had to be, we figured, about two hundred years old, at least. And that would put it right in period with some of the historic old, pre-Revolutionary houses in the area which were built of the same sandstone. We thought that they might be some sort of ovens (although there was no trace of fire) or root cellars. But regardless of their original function, they are still mounds, and quite covered by vegetation, and they are in the very same forest where, a decade earlier, I had seen the Faeries.

Tradition tells us that, aside from Faery Mounds or Faery Hills, the type of place we are most likely to encounter a Faery is in a Faery Ring. These Rings, unlike those of standing stones, are not at all confined to Northern Europe and the British Isles. They are likely to spring up anywhere. Like the mounds of Europe, though, they are of two types. One is the ring of mushrooms, some as large as dinner plates, that appear suddenly, overnight. The other, more subtle type, is a ring of grass that appears to be thicker, deeper green, more lush and faster growing than the rest. This Faery Ring of grass will not disappear when mowed. Instead it will remain a deeper green, and in a few days be taller and thicker again than the grass around it. But like the Faery Ring of mushrooms, the rings of grass are caused by an underground network of the fibrous parts of fungi called "mycillium." There is another term, the Faery Throne, and

Ring of Mushrooms

this is probably the small, circular (one to two feet in diameter) tufts of a certain type of grass that sheep will not eat, and so it will grow quite luxuriously in an otherwise well-clipped pasture.

But rational explanations aside, there is an aura of magick and mystery about these Faery Rings—and there is a very real connection between mushrooms and Faeries. Once again the connecting link is shamanism. The shaman in many different cultures ingested some type of mushroom as part of a ritual that enabled him to enter the spirit realms. When I first started out on the Wiccan path, a Witch told me that eating mushrooms helped to develop psychic abilities. I forced myself to acquire a taste for them, and I think perhaps she was right.

There are several types of trees that are traditionally associated with Faeries, too. The first of these is the oak, and in particular, a hollow oak. For this reason, acorns can be worn as amulets to attract Faeries. The oak to ancient European people symbolized all of the attributes of the Horned God, or Spirit Father, and for this reason the trees were held sacred, considered to be a link between this world and the world of the spirit. Probably for this reason, too, these ancient people used hollow logs as coffins for their dead nobility, and it is these same coffins that lie at the heart of many of the burial mounds called Faery Mounds. Also, it was on a fallen oak log that I used to sit when I saw Faeries.

An Ancient Oak

A Witch Broom Tree

The hackberry tree is subject to bacterial disease which causes it to grow tufts of twigs called witch brooms. These witch brooms really resemble the traditional Witch's besom, and small ones make wonderful amulets that can be used as links to Faery realms. But, above all, a hackberry tree, or any other tree for that matter, that grows a witch broom is traditionally a place where Faeries may gather. Yet most all the trees associated with Faeries, probably the strongest association is with the hawthorn tree. This tree is also known as whitethorn or may, and its pink and white blossoms were used to adorn the ancient altars from Greece to Ireland. In the British Isles it is often found growing near sacred springs or wells, and the Faeries associated with these trees will, under certain circumstances, grant wishes.

The traditional way of making a wish at a hawthorn tree is to leave strips of cloth, symbolizing your wish, in the tree. At the time of the Full Moon, go to a hawthorn tree and bring with you strips of colored cloth, choosing the color appropriate to each wish you want to make. Stand silently before the tree and attune yourself to it. When you feel you have attracted the attention and approval of the spirit of the tree, take one colored strip of cloth at a time and hold it, concentrating on your wish and visualizing a logical way in which it might come true. Then, with the words appropriate to the color and the wish, hang the cloth in the tree by piercing it on one of the thorns and chanting your wish.

For protection, use a blue cloth and words like:

> *With this thorn will this charm*
> *Protect my family from harm.*

For prosperity, use a deep bright green and words like:

> *Spirit of this hawthorn tree*
> *Grant to me prosperity.*

For love and romance, use pink or rose strips of cloth and chant words like:

> *Charm of rose and hawthorn tree,*
> *Bring my true love unto me.*

To attain occult knowledge, use deep purple or indigo cloth and intone words such as:

> *In darkest night the hawthorn tree*
> *Reveal to me a mystery.*

Make as many wishes as you like, being sure to use different words each time so that each wish is a separate ritual—and make the wording as specific as possible for each enchantment. If you have an urgent need, use several strips of the same color, repeating the same chant again.

Wish Cloths Hanging On A Hawthorn Tree

When you have finished, leave an appropriate gift for the spirit of the tree. And when your wish has been granted, go back to the tree with an additional offering as a "thank you."

In some traditions, colored eggshells are also hung on hawthorn trees as tokens of wishes made; and since hawthorn trees often grow near sacred or wishing wells, this sounds remarkably like the Ukrainian tradition of setting colored eggs adrift in streams and rivers as a sign to the Blazhennie, or "Kindly Ones," that spring has returned.

Forests and wild places far from towns and cities have always been regarded as places likely to be inhabited by Faeries and Nature Spirits. The shaded forest floor, clad in hay scented fern, where the tall, stately oaks give way to the silver barked beech, and humming birds sip nectar from the wild pink rhododendron; or the moss-covered banks of a woodland pool, where sunning turtles slip silently from a log, seeming to vanish at the sound of an approaching footstep—only to re-appear on the log again, as if by magick—here are Faeries, their presence to be sensed, if not seen. And like trees, there are certain plants more often associated with them than others. Ferns and Faeries naturally go together, but there are some ferns with even stronger associations than the rest. One of these is bracken, whose large, lacy triangular leaves form a second canopy just two feet above the floor of the yule scented pine forest. The sight of the scarce maidenhair fern, so named for its thin, black stems that support the semi-circular fronds of primitive leaflets, almost always bring the Faery-folk to mind. And moonwart, a fern so rare as to seem more mythological than material, is also associated with Faeries. Ebony spleenwort and maiden hair spleenwort, both of elfin proportions, also seem to belong in this group. Mushrooms, toadstools, liverworts, and club mosses, all convey the feeling of the Faery-folk.

Among the flowering plants, the large waxy, umbrella-like leaves that hide the blossoms of the May apple, the green-white flower spikes of snakeroot that seem to sway and meander above the forest floor on invisible stems, and the tiny flower clusters and heart-shaped leaves of Canada mayflower that perfume the air and carpet the floor of the forest, all seem to be especially favored by the Faeries.

Not only the forests, but also the moonlit meadows, springs, wells and streams, all have resident Nature Spirits. Certain type of Faery-folk prefer certain environments. For example, trolls are believed to dwell under bridges, while dwarfs prefer caves and mines.

If you don't wish to visit a Faery forest, but prefer to create an environment for them in your own backyard, begin gathering and planting trees, ferns, and wildflowers that you feel are especially appropriate and best adapted to the type of environment you are able to provide. Many nurseries and mail-order catalogs sell a wonderful variety of less common and endangered species of wild flowers and ferns. Wood chips, straw, pine needles, and leaves all are excellent mulches, and certain ones are necessary to certain plants; but they also encourage the growth of some strange and wonderful mushrooms that the Faeries might find attractive. A piece of moss-covered log will also do this.

Once the garden has been started, you might want to ritually dedicate it as a Faery garden sanctuary. Begin describing the boundaries of the garden with an athame. Then sprinkle the perimeter with a branch of fir dipped in salted spring water. Finally, describe the boundaries of the garden with a stick of burning incense, which can be left in the ground to burn out afterward. Then with a wand of hazel slowly walk about the garden and greet each species of plant with words like:

> *Spirits of the Jack-in-the-Pulpit*
> *I welcome your presence in this garden.*

Feel your love flow from your heart, down your arm and out through your wand, directed toward the plant. Address each plant (or grouping of plants) tree and stone, this way being sure not to overlook any because it is said that Nature Spirits are easily offended. You might wish to conclude the ritual with words like:

In the name of the Goddess
(most of the names of the Goddess in her aspect of
Goddess of the Moon are also names of the Queen
of the Faeries)
And the God (in his aspect of Lord of the Greenwood),
I declare this garden a sanctuary
For the Spirits of Nature
And the Children of the Gods.

It would then be appropriate to leave a gift to attract the Spirits; cookies, soda, ale, or cream are all appreciated. So are bright and shiny things like rings or beads. Certain stones, too, are favored by Faeries. Moonstone (feldspar) and quartz crystals, and especially the twin crystals of staurolite that form perfect solar crosses (called Faery crosses) are attractive to Faeries. Selenite, named for the Moon Goddess Selene, is also a favorite of Faeries. It is the crystal form of gypsum from which plaster is made, and these crystals grow in caves. Selenite is the only mineral that habitually forms curved crystals. Wearing these stones as amulets also opens a channel that might help one to see Faeries.

A Troll Bridge

Another environment suitable to Faery-folk is a dollhouse. I had one as a child and knew it to be inhabited by Spirits. For that reason, I would never have dolls in the dollhouse. They would have been an invasion of privacy. When I was about twelve years old, my mother gave my dollhouse away. Somewhere she got the ridiculous idea that I would outgrow such things. I have another dollhouse now, much more expensive and once again it is inhabited by Spirits, especially the attic and the kitchen.

If you have a dollhouse or other such miniature environment, you have a perfect place where you can meet the Spirits on their own territory. Here is a fun exercise to try: Light candles in front of the dollhouse so that every room is lit by them, even if it is electrified. Then sit on a comfortable chair very close to the dollhouse so that it is at your eye level. Gaze into each room and imagine what it would be like to sit on the chair or lie in the bed, eat from the dish or drink from the cup. Then close your eyes and let your spirit enter the house, asking, "May I come in?" Listen for an answer and as you move through the rooms be aware of any presence you may encounter. When your visit is finished, blow out the candles and leave a gift for the folks that live in the house. Afterward watch for signs that there is a presence. Obviously, such things as objects being moved would suggest this. Try to learn the entities' likes and dislikes in order to make them happy, and in so doing, befriend them.

But for most of us it is not enough to sense the presence of Faeries. We wish to see them as objective reality. In order to do this, we may arm ourselves with amulets and moonstones and Faery crosses, anoint our eyelids with specially prepared oil, carry herbs attractive to Faeries, and sit within a Faery Ring or forest. But it is still necessary to achieve an altered state of consciousness, because it is on the "inner planes" (or astral, or spirit realms) that real magick takes place, and where Faeries actually exist. But this altered state of consciousness need not be the deep, deep state of meditation sought by Eastern mystics—just a slight shift in focus will do. I have not only seen Faeries with this slightly shifted awareness, I once read an entire album jacket in a busy record store in this state, until Dan interrupted me and pointed out that the album jacket was written entirely in Russian! I prefer to call this state a shifted focus or awareness because it is very much like shifting the focus of the eyes to gaze through something rather than at it, in the same way one gazes into a crystal ball or scrying mirror. For this reason, Faeries are seen with the eyes wide open, not closed.

Once this state is achieved, and assuming Faeries are present, there is any number of ways they might appear. One of the most typical is a tiny pinpoint of blindingly white light. This pinpoint might remain as such, or it can expand in human form to any size, although they usually remain small. They may appear somewhat transparent and seem to float, and they may appear to be part human and part plant, or clad in leaves and petals and butterfly wings; but I believe that the human part of their appearance might have more to do with our perception of them as being like us. At other times, especially in memory, they may appear as clouds or nebulas of millions of tiny pinpoints of light, shifting and shimmering colors of the rainbow. Or, they may appear as a sudden movement seen out of the corner of the eye, or heard as a giggle. Or, they may choose to be seen as a bird or butterfly, in which case they may do something obvious to let you know that they are what they are. Once Faeries have been seen, the next step is to befriend them or gain their trust. The only way to do this is to feel only love and joy for them.

There is much practical knowledge to be gained from knowing the Faery-folk. They have knowledge of all the healing and the magickal properties of herbs, stones, trees and animals. They have what is traditionally called, "The Sight," and can predict the future and in certain circumstances, transmit the ability to others. They are credited with being able to perform incredible feats of magick, often in very little time—suggesting that time in the Land of Faery is different than it is here.

Many years ago, when I was working on my first quilt, I decided that I would like to have it finished by a certain date because we were planning an open house on that date, and I had invited over a hundred people. I really wanted to have the quilt on the bed when they arrived, so every night I worked on the quilt, and every night I quilted one square. Then, two weeks before the date, I counted the number of squares left to do and found that there were fifteen of them, and only fourteen nights left. I quilted as much as I could, but all I could do was one square a night. Each night I counted the squares, and each night there was more than I had time to do. And then, just two night before our open house, I sat down to my quilting frame and counted again and there were only two more squares left to do!

The Faeries also know the whereabouts of buried treasure, precious metals and jewels. But the most valuable knowledge to be gained from the Faery-folk is that they do exist, and that the Land of Faery is every bit as real as the material world.

It might be noted that the magickal abilities of the Faeries are the same as those of Witches, i.e., the knowledge and use of healing herbs, stones, animals, etc.; having "The Sight," or the ability to see into the future; the ability to work magick in accordance to one's will, and the ability to locate hidden treasure or minerals (dowsing or "water witching"). This suggests that either Witches gained their knowledge from the Faeries, or that Faeries and Witches obtain their knowledge from a common source. Most likely, Witches obtained their knowledge and methods by an oral tradition handed down from earlier races or ancestors who had received them directly from the Spirits of Nature. With the coming of the new religion, Faeries were labeled demons and devils, and their magicks evil. (Actually, the word "devil" may come from the Sanskrit word "deva," meaning god or good spirit.) Witches, of course, were condemned along with the Faeries because of their association with them, which was called "intercourse with the devils." Of course, intercourse originally meant interaction, or more literally, "running between," as in travelling between the worlds. Like so many other things, this became perverted by the new religion into copulation with (their) Devil. For this reason, a great number of charms were recommended for protection against the evil magick of the Faery-folk.

No such protection is actually needed, since the Faeries are, in fact, "The Good People." But many of these ancient charms are excellent charms for protection against evil in general.

One such charm is to gather the leaves of elder on May Eve and hang them over the doorway. Though this was a charm to protect against Faeries, elder is a tree favored by the Faery-folk and probably invites their blessings and protection. When gathering the leaves at dawn on the first morning of May, point your wand at the elder bush and say words such as:

> Elder leaves come with me
> Magick as the number three.

Then tie them with green yarn and hang them over the doorway, saying words like:

> Elder over the doorway
> Fortune over the threshold.

Faeries are not at all evil, although they are very playful in a child-like way, and their games might be considered annoying to one who does not love them enough to have patience with their games. Their feelings are also easily hurt due to the innocence of their purely spiritual nature, and their ways of getting even when coupled with their immense magickal power, could seem cruel and vindictive; but their motivations are never evil. Even so, if you have injured the feelings of a Faery, it is said that a charm made of iron is the best protection.

Neither the existence of Faeries, nor belief in them, is confined to the British Isles or Northern Europe. Certain Indians of North America believe in a class of Nature Spirits that inhabit natural hills, sand dunes, and forests. In Africa, there is a class of Nature Spirits closely akin to tree Spirits, who, under certain circumstances, will mislead a man so that he becomes lost in the forest. That this trait shows up in countries as different from one another as Africa and Britian—where a person can wander, lost for hours, pixie-led by the Faeries—should be evidence enough of their reality.

In the Arabian countries, they are the Djinn, and to the Polynesians of Hawaii they are the Menehune who are credited with building ancient structures of unknown history. Here again, like the Faery-folk of Europe, they seem to be thought of at once as an ancient race of mortals and as a class of Nature Spirits who dwell in the forest, perform magick by moonlight, and under certain circumstances, are able to be seen by humans. There is another curious parallel: The Hawaiian name "Menehune" for these little people is very much like "Huna," the Hawaiian word for magick; or "Kahuna," meaning "magician," or more correctly, "shaman." This is identical to the Faery-Witch connection in Europe.

To the ancient Egyptians, the dwarf Bes was the guardian of children and he blessed the home with happiness. To the Romans and the Etruscans, Faeries and Witches alike were presided over by the Goddess Diana or Tanit. The red-capped Italian imps resemble, at least in attire, the gnomes and elves of Northern Europe. Greek myth recognizes all manner of Nature Spirits, including Fauns, Nymphs and Sprites. To the French, they are the Fee, and in the Ukraine and other countries of Eastern Europe they are the Blazhenni, or "Kindly Ones."

Even the Faeries of Northern and Western Europe have many different names and functions. The name "Faery" is an English one; the Irish call them the "Sidh" (pronounced "shee"), and the Scottish call them "Siths." In Cornwall, England, they are also called "Pixies," a name supposed to be derived from the ancient tribe known as the Picts. Pixies are associated with the Earth and Nature, and are believed to live in forests, hollow hills, caves, mines, and beneath the roots of trees. Also, because of their association with the earth and nature, they traditionally wear and are attracted to earth colors: browns, tans, greens, and rust. One group, the Brownies, wear brown (or have brownish skin), and prefer a friendly house or cottage to the forest. If they are treated well (and they don't ask for much, just a bit of bread and some cream), they will make themselves very useful around the house and be very protective of the family. Brownie is a Scottish name, but to the Germans they are "Kobalds, to the Danes, "Nis," and to the French, "Lutin."

In the countries of Northern Europe, the Faery-folk are called Elves, and their function is to inspire and teach the ancient wisdom to those that are capable of perceiving them. They are the Shining White Ones, in contrast to the Dark Dwarfs. Dark Dwarfs are not necessarily evil; they are sometimes called Gnomes and Trolls. While Elves usually dwell in forests, Trolls and Gnomes generally dwell underground, in caves, mines, and hollow hills. They are the shapers and the forgers of things before they appear on the material plane, and they know the whereabouts of mineral wealth and guard great treasures. It was these Dwarfs that forged the necklace of the Goddess.

There seems to be an American version of these guardians of the mines. Called Tommyknockers, they probably originated in the tin mines of Cornwall, England. Today they are believed by some to warn of mine disasters, and occasionally indicate, by their knocking or other eerie sounds, the most profitable places to dig. Still, others believe that they are the ghosts of miners killed in mining accidents, who continue to haunt the shafts and tunnels of the mine.

Some Pagans today consider Faeries as being identified with, or creatures of, the Element of Earth. But this idea was developed by Paracelsus, the sixteenth century alchemist who assigned Gnomes to the Element of Earth, Sylphs to the Element of Air, Salamanders to the Element of Fire, and Undines to the Element of Water. Certainly Faeries are of the earth in that they are Spirits of Nature, and as such are children of the Earth Mother. But the idea of Spirits of the Elements is really more a concept of Ceremonial Magick, not of the Old Religion—and, as I said earlier, the important thing about Faeries is THAT they are, not what they are.

There is a wealth of European folk tales also known as faery tales that still have much to tell us about the Spirits of nature. The first one that comes to mind is the tale of Rumplestiltskin. This Dwarf (Troll or Gnome) came to the rescue of a miller's daughter after the miller had promised the king that she could spin straw into gold. The king declared that if she could do this, he would marry her, but if she could not she would be executed. Rumplestiltskin spun the straw into gold for the girl in exchange for a small trinket. He did likewise on the second night. But on the third night, he agreed to turn straw into gold only in exchange for her first born child. With the straw magickally converted to gold, the king wed the miller's daughter and made her his queen and eventually a child was born. The Dwarf returned to complete the bargain, but the queen could not part with her child. Instead she was given an alternative, that if she could discover the Dwarf's name, the bargain would be broken and she could keep her child. She did, through trickery, learn his name; and she called him by it—"Rumplestiltskin." He became so infuriated at this that he stomped and stomped until he stomped himself into a hole in the ground.

This simple little tale actually tells us a great deal about Faery-lore: first, that Faeries are willing to help people; second, that they are fond of trinkets; third, that they are able to perform wonderful magick—and as in this case of spinning straw into gold, they are able to transform the mundane into the spiritual; fourth, that the third time is the charm; fifth, that this particular Faery, a Dwarf, was of the underground Gnome or Troll variety; sixth, and most importantly in this tale, is that to know a Faery's name is to bind the Faery, or break his spell. (The magick in a name is in its being kept secret, which is why Dan and I use our Craft names only in the Circle.)

A purely American folk tale that still carries with it traces of Faery-lore is the tale of Rip Van Winkle, who, in the days just prior to the American Revolution, wandered off into the Catskill Mountains where he fell asleep. Apparently, he did so on a Faery Mound because he slept for twenty years. While he slept, he visited the ghostly crew of Henry Hudson's ship, The Half Moon, who had apparently become Nature Spirits that caused the sudden thunderstorms of the Catskill mountains and the Hudson Valley by playing their games of Ten Pins.

May in this part of the country is sheep-shearing time, and this is the cause for celebration to a Witch, because both wool and spinning have some significance in magick and Witchcraft. One old charm from Devonshire to cure warts required that the patient bring in a blackthorn, milk from a red cow, and wool from a white sheep. The Witch presumably skewered the bit of wool onto the blackthorn, and then dipped it in the milk with which she then bathed the warts.

Wool is also the easiest fiber to spin and to dye for magickal cords and many other uses. (Cotton and flax are both plant fibers, and so they contain cellulose which causes them to resist most dyes.) Spinning or a spindle, of course, is a symbol of the Triple Goddess of the Moon.

For two days before sheep shearing, the sheep must be kept dry because damp wool dulls the shears (which can then cut and scrape the sheep), so our sheep are kept in their shelter for that time. Then, on the morning of the shearing, they cannot be fed. After the sheep-shearer arrives it is only a few minutes before the entire fleece is removed, and they emerge, lean, sleek white animals, prepared to tolerate the coming summer heat. And so, the sheep-shearing is as much a celebration of their liberation as it is the harvesting of their wool, which will be spun and dyed and made into clothing that will protect us from the cold, as well as many magickal objects.

To begin the celebration, they are let out to graze the fresh green grass on the hillside. We spend the afternoon with them, relaxing on the grass in the shade of a tree, bundles of fresh fleece nearby as I card wool and spin it on the drop spindle. Our meal is a picnic on the grass. Then, when we bring Rowena, Rowan (Buckethead) and Willow in for the evening, we take the bundles of fresh fleece into the house, where we bless them by sprinkling them (lightly, so that they won't get moldy) with salted water, censing them with incense, and encircling them with a lit candle. We also give thanks to Faunas for the sheep and the fleece.

Faunas (Pan to the Greeks) is the God of Wild Creatures, an ancient God who is probably a direct descendent of the ancient and nameless God whose image adorns many an ancient and sacred cave. His twin sister is Floralia, Goddess of Flowers, whose feast day (the Floralia) coincides with Beltane both in terms of the time of year that it was celebrated and in what was being celebrated: the bursting into blossom of all of

Nature. Almost every one of the major Wiccan festivals has a Roman counterpart, which in turn had its origins in Ancient Greece—and no doubt the countries of Old Europe.

Beginning at Imbolc, a festival of fertility in Western Europe, the Roman and Eastern equivalent is the Lupercalia, a celebration where in the Lupercali, the goatskin clad priests of Dionysus (Pan), ran through the streets of the city using goatskin thongs to strike the palms of women who wished to bear children.

In ancient Rome at the time of the Vernal Equinox, the eunuch priests of Cybele held a five day festival during which Attis, the consort of the Great Goddess, symbolically died and was mourned for several days; he was then resurrected, to the great joy of his worshippers. This corresponds to the celebration of the resurrection of all of Nature, and the return of the Sun God at this same time in other part of Western Europe.

As mentioned above, the Floralia of ancient Rome corresponds to the Beltane of Western Europe. It was the time of the celebration of Nature in full blossom, a time to clean and purify the temples and to make offerings of flowers at springs and rivers.

In June, the ancient Romans celebrated the Vestalia in honor of the Goddess Vesta. Vesta is the Roman Goddess of the hearth and her symbol was the sacred flame, so that Vestalia was a festival of Fire very much like the Midsummer Fires of Western Europe.

In August, at the time of the grain harvest, there was a celebration of joy for the reunion of Demeter, Goddess of Grain, and her daughter Persephone, or their Roman counterpart, Ceres and Prosepina. This equates perfectly with the Lammas festival in honor of the Grain Goddess or Corn Mother.

Although the Bacchanalia, the festival of Bacchus, the God of Wine, took place in the Spring, as did the rites of his Greek counterpart, Dionysus, Fall was also a time to honor him when the grapes were harvested and the wine was being pressed.

The final Roman holiday of the solar year was the Saturnalia. The celebration lasted for several days beginning on December 21 and reconciled the difference between the solar and the lunar calendars. Saturn is a God of Death, and is often portayed as carrying a scythe—an image which has carried over into the present day with the symbolism of Father Time, or the old year of New Year's celebrations who makes way for the diaper-clad infant of the incoming year. Zeus is the father of the Gods, but Saturn was the father of Zeus. This suggests an unbroken lineage, in spite of some minor changes, in a religion that began before the Golden Age of Greece, and whose fragments have filtered down to present day celebrations in such symbols as Father Christmas and Father Time.

THE SABBATS & ROMAN HOLIDAYS

WESTERN EUROPEAN SABBATS	ROMAN HOLIDAYS	PURPOSE OF THE ROMAN CELEBRATION
IMBOLC	LUPERCALIA	A FERTILITY RITE
VERNAL EQUINOX	BACCHANALIA	CELEBRATION OF RESURRECTION
BELTANE	FLORALIA	CELEBRATION OF THE FLOWERS THAT PROMISE FRIUT
MIDSUMMER	VESTALIA	REKINDLING OF THE HEARTH FIRES
LAMMAS	FESTIVAL OF DEMETER & PERSOPHONE	REUNION OF THE GRAIN GODDESS & HER DAUGHTER
AUTUMN EQUINOX	WINE HARVEST	IN HONOR OF THE GOD OF THE VINE AND OF RESURRECTION
SAMHAIN	FESTIVAL OF POMONA	HARVEST OF FRUITS & NUTS FOR WINTER
YULE	SATURNALIA	END OF THE OLD YEAR BEGINNING OF THE NEW

In preparation for our own May Day rites, there are many things to be done. The first of these preparations may have begun as early as the pruning season in March, when nine kinds of wood for the Beltane fire were gathered and bundled. The bundle might contain three pieces of each type of wood, and the different kinds might include: birch for the Goddess, oak for the God, fir for birth, willow for death, rowan for magick, apple for love, (grape) vine for joy, hazel for wisdom, and hawthorn for purity and for May. These pieces might be as small as match sticks for burning in a cauldron, or might be large pieces of wood for an outdoor fire. Wood that was cut and collected in March is dry enough to burn well.

For a good sized coven able to celebrate the Sabbat rites outdoors, each coven member might prepare their own bundle for a really spectacular blaze. In any case, wood for the Beltane Sabbat, like the Yule log, should be adorned for the sacred rites. Streamers of white ribbon and bouquets of wild flowers are ideal.

One of the more important aspects of the Beltane rites is the crowning of the May King or Queen. In some traditions, only a May Queen is crowned, but Beltane is a celebration of the Sacred Marriage and so a Queen without a King is not appropriate. Equally important to the Queen is her crown.

One of the keys to a good Pagan ritual is simplicity, and a simple way to make a good crown for the May Queen is to cut up two 12-18 inch branches of apple, which at this time of year is usually in bloom. Put the branches together end to end, so that the two base ends are overlapping each other by 6 inches, and so the tips of the branches are pointing away in either direction. Secure the two base ends together with twist-ties in two places. Then slowly and gently bend the two tips together to form a circle. It may be necessary to crack the wood in several places in order to form a nice circle. Adjust the size by overlapping the branch tips and then secure the front of the chaplet with twist-ties in at least two places. More flowers can be added, if desired, with floral wire, and ribbons might be a nice touch.

For the King's crown, since he represents the God in his aspect as the Lord of the Greenwood, or the Sun God returned, green leaves of the oak or laurel are appropriate. Birch is symbolic of the Goddess, but as it also symbolizes a return from death, birch is also a good choice—or a combination of these. Which ever type of wood is chosen, the King's crown can be made in the same manner as the Queen's.

Probably the most popular object of the Beltane rites is the Maypole. The most traditional Maypole is a fir tree which has been stripped of all but its uppermost branches. It may range in height from a few feet in height to well over a hundred. It was generally cut by the young men of the village on May Eve and erected in the village square to be danced around on May Day. Some Maypoles were left up permanently.

Beltane Altar

Beltane Fire

Not every one today can have a fifty-foot Maypole. For those who, for some reason or another, have to hold their Beltane rites indoors, a pine dowel three or four feet in height inserted in a block of wood and placed on the altar can suffice. Lengths of 1/4 inch of ribbon can be thumb-tacked to the top, and the ends of the ribbon might be adorned with nosegays of Spring flowers. Larger Maypoles for outdoor rituals should be cut a few feet longer than the desired height (approximately 1/4 of this height) in order to have enough of the pole in the ground to stabilize it. Before such a pole is erected the ribbons should be attached to it by tying it just below the tuft of foliage at the top. Each covener might wish to bring a ribbon of a specific color, according to a certain blessing they might wish for; but the traditional colors for these ribbons are red and white. The reason for this might be found in the origin of the May-pole, which is connected to the Spring Rites of the cult of Cybele and Attis. Here an evergreen tree, representing the dead Attis, was wrapped in white woolen cloth and splattered with blood from the slashed arms of the priests of Cybele. This was performed in order to bring about the God's annual resurrection. In this ritual, we have the traditional elements of the Maypole, the evergreen tree wrapped in white ribbons, representing the shroud of death, and red ribbons representing the life-giving blood.

A Laurel Crown for the King of May

The Maypole may have even more ancient ties. To the shaman in just about every culture, there was one tool that was indispensable: it was the staff that symbolized his calling and might be a tree trunk propped up to the smoke hole of his tent. In every case, the wood used was considered to be an offshoot of the World Tree which connected the world of the living with the spirit planes. Possibly for this same reason, branchless trunks of fir trees have been found among the offerings left in the wells that were sacred to the Druids.

The Maypole represents the male principle in the Divine Marriage between the Spirit Father and the Earth Mother. It is also the Witch's broomstick at Halloween, and upon which the Crone rides up the chimney and past the moon to spirit realms. The Maypole at Beltane, and the Witch's Besom at Samhain, stand across the Wheel of the Year from one another, the one symbolizing the male principle in the Divine Marriage, and the principle of Death in Life; the other, the principle of Life in Death.

For these reasons, the erecting of the Maypole should be carried out with ceremony and reverence. Once a tree has been selected, cut down, and had the branches removed, it might be ritually carried as in a procession to the site of the Sabbat rites. Next, a hole must be dug for the pine to be placed in. When it is deep enough, pour an offering of salted water into the opening, with words like:

Earth Mother, may this offering
Prepare you to receive
This symbol of your consort, our Lord.

Next, you might wish to anoint the Maypole itself, using altar oil, or an oil especially prepared for this night. An oil containing myrrh, (artificial) musk and sweet woodruff would be appropriate. Anoint the pole with oil at intervals, making the sign of the solar cross or else the Rune, ⚥ ; and at each anointing intone words such as:

Blessed be this tree,
Vehicle of our Lord
Which shall soon enter
Our Mother, the Earth.

Then, when the Maypole has been erected, light the Beltane fires and begin the celebration. Another way of symbolizing the Sacred Marriage was to place a circlet of flowers over the top of the Maypole. As the ribbons tightened and entwined the pole, the wreath was slowly lowered so that the pole, which is the Lord slowly penetrated the circle of flowers, which is the Lady. Here at Flying Witch Farm, we hold a similar rite: following the Beltane Sabbat, the chaplet of flowers is placed over a stone which we have come to call the King Stone, and which stands at the center of a small garden dedicated to the Horned One. This small standing stone is a sort of permanent Maypole.

Due to its resemblance to the Maypole and all that the Maypole represents, asparagus has been a traditional food for May Day celebrations. But, the plant is not grown in Europe the way it is grown here. In this country, it is simply allowed to grow and the green shoots harvested; but in Europe it is mounded up with mulch which causes the asparagus to grow short and thick, and without chlorophyll so that it is completely white. These shoots are then served in a white cream sauce.

Another traditional part of the May Day feast is May wine or the May bowl. This is a bowl of white wine containing strawberries and sweet woodruff. A recipe is given in *Wheel of the Year*.

When the Beltane fires have burned to ashes and the May bowl has been emptied, it is time to look forward to the season of growth that lies ahead.

All about us Nature flourishes. The hens in their pen preen and dust-bathe in the afternoon sunlight, and a falcon hovers above a newly planted field of corn. A gentle breeze blows the last of the blossoms from the apple trees in a shower of pink and white petals. Slowly, seeds sprout and fruits swell, and slowly our Lord, in his aspect of the Sun God, moves toward the zenith of his path and the height of his power.

The May Queen's Crown on the King Stone

Chapter Four
MIDSUMMER

MIDSUMMER

The wildflower blossoms of May fade in the hay-scented breezes of June, and ferns unfurl giving the shaded woodland garden the lush, green appearance of a tropical rain forest. Along the stone wall, at the back of the vegetable garden, tall spikes of iris stand above clusters of sword-blade leaves. They burst into blossom of every conceivable combination of purple and yellow pigment—and a few too strange to be believed, as exotic as jungle orchids, with names like "Rocket" and "Millionaire," "O Suzanna" and "Ecru Lace." They stand proudly in the noonday sun, while secretly, in the crevices of the stone wall behind them, spiders lie in ambush; or spin silken traps and wait to pounce menacingly on a careless moth or preoccupied gardener.

As the month progresses, the afternoon hours become uncomfortably hot, but evenings are still spent outdoors, on the back porch where fireflies twinkle in the grass and warm animal smells drift down from the sheep pen and chicken coop.

At Midsummer it is traditional to make amulets of protection out of various herbs for homes and animals. Boughs of rowan were hung up over the entrances to stables and cow barns, sheep and goat pens and chicken coops, as protection against any evil magick which might cause harm or disease to the livestock. Today not everyone keeps horses, sheep or cattle, but anyone who has a pet a dog, cat, parrot or toad, may wish to hang a sprig of rowan over their "place" to give the special protection of magick to a beloved pet or companion.

Rue is also an herb of protection. As rowan protects against evil magick, rue protects against poison and disease; although rue itself, if ingested in excess, can be a poison. It is native to the Mediterranean countries of Europe, and was such an important medical herb in Italy that replicas of it were made in silver to be worn as amulets against the Evil Eye. Italian Witches also sewed sprigs of rue into a small pouch along with bits of bread, a pinch of salt and a couple of anise seeds, using a red thread and saying words like:

> Herb of rue, let this charm
> Protect my family from harm.

Gathering Vervain

ANCIENT WAYS

In England, rue was believed to be protection against the spells of Faeries; and Witches in France included it in their flying ointments, but it had to be accompanied by these words:

By yarrow and rue
And my red cap too,
Hie over to England!

Rue is an herb that grows nicely in this country, although it dies in winter. Its medicinal properties, those of an emmenagogue, which stimulates the action of the smooth involuntary muscles, are lost when the herb is dried (but might be preserved by freezing). Its magickal properties for protecting against poison and disease, evil magick and the mischief of Faery-folk, however, are longer lasting, and for this purpose it is traditionally gathered at Midsummer.

An herb that is practically synonymous with Midsummer is St. John's wort. In fact, its name came from St. John's Day, the name given to the Summer Solstice by the Church in an attempt to abolish Pagan celebrations. St. John's wort is ruled by the Sun. Its flowers are the bright yellow that symbolizes the Sun, and the arrangement of its foliage show the four spikes of the Sun Wheel. The plant, too, yields a sunny yellow dye. St. John's wort has the power to bind spirits, and it is traditionally gathered at Midsummer and hung for this protection.

An ancient Chaldean magickal text gives this charm for protection:

Fleabane on the lintel of the door I've hung,
St. John's wort, caper and wheat ears.

Here at Flying Witch Farm, we make little amulets out of a sprig of rowan, a sprig of rue and some St. John's wort. If the St. John's wort isn't ready yet, and it isn't this far up the Delaware, then we use a pinch of herb gathered last year and put it in a little red pouch. This we tie together with the sprigs of rowan and rue using red yarn. We hang one amulet in the sheep's stall and one in the chicken coop, one over the dog's bed and one over the front door with these words:

Herbs of the Sun, work your charm
Protect these animals (or this house) from harm.

As we hang up the new amulets we take down the old ones which are very dry and burn nicely on the Midsummer fire.

Woodbine (woody nightshade or bittersweet) is also hung over stable doors for protection, and Scottish Witches would pass a patient through a wreath of it nine times as part of a healing charm.

There are a number of herbs which are traditionally gathered at Midsummer. Vervain is an herb closely associated with the Summer Solstice, and as magickally powerful as St. John's wort. Its magick is the magick of purification, and it has the power to banish evil or negativity. It is traditionally gathered Midsummer morning with the left hand.

The Greater Key of Solomon contains instructions for making an "aspergillum," or magickal sprinkler, using a sprig of vervain and eight other herbs, including sage, mint, basil, and fennel. But in Pagan times, vervain was usually used alone to dispel negativity and invite joy into the home. The Key of Solomon requires that the herbs be bound with yarn spun by a maiden, but the Pagan knows that the Mother is as pure as the maid, and does not acknowledge the symbolism of the new religion. The aspergillum of the ceremonial magician has a wooden handle inscribed with signs and symbols, but a simple Pagan water sprinkler can be made with vervain alone, or with vervain, rosemary and hyssop, which also have magickal purifying properties. Tie the bunch of herbs together with pure white yarn, spirally binding the stems together to form something of a handle.

This can be used to cleanse and purify objects such as jewelry purchased at an antique shop, or a second hand crystal ball. It can also be used to banish the negative feeling that seems to linger in your home after it has been visited by people with very unhappy attitudes.

Sprig of Rue Amulets
(by jeweler Robert Place of Saugerties, NY)

To use this tool, dip it in a bowl of spring water and sprinkle the article; or walk through the rooms of your home with the bowl of water and a bundle of herbs, sprinkling as you go, and saying words like:

By rosemary, hyssop and vervain
Evil spirits, be gain, be gain!

This is not to be confused with the consecration of the Magick Circle by the Element of Water, which is performed only with a bowl of water and the fingertips. The purpose of this ritual is to charge the Circle with the magick of the Element of Water, not to purify it with the magick of any herbs.

Finally, it is sometimes instructed that after gathering vervain, an offering of honey should be made to the Earth; but in fact, honey attracts ants which could eventually harm the vervain. An offering of water or plant food would be far more appropriate.

Mistletoe, sacred to the Druids (as was vervain), was also ritually gathered at Midsummer. At this time of year, it is without berries and is valued as an amulet of protection (at Yule it is with berries and is an amulet of fertility). Mistletoe was the only creature that could kill Balder, the Sun God of Germanic and Nordic peoples. It is suggested in ancient texts that it has power over life and death. On the day of Midsummer, at high noon, when the God of the Sun is at the peak of his power, the sacred mistletoe was cut in the oak groves of the Druids. As everyone knows, this was done with a golden sickle, and the precious herb fell onto white linen so that its magickal power would not be grounded.

Today many Pagans and Wiccans use a white handled knife to cut sacred and magickal herbs, but the origin of this knife is in ceremonial magick and not in Paganism. As we are in the process of stripping away the masks and disguises of the new religion to reveal the true Pagan face of our own traditions, so we should be removing the concepts and paraphernalia of ceremonial magick, or at least recognizing them for what they are.

A truly Pagan device for the gathering of herbs would be a tiny sickle of brass (bronze), formed in the shape of a crescent moon. The blade could be made easily enough by cutting the crescent blade out of heavy gauge sheet brass available at many hobby shops. The blade need only be about three inches long. The cutting side can then be beveled with files, and finally brought to a sharp cutting edge with a whetstone or an old fashioned knife sharpener. Once the cutting edge has been established, the blade can be inscribed with Runes or symbols, and a wood handle might be added for comfort.

Another would be a blade of flint or obsidian, or of stag antler. This, as well as the blade of bronze, would need to be kept in a leather sheath when not in use to protect its fine, sharp, cutting edge. A quick cut with a

Herbs Drying in the Attic

sharp edge is the most humane way to sever the leaves or sprigs, as it also allows the plant to heal quickly and without infection. In some vineyards, where a great deal of pruning is done, pruning shears are periodically washed in isopropyl alcohol to prevent the spread of bacterial infection.

One final reason for the use of bronze or flint over the white handled knife is the fact that the early instructions for gathering herbs specifically forbids touching certain kinds of plants with iron or steel. Though these instructions are obviously the product of the Iron Age, such instructions have an air of antiquity about them, and seem to suggest a tradition that predates the Iron Age.

Another herb that is traditionally gathered at Midsummer is lavender, whose tiny purple spikes of aromatic blossoms now rise above the dusty gray foliage. Ruled by Mercury, the flowers of lavender are the basis of many an herbal incense blend and bath mixture. The plant was not native to Egypt, but was grown in the temple gardens there and it was burned as an offering by the ancient Greeks. Dried blossoms are still today used to make traditional incense for Midsummer rituals.

It was also traditional to gather the fern seed on Midsummer's Eve for the purpose of making one's self invisible. Ferns, however, are non-flowering plants, and as such, do not have seeds. They do have spores, though, which in a sense are seeds. These are so tiny as to be invisible.

They are contained in tiny organs which are arranged in neat rows on the underside of leaves of certain species of ferns. Gathered on Midsummer's Eve and worn in one shoe (still attached to the fern leaf), they will aid a person to go about unnoticed if they wish to. Also, the root of the male fern with the embryonic leaves still attached, dried over the Midsummer fire, is the "lucky hand" amulet.

An old Anglo-Saxon herbal gives a lengthy poem called the "Nine Herb's Charm." It tells of the virtues of nine of the herbs believed to be the most powerful medicinal herbs of that time. Today the identity of some of the herbs are in doubt. Nevertheless, the first of the nine herbs that the poem praises is mugwort. This is one of the herbs most highly valued by modern Witches for its magickal powers. An infusion of the herb is used to bathe crystal balls, scrying mirrors and some amulets on the night of the Full Moon in order to recharge or enhance their ability to give psychic visions. Little pouches containing mugwort and bay leaves help to induce prophetic dreams. It was also believed in times past that to wear a leaf of mugwort in one's shoe on a journey (or under the saddle, if going by horseback) would make the trip less tiring.

The second herb of the charm is plantain. A common weed today, it was once considered one of the very few herbs that could mend broken bones. It was brought to this country by some of the very first white settlers, and it spread so rapidly that the Native Americans called it "White Man's Footprints"; however, many botanists believe that the plant was indigenous to North America.

Stime is the name given to the third herb of the charm, which has been interpreted as the Moon-ruled watercress. While watercress was eaten by the Romans because it was believed to be a brain stimulant, the Greeks before them considered it a brain subduer.

The next herb in the charm is cock-spur grass, which is still used by some herbalists.

Mayweed is the fifth herb of the charm. It is a type of wild chamomile that prefers to grow in the poorest of soils, where almost nothing else will grow. It has some value in medicine, but it is more likely that the charm in the ancient herbal was referring to chamomile.

The mysterious name "wergulu" is given to the sixth herb of the charm. It has been interpreted as referring to the stinging nettle. If an herb can be defined as a useful plant, then stinging nettle belongs in every herb garden. No herb has had more uses than this one. The fibers of its stems have been spun and woven into fabric to make it more durable, some say even more durable than linen. It has also been made into rope and paper. It has been eaten as a green vegetable and as a soup green. Dried like hay, it has been fed to livestock and is said to increase egg production among hens and milk production among cows. The painful sting of the living plant, when planted as a hedge, however, forms a boundary that few domestic animals will cross. It is the food plant of some of our loveliest native butterflies, including the Red Admiral and the Painted Lady. And the seeds are a favorite food of several song birds. A tea brewed of the foliage is a tonic and a natural insecticide for seedlings in early Spring. It is also a healthful tonic for humans. The root yields a yellow dye for woolens, while the upper part of the plant produces a green dye. It has been used as a poultice to stop bleeding.

The painful sting from the lightest touch of the nettle has caused it to be used in harmful magick, but the sting is lost when the herb is dried.

Apple is the seventh herb named in the ancient charm. Its fruit eaten once a day is said to keep the doctor away, and apples have been used to cure warts in remedies that are more magickal than medicinal. When cut in half horizontally the apple reveals a five-pointed star, and its wood and blossoms have been used in love charms.

The eighth and ninth herbs of the charm, thyme and fennel, are mentioned together. Both herbs have some value in aiding digestion, and both have the property of magickal protection. Thyme also is an ingredient in anointing oil prepared to enable one to see the Faery Kingdom.

Like Samhain, Midsummer's Eve was a time for divining the future, especially for young girls who were interested in marriage. One method was to gather the buds of houseleek and name one bud for each eligible young man. The bud most opened on Midsummer morning predicted the name of the future bridegroom.

In Denmark at Midsummer two sprigs of St. John's wort were set between the roof rafters of a house, and if they grew together there would be a marriage.

In some countries, a plant of orpine was set on the windowsill of a young woman's bedroom on Midsummer's Eve. The next morning, its stalk would point in the direction from which her true love would come.

A method for dreaming true that can be done anytime, not just on Midsummer's Eve, is to gather a bouquet of nine different kinds of flowers, one of each. With the left hand, sprinkle them with oil of amber (i.e., oil in which an amber stone has been soaked). Then bind the blossoms to your forehead (under the night cap) and get into a bed made up with fresh linen. You will be sure to dream true.

As it is traditional to burn nine kinds of wood for the Beltane fire, it is also a custom to throw nine kinds of herbs onto the Midsummer fire. Many of the herbs that were traditionally offered in this way have been mentioned above: St. John's wort, rue, vervain, mistletoe, and lavender. The last one being an especially lovely incense. To these may be added feverfew, a daisy-like flower that, as the name implies, reduces inflammation; meadowsweet, which in ancient times was also called bridewort; heartsease, the tiny three-colored pansy; and trefoil.

There are several plants that in earlier times were called trefoil, and all were sacred to the Triple Goddess. Among these were oxalis (a type of sorrel), clover, and the shamrock. It is said that St. Patrick used the shamrock to demonstrate to the Irish people the three-in-one concept of the Christian trinity; but of course, the Tuatha de Dannan, the Children of the Goddess, were already familiar with the idea.

But it is the clover that is the trefoil of the Midsummer fire. Most clover leaves have three heart-shaped sections, but there is the rare and lucky four-leafed clover that, like the foliage of St. John's wort, or the seed pods of rue, are the four part radial symbols of the Sun Wheel. The four-leaf clover is collected anytime as a lucky amulet:

One leaf for fame, one leaf for wealth,
One leaf for love, and one for health.

But if you find one with five—"let it thrive"; and if you find one on Midsummer's Eve, offer it on the Sabbat fire!

The Nine Herb's Charm tells us something of the healing properties of certain herbs, and the nine herbs for the Midsummer's fire tells us something about the magick of herbs. But they also tell us of the magick of the number nine. Nine is the number of completion. It is the last number of a cycle, the number ten being the beginning of a new cycle, or the same cycle on another level. Nine is also three times three, and three is a number sacred to the Goddess.

The number one is the number of unity, it is often associated with the Sun and the masculine principle in Nature. It also relates to our stage in life as a newborn, and therefore to the Sun and to the Divine Child. The number one, of course, is preceded by the number zero, a circle. The number one is symbolized by a circle with a dot in the middle.

The number two is a number of duality. It has been associated with the moon and its waxing and waning. It also corresponds to that stage in human development when we become aware of others. It represents the Goddess and her consort, and all pairs of complements, balance, and harmony. The number two is symbolized by the solar cross.

The number three is sacred to the Goddess and reflects her threefold nature of Maiden, Mother, and Crone. For this reason, ingredients in a magick charm are often three in number and spells are repeated three times. The third time's the charm. A triangle symbolizes the number three.

Four is the number of the Earth plane, of the four directions: North, South, East, West; of the four elements: Earth, Air, Fire, Water; and of the four seasons: Spring, Summer, Autumn and Winter. It is also the number of the greater Sabbats, and of the lesser Sabbats. The number four is symbolized by the sun wheel or the square.

1	2	3	4	5	6	7	8	9
A	B	C	D	E	F	G	H	I
J	K	L	M	N	O	P	Q	R
S	T	U	V	W	X	Y	Z	

Letters of the Alphabet and Their Numerical Equivalents

The number five is the number of man. It represents the five senses of sight, sound, smell, taste and touch; the five fingers of the human hand, and the five appendages; the two arms, two legs, and the head. It also represents the four elements of the number four plus Spirit, which makes up five and all life, which is represented by the pentagram.

Six is a number of the Goddess because it is a multiple of three, and it is often associated with the Goddess in her aspect as a love and fertility goddess, Venus or Freya. The number six is the total of three and the numbers that precede it, one and two. This process of adding numbers together to better understand their significance is a practice much used in ceremonial magick, but seemingly forgotten in the natural magick of Wicca and Paganism. It was, however, part of the magick of Pagan Europe because the practice of repeating a charm once, then twice, then three times (a total of six), is still a part of many an old European spell, as will be discussed later in this chapter. The number six is symbolized by the six-pointed star, among other things.

Seven is a mystical number, a number of Spirit, and represents the various planes of existence, including the material or Earth plane. It also corresponds to the psychic centers called "chakras," which are associated with points along the central nervous system of the human body. The seventh, or the highest chakra, is receptive to the highest spiritual planes. The number seven also corresponds to the seven days of the week, and one week represents one phase of the Moon, or New to the first quarter, first quarter to full etc., so that the number seven is also a number of the Moon.

The seven days of the week are of great importance to ceremonial magicians, who recommended that certain types of magick be performed on particular days of the week, according to certain planetary influences. While we Pagans and Wiccans may not be as concerned with planetary days and hours as we are with phases of the Moon, it is important to be aware both of the Pagan origins of this tradition, and the names of the days of the week.

The first, of course, is Sunday, which is named for and sacred to the Sun God, and the Sun that symbolizes him. It is a good day for power magick, for health and vitality.

The second day of the week, Monday, is named for the Triple Goddess of the Moon, and this day is sacred to her. It is a good day for intuition and all sorts of magick concerning psychic ability.

Tuesday is named for the Anglo-Saxon and Norse God Tiew, and ancient Father-God or Spirit-Father. Ceremonial magick associates Tuesday, or Tiew's day, with Mars; but he is more closely linked with the Roman Jupiter or the Greek Zeus, the Father of the Gods. Among ancient languages, Z, D, and J are frequently interchangeable, so Zeus is Deus, meaning God. Jupiter is Zeus-Pater, meaning Father-God. D and T are also interchangeable, so Deus becomes Tiew. Tiew's day is best for magick associated with gifts form the Gods, or the kind of money spells usually associated with Jupiter and performed on Thursday.

Wednesday is named for the God Woton, or Odin. Odin is a God of Transformation and Resurrection, and it is he who gives us the Runes. Odin is also a shamanic god, and so his day, Wednesday, is perfect for all kinds of magick (especially shamanism), and anything dealing with the written word.

Thursday is named for the Norse God Thor, the God of Thunder who, with his stormy nature and thunderbolts, superficially resembles Zeus. But he is really an ancient war God more closely linked with Mars and martial attributes of conflict, strife, courage, power and victory. His day, Thursday, is more suited to magick concerning these things than is Tuesday.

Freya, the gentle Goddess of Love, Beauty, and Fertility, gives her name to Friday, traditionally a day of sorrow and tragedy. But this is probably due to the influence of the new religion and the events of Good Friday. For Pagans and Wiccans it should be a day for love spells, fertility charms and "all acts of pleasure."

The seventh day is Saturday, named for Saturn, the Roman God of Death and Agriculture. As a God of Death, it is suitable that he gives his name to the final day of the week. But Saturn is also the father of Zeus, and every ending is a new beginning. Saturday is perfect for magick dealing with new beginnings and firm foundations. Seven is represented by the seven-pointed star.

Eight is a number of power. It represents the Sun and the eight solar Sabbats, the solstices and the equinoxes, and the turning points in between. It is symbolized by the eight-pointed star.

The number nine completes the cycle.

The letters of the alphabet also have numerical value which can be determined by using the chart.

The knowledge of numerology can be applied to the practice of magick in many different ways. For example, the number of herbs or candles to be used for a charm would depend on the kind of magick intended.

Other numbers that have great significance to Pagans and Witches are: thirteen, the number of lunar months in a year, and therefore the ideal number of Witches in a coven; thirty-nine (three times thirteen), and one hundred and sixty-nine (thirteen times thirteen). These numbers are naturally all sacred to the Goddess.

The time of the Summer Solstice is traditionally a time when charms and spells were performed for the purpose of protecting livestock and the barns in which they live, as well as the farmhouse. No one has done so more colorfully than the group of people who have come to be known as the Pennsylvania Dutch. These people, who migrated here in search of religious freedom early in the 18th century, include the Amish, Mennonites, Quakers, Lutherans, Reformed, and French Huguenots. Among the rolling hills of Lancaster and Lehigh Counties, and the deep, haunted valleys of Burks County, they erected the enormous forebay barns, and cleared the fertile farms for their new homes; but they also brought with them from the old countries of the Rhine Valley a system of folklore, magick, and tradition that has been greatly overlooked by many on the Pagan path.

Probably the first thing that comes to mind when the term Pennsylvania Dutch is mentioned is the colorful and beautiful works of folk art known as Hex signs. Incidentally, not all of the Pennsylvania Dutch use Hex signs. The Amish and the Mennonites are "plain folk" who do not ornament their barns, their homes or themselves. It is the "gay folk"—the Lutheran, Reformed, and others—who produce these colorful rosettes enclosed in Magick Circles, to protect their barns and livestock. These Hex signs come in a colorful variety, almost as wide as the designs of the Pysanky, and each symbol has a specific meaning. The six-pointed rosette is for protection, and the five-pointed star enclosed in a circle—a sign more familiar to most Pagans—is a charm for good luck. A four-pointed star is a sun symbol, while the tear shape is a rain symbol. Oak leaves and acorns give strength of both body and character. The eagle, often two-headed, is also a strength symbol, while the distlefink or

A Hex Barn

thistle-finch (gold finch) is a good fortune symbol. The eight-pointed star is for abundance. Hearts symbolize love, while "laced" hearts—those with scallops around them—insure love in marriage. Doves, unicorns and tulips express virtues of peace, purity and faith, hope and charity, respectively. Most of these symbols can be combined with others for more specific meanings. For instance, a sun symbol combined with a rain symbol would be a charm for fertility. Symbols can be repeated several times to multiply their power. For example, a five-pointed star surrounded by five more five-pointed stars between its points is a powerful Hex for luck and successs.

Numbers, too, play a significant part in Hex signs. Basically, three and multiples of it are feminine, while four and multiples of it are masculine.

But the most popular of all Hex signs is the six-pointed rosette for protection. It is the basis of most other Hex signs, and it usually forms the center of other designs. It is also based on a mathematical law which is one of the building blocks of nature: the relationship between the radius of a circle and the circle itself, as seen in beehives, ice-crystals, etc. Here is how the six-pointed rosette is formed: using a compass, draw a circle of the desired size. Then, without changing the radius of the compass, make a mark anywhere on the circle. With the point of the compass on that mark, mark the circle with the radius. Then put the point of the

HEX SIGNS

6-POINTED ROSETTE
PROTECTION

5-POINTED STAR
LUCK

4-POINTED STAR
A SUN SIGN

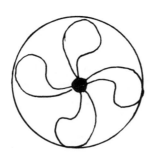

TEAR DROPS
A RAIN SIGN

OAK LEAVES
STRENGTH

DISTLE FINK
PROSPERITY

SUN & RAIN
FERTILITY

ROSETTE & HEARTS
LOVE

8-POINTED STAR
ABUNDANCE

compass on the new mark and mark the circle with the radius again. Continue this around the circle and you will find that the circle will be divided into exactly six parts by its own radius. Now, still without changing the radius, place the point of the compass on any one of the marks on the circle and draw an arc from one point on the circumference, through the center of the circle, to a point on the other. Continue doing this at each of the six points on the circle and you will have drawn a geometrically perfect six-pointed rosette, the basic Hex sign. And this raises an interesting question. The name "Hex" sign, of course, comes from the German word "Hex," meaning "Witch" (today some Pennsylvania Dutch prefer the word "jinx"); but the Hex sign is a six-sided figure, or Hexagram, from the Greek word for six—yet there is no significant connection between the Greek Hex for six and the German word for Witch— or is there?

The number six is a powerful number in the geometry of nature, and as the six-pointed rosette is the basis for most Hex signs, so the Rune "haglaz" ᛉ (ninth in the Rune row) is sometimes referred to as the mother of all Runes.

Not far from the Flying Witch Farm, among the wooded rolling hills and open farmland of Northhampton Co., one hill stands out from all the rest. The name of this treeless rocky peak is Hexenkopf—The Head of the Witch. How this hilltop earned its name, and the mysterious power it contains, is a story that is closely linked to the Hex signs of Lancaster Co., and is even less well known.

Along with the painted Hex signs, the Pennsylvania Germans brought with them a system of healing magick called "Pow Wow." In spite of its name, it had nothing to do with Native American practices. It is entirely Germanic. It is my belief that the term comes from the word "power," because in the South those who have the ability or know some of the charms or incantations are said to have "The Power."

It is also almost entirely Christianized, almost—but not quite. Here and there among the charms, spells, and incantations, there are hints still to be discovered by the serious researcher of the great antiquity of this body of practice.

For example, an incantation from West Virginia to cure burns invokes the guardian angels of the four directions. Another, a cure for worms from Pennsylvania states:

> *Mary, God's Mother traversed the land*
> *Holding three worms close in her hand.*

The image of this Mother of God holding worms, or rather snakes, in her hands immediately brings to mind the Minoan Goddess who holds snakes in her hands, as the word worm was often applied to snakes and serpents, and even dragons. A similar image appears even

HOW TO FORM THE SIX-POINTED ROSETTE

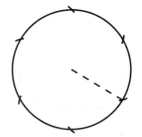

A CIRCLE DIVIDED
INTO SIX PART
BY ITS RADUIS

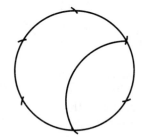

AN ARC DRAWN FROM
ONE POINT ON THE
CIRCUMFERENCE
TO ANOTHER

A GEOMETRICALLY
PERFECT SIX-
POINTED ROSETTE

SOME SIX-SIDED FIGURES

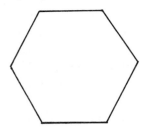

HEXAGON

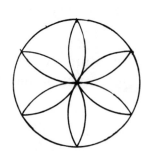

HEX SIGN

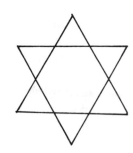

STAR OF DAVID

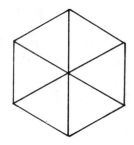

HEXAGONAL
CRYSTAL SYSTEM

SNOWFLAKE

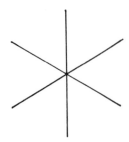

HAGLAZ RUNE

earlier in the Goddess figures of old Europe, and a bit later on a stylized model of a funereal boat in a mound burial in Denmark, ca. 800 B.C.E. In this figure, a Goddess is seated in the center of the boat with a snake on either side of her.

But the incantation continues:

> *One was white, the other was black,*
> *The third was red.*

These are the three colors, red, white and black, which are traditionally associated with the Triple Goddess.

A remedy for fever begins with the words: "Good morning, dear Thursday!" and the instructions that follow explain that the charm must be begun on a Thursday. Thursday, of course, is sacred to the God Thor, and so the "dear Lord Jesus" invoked later in the same incantation was probably originally the God Thor.

When a researcher from the Lutheran Theological Southern Seminary was doing research on this form of healing in South Carolina, he came across a woman who used an incantation that invoked Thor. The incantation worked—to the dismay of the researcher!

Aside from incantations, there are other instructions that link the practice of the Pennsylvania German Pow Wow to traditional Wicca. For example, many of the charms must be applied three times, as in the saying "The third time's the charm." Usually a second application is made a half hour after the first, and a third one made one hour after the second.

Most incantations are followed by the practitioner making the sign of the Solar Cross in the air three times with the hand folded into a fist and the thumb held upward. So an incantation which repeats the magickal number of three times is accompanied by the Pagan sign of the Solar Cross, made the sacred number of nine times.

This marking of the Solar Cross with healing incantations is not confined to the Pennsylvania Germans. In England in 1528, Elizabeth Fotman was accused of Witchcraft and confessed that she took a rod and put it up to the horse belly that "was syke of the botts and made crosses on the caryers horse belly, and that the horse rose up and was hole." Other women accused of Witchcraft were also guilty only of healing animals with their charms.

In the early years of the 19th century, a book was written by a man named John George Hohman who lived in the vicinity of Reading, Pa. The book is entitled *Pow Wows: The Long Lost Friend* and subtitle, *A Collection of Mysterious Arts and Remedies for Men as Well as Animals*. In it, Hohman states clearly that what cures man also cures animals (so the reverse might also be true). The book also states that anyone who owns the book and does not use it to save an eye or limb is guilty of the loss of the limb.

Another curious note in the preface states that the word "Amen" at the end of an incantation means that the Lord will make come to pass that which was asked for. In other words, "So Mote It Be."

Prior to the writing of *Pow Wow*, the charms and spells were passed down by word of mouth and never committed to paper, except in the case of a practitioner who knew too many charms to remember them all—and so wrote "Papers" of them. The methods by which these incantations were passed on verbally is also purely Wiccan. A practitioner (or "user," as they were so called) was only permitted to transmit the knowledge to a member of the opposite sex, and only to three individuals in his lifetime. The penalty for violating these laws was the loss of "the Power." The first of these two conditions is based on the law of polarity and the flow of energy between opposites, a law that has largely been forgotten in recent years due to so much information being transmitted in the form of printed books. But, when a charm is verbally transmitted form one person to another of the opposite sex, much more than just knowledge was given. This is why it is said that only a Witch can make a Witch.

The other part of this tradition, teaching the charms and spells only to three persons in a lifetime, reaffirms the almost forgotten law that states, "power shared is power lost"—one of the primary reasons for secrecy, even in pre-Christian times.

A Pow Wow Doctor's Cabin

Hohman's book is a collection of Gypsy lore as well as Pennsylvania German Pow Wow and folk remedies, and really deserves serious study by anyone on the healing path.

Here are a few of my favorite remedies adapted for Pagan use: to prevent a person from killing game, speak the person's name, and then say:

> *Shoot whatever you please,*
> *Shoot but hair and feathers*
> *And with and what you give*
> *To poor people.*
> *So Mote It Be.*

Here is a charm for worms which begins:

> *Mary, God's Mother [The Mother Goddess] traversed the land*
> *Holding three worms close in her hand.*

The charm ends with these instructions: "This must be repeated three times, at the same time stroking the person or the animal with the hand, and at the end of each application, strike the animal or person's back, once at the first application, twice at the second, and three times at the third. Then set the worms a time to leave, but not more than three minutes."

Some charms give the disease, or spirit of the disease, an alternative place to dwell. This is the secret of the Hexenkopf, the Witch's Head. In the nineteenth century, near this unusual hill lived several Pow Wow doctors. The cabin of one of them still stands on a lonely knoll overlooking a wooded valley. All of these doctors, the Sailors and the Willhelms, used the hill called Hexenkopf as a vessel into which to drive the spirits and creatures of disease.

In ancient times, when tribes and clans gathered to celebrate the Sabbats, there can be little doubt that the telling of tales was a major part of the celebration. Particularly important were the tales that described the nature of the aspect of the deity being celebrated. These kinds of tales, which often come to be known to us in the form of myths and legends, tell us of a different kind of truth than historic truth, and of a reality other than physical reality. One such tale especially appropriate at the time of the Summer Solstice is the Legend of King Arthur. From the Roman chroniclers of ancient Wales to the poets of the Victorian era, much has been added to the legend of Arthur, and these additions clarify rather than cloud the myth.

The historic facts about Arthur are simple enough. There was in fifth century Wales a warrior chief named Arthur, who twelve times met the Saxon invaders in battle, and twelve times was victorious. But the legend of Arthur, that is where history and myth come together, tells a much more important story. It tells the story of a Pagan Sun God.

Uther Pendragon, the rightful heir to the throne, in addition to his having just won it in battle, was filled with desire for the beautiful Igraine, wife of Gorolis. His friend and advisor, the wizard Merlin, agreed to help Uther to possess Igraine. Having had a vision of the coming of a king and a glorious future for the land, Merlin recognized his opportunity. He used his magick to shape-shift Uther into the likeness of Igraine's husband, Gorolis. That night, as Uther and Igraine loved, Gorolis was killed at his encampment at Dilmilioc. At this time Arthur was conceived. His death/birth theme is a bardic type of formula used to indicate the divinity of the child.

In another version of this myth, Merlin and his master Bleys perform a spell to bring forth the infant Arthur from a storm tossed sea. The sea is a symbol of the Mother Goddess, and many an ancient God entered the material world by simply drifting ashore. But to some early Celts, the sea was also the site of the Underworld; so this myth suggests a return from death.

THE SWORD
(Made by Garry Vann Ausdle, Nelson County, VA.
Photo by Weyer of Toledo)

In Tennyson's *Idylls of the King*, Arthur's birth is surrounded by as much Pagan symbolism as is his conception, as Yule (i.e., the death of the old solar year and the birth of the new one) was the time chosen for Arthur's birth. This repeats the death of the father/birth of the son theme basic to many pagan belief systems, and in some Pagan traditions, represents the birth of the Divine Child—the Sun God. Tennyson says:

> *And with shameful swiftness afterward*
> *Not many Moons, King Uther died himself,*
> *And that same night of the New Year*
> *By reason of bitterness and grief*
> *That vext his mother, all before his time*
> *Was Arthur born.*

The motif of the changeling or the kidnapped child in myth also usually indicates the child's divinity.

Merlin hid Arthur away, or possibly left him in the care of a Knight named Anton or Ector, who saw to Arthur's schooling and welfare.

When Arthur was about fifteen years of age, he drew the sword from the stone, a feat that could only be performed by the rightful King. His kingship thus confirmed, Arthur was crowned. As King he fought many battles and united the land. In one of these contests he shattered the sword that he had drawn from the stone. Merlin took him to the edge of a lake and an arm clothed in "white samite" appeared. It rose from the lake, holding aloft the jewel encrusted magickal sword, Excalibur. The sword was a gift from the Lady of the Lake, variously known as Vivian, Niniane, or Nimu. Arthur rowed out and took the sword:

> *The blade so bright that men are blinded by it—on one side*
> *Graven in the eldest tongue of all this world,*
> *"Take me" but turn the blade an ye shall see*
> *And written in the speech ye speak yourself,*
> *"Cast me away" and sad was Arthur's face.*

"What should I do?" Arthur asked. And Merlin said, "Take it, the time has not yet come to cast it away."

Excalibur is, of course, Arthur's sword or blade of power—his athame. But who is the Lady of the Lake? Traditionally, only the Mother can arm the son, but it is the Crone that bestows magickal power.

Arthur fell in love with Guinevere, daughter of King Leodogran. He sent one of his knights to fetch her to be his bride:

> *For that was later April—and returned*
> *Among the flowers of May with Guinevere,*
> *And before Britain's stateliest altar-shrine the King*
> *That morn was married while in stainless white.*

> *Far shone the fields of May thro' open door*
> *The sacred altar blossomed white with May.*
> *The Sun of May descended on their King*
> *They gazed on all earth's beauty in their Queen.*

That the wedding took place in May suggests that this is a sacred wedding, of a God and a Goddess. Celtic Pagan tradition held that during the month of May mortals were forbidden to marry. May was the month for Sacred Marriages, and June for mortal ones. The "Sacred altar blossomed white with May" refers not to the month, but to the white blossoms of the hawthorn tree with which Pagan altars were decorated at this time of year. The line, "The Sun of May descended upon their King," reaffirms that Arthur represents a solar deity, and Guine-vere as Queen of May represents the Maiden aspect of the Goddess.

Following the wedding, the Knights sang a song that began:

> *Blow trumpets for the world is white with May*
> *Blow trumpets for the long nights have rolled away*
> *Blow thro' the living world—let the King reign!*

This song would certainly suggest the celebration of victory of the Sun God over the darkness of the winter months.

After the wedding, Arthur was given a gift of the Round Table by his father-in-law, Leodogran. The table had originally been designed by Merlin and could seat 140 men (or 150 depending upon the author). The Round Table is, of course, the Pagan's Magick Circle.

Arthur gathered about him the Knights of the Round Table. A list of their names is given in the story of "Culhwch and Olwen" in the *Mabinogian*.

Here in the story of Culhwch and Olwen, the antiquity of the tale is attested to by the repetition of a bardic formula by Culhwch, the hero of the tale. He is told of 39 tasks he must perform in order to win the beautiful Olwen. To each he answers, "It will be easy for me to get that, tho' you think otherwise." And each time his opponent replies, "Tho' you get that, there are other things you will not get." The magickal quality of this tale, and the identity of Olwen, are suggested by the number of tasks—39—or three times thirteen—a number sacred to the Goddess. Among the Knights in this earliest tale of King Arthur's court, there are a few familiar names like Kei and Bedwyr (Sir Kay and Sir Bedevere). Many of the names are possibly historic, and many of the Knights have supernormal or shamanistic powers.

Lancelot, Galahad, and Percival are more recent additions to the legend, but even Lancelot has some of the earmarks of a deity. As an in-fant, he was snatched from his mother's arms as she mourned over his father's corpse on the battlefield.

Here again is the ancient Pagan theme of Death of the Father/Birth of the Son, as well as the changeling child. His abductor was Vivian, hence his name—Lancelot of the Lake.

In another tale, Lancelot must cross a sword bridge in order to reach Guinevere's chamber. Like the rainbow bridge Bifrost in Norse Myth, the sword-blade bridge is a bridge to the Otherworld—and Guinevere, its Queen, a Goddess.

One of the earliest of the Knights associated with King Arthur is Sir Gawain. In the story of *Sir Gawain and the Green Knight*, Gawain is invited by the Green Knight to take the first swing of the axe in a challenge—though Gawain succeeds in chopping off the Green Knight's head, the Green Knight merely picks up his head and puts it back on his shoulders. Poor Gawain is then forced to keep the bargain they had made—to meet one year from this night, on the eve of the New Year, to give the Green Knight his turn to return the blow. The Green Knight represents the Holly King of the dying year (as is magnificently portrayed by Sean Connery in the lovely Stephen Weeks film, "The Sword of the Valiant"). While Gawain is likely to be a solar deity, the Oak King of the New Year. In Malory's *Le Morte D' Arthur*, Gawain predicts his own death will fall at noon, the hour when the Sun's strength begins to wane.

And so Arthur surrounded himself with Knights, many of whom had supernormal powers and some of whom were earlier Gods. King Arthur reigned and the land flourished and prospered because his powers were the powers of the Sun.

The two most important objects in the tales of King Arthur are the sword Excalibur and the Cup (cauldron) or Grail. To Pagans, these symbolize the athame and the cup, male and female, God and Goddess.

At one point, some of the Knights went on a quest to find the Holy Grail, which according to Malory was the cup which was used by Jesus in the Last Supper. Aside from *Le Morte D' Arthur*, in the 1640s Thomas Malory also wrote *A History of the Holy Grail*, but the first actual mention of the Grail in connection with King Arthur is by Cretien de Troyes in 1180. According to Richard Barber in his introduction to *Yvain, or the Knight with the Lion*, "What Chretian himself intended by the Grail we may never know. Such evidence as there is points to a dish of plenty for which Chretien himself chose a rare French word 'graal' from the late Latin 'gradalis.' Such all providing dishes or cauldrons are fairly frequent in Celtic literature."

In the tale of "Branwen, daughter of Llyr" in the *Mabinogian*, a cauldron is brought to Britain from Ireland by a pair of giant warriors. It has the power to bring warriors slain in battle back to life. In the tale of "Culhwch and Olwan," handsome and generous King Arthur and his Knights help Culhwch to obtain a magickal cauldron from the steward of the King of Ireland—one of his 39 tasks. And, Taliesin became a wizard

The Cup

when he was touched by one drop of the brew from the Cauldron of the Goddess Cerridwen. One of the thirteen magickal treasures of Britain was the Cauldron of Dyrnwch.

Arthur had about him not only the bravest Knights but also the wisest wizard—Merlin. Merlin is the Latin form of the Celtic "Myrddin," and his story is as mystical as Arthur's. During the Dark Ages, there was a King Vortigern who had usurped the throne, and who was hated by the people. He attempted to build a tower in which to protect himself, but the tower kept collapsing. He was advised by a court magician to find a boy child that had no father. This would end the problem. After years of searching he found a boy whose mother vowed that she had never known a man but was made pregnant by a spirit. The boy was Merlin, a child of the union of Spirit and Matter. (A Christianized version has it as the union of a demon and an unconscious nun.) Merlin told Vortigern that an underground lake was causing the tower to collapse, and that draining the lake would solve the problem. But when the lake was drained, there emerged two dragons—one red, one white—that engaged in a terrible fight. One killed the other and fled. An earlier version of this appears in the *Mabinogion*, in the tale of "Lludd and Llevelys," a Sun God imprisoned the two fighting dragons in a stone chest.

Inspired by the sight of these two dragons, Merlin developed the ability to prophecize. He predicted the death of Vortigen and eventually Uther attained the throne and fathered Arthur.

Geoffrey of Monmouth in his *The History of the Kings of Britain*, written in the early 1100s, credits Merlin with the building of Stonehenge. Geoffrey's work is more fiction than fact, and it is he that first called Arthur a King. This linking Merlin to the pre-Christian Pagan shrine shows us that even then, Merlin was not believed to be of the new religion.

When he was one hundred years old, he began having premonitions of the end of Arthur's reign. He also became involved with a beautiful young woman. But here things tend to get confused; some writers say she was Vivian, the Lady of the Lake. Others say that she was Arthur's sister, Morgan le Faye. Whoever she was, Merlin eventually taught her a charm which would result in the death-like state of its victim. Tennyson says:

> Then in one moment, she put forth the charm
> Of woven paces and waving hands,
> And in the hallow oak he lay as dead,
> And lost to life and use and name and fame.

In some versions, Merlin is imprisoned in the hollow oak, while in others he is encased in an "island of glass." The ancient pre-Celtic people of Western Europe buried their dead in hollowed oak logs, possibly because of the preserving qualities of the tannins in the wood; but more likely because of a belief in an Oak God and in an afterlife. (This idea bears stunning resemblance to an Egyptian myth in which Isis preserved the dismembered parts of her beloved Osiris in a hollowed tree trunk to give him eternal life.) The oak tree also suggests that Merlin was a Druid.

The island of glass may also lend itself to an interesting interpretation: according to *The Atlas of Mysterious Places*, "Glastonbury Tor was once almost an island for the sea-covered lowlands of Somerset Levels." "Glas" is a Celtic word meaning green or blue. "Tinne" is the Celtic name for holly, a sacred tree (but in ancient times the sacred tree was the evergreen oak). "Bury" means hill, so Glastonbury (glas-tinne-bury) means Hill of Sacred Trees. Possibly in ancient times there was a sacred grove on the Tor, which was then an island. An island of glas, then, would be the perfect place to keep the enchanted priest Merlin. Legend today holds that the summit of Glastonbury Tor is the entrance to Annwn—the Otherworld. And this is where Merlin waits for the spell to be broken.

The women in Arthur's life are: Igraine, his mother; Guinevere, his wife; Vivian, The Lady of the Lake; and Morgan le Faye, his sister. Since

Vivian and Morgan are also frequently confused, or their identities interchangeable, they can be considered one entity.

It is also Morgan/Vivian who brings about the end—at least for a time—of Merlin. Niniane or Vivian, the other half of this duality, gave Arthur Excalibur, the sword of power; the right to bestow magickal power also belongs to the Crone aspect of the Goddess.

Robert Graves says that "le Faye" means "the Fates," but Faery is a better interpretation. She is certainly Morrigan the Celtic Goddess of Death. In an ancient French tale, Ogier the Dane, a Knight of Charlemagne's in his hundredth year, married Morgana the Faery, who gave him back his youth. He lived for two hundred years in her Castle of Forgetfulness and then returned to the French court. There he wanted to marry another woman, but Morgana made him return to her castle. In this French version of the story of Merlin and Morgana, she most certainly is the same Death Goddess, and her Castle of Forgetfulness, Caer Arrianrod. But, above all, it is Morgan's son Mordred who brings death to Arthur. According to the unknown author known as the Gawain poet:

> *So Morgana the Goddess she accordingly became*
> *The proudest She can oppress*
> *And to her purpose tame.*

Igraine, Arthur's mother, is most certainly the Mother Goddess. Guinevere, Arthur's bride in May—Goddess of Love and Beauty—is the Maiden. And his sister the dark enchantress, Morgan le Faye, is the Crone. All the women in Arthur's life are aspects of the Triple Goddess.

The final symbolic episode in the life of King Arthur is its conclusion by death in a battle after a reign of 39 sacred years. The night before the battle, Arthur had a dream. According to Malory:

> *King Arthur dreamed a wonderful dream, and in him*
>   *[the dream] seemed*
> *he saw upon a scaffold a chair, and the chair was fast to a wheel,*
> *and thereupon sat King Arthur in the richest cloth of gold*
> *that might be made.*

As the dream went on, the wheel turned so that the chair was upside down, and the King fell into "an hideous black water and therein were all manner of serpents." Initially, the symbols are obviously Sun symbols—i.e., the solar wheel and the "richest cloth of gold." And then the King or solar deity falls from his throne into darkness at the turning of the season.

The foe that Arthur is to meet in battle at daybreak is Mordred, son of his sister Morgan le Faye. According to some authors, including Malory, Mordred is also Arthur's son. There is a wonderful scene in the outstanding 1981 British film "Excalibur" (starring Nigel Terry), in which Morgana uses Merlin's magick to shape-shift into the likeness of Guinevere so that she may trick Arthur into begetting Mordred.

The battle, according to Malory, takes place in Salisbury. What more perfect place for the ritual death of the Sun God than at this ancient temple of the Sun?

According to Tennyson, the battle was fought at Lyonesse. The "Lost Land of Lyonesse" is traditionally said to have been between Land's End in Southwestern England and the Scilly Is. This is the westernmost point of Southern England. And since West is where the Sun sets, and the western point on the Circle in the Wiccan-Pagan tradition symbolizes death, it is a most appropriate site for the death of the Sun God.

The morning of the battle dawned dense with fog, and many were killed on both sides. Arthur received a fatal wound from Mordred, and at the same instant Excalibur struck its final blow killing the King's nephew/son.

Then, according to Malory, Sir Bedevere carried the wounded King to a nearby ruined chapel. We could take this to mean Stonehenge, which in Malory's day was understood to be a Pagan temple, and was even more of a ruin than it is today.

Arthur asked Bedevere to take Excalibur to a nearby body of water and cast it in, and to come back to him and report what happened. Twice Bevedere had not the heart to throw the sword into the lake, but the third time he did. And an arm "clothed in white samite" rose from the lake to grasp it—brandishing it thrice before disappearing beneath the waves. When Bedevere reported this to Arthur, the King asked to be carried to the water's edge.

"Then saw they how there hove a dusky barge," and on the deck of this barge, "Black-stoled, black hooded, like a dream, Three Queens with crowns of gold." And the dying King's body was placed on the barge in the laps of the Queens, to sail—

> To the Island-Valley of Avilion
> Where falls not hail, nor rain, or any snow,
> And bowery hollows crowned with Summer see,
> Where I will heal me of my grievous wound.

This most certainly is the Pagan Summerland, the three Queens the Triple Goddess, and the barge at once a symbol of the Goddess and the Solar Boat.

> "And then the new sun rose, bringing the New Year."
> —Tennyson.

And Malory says, "And many men say that there is written upon his tomb this—*Hic jacet Arthurus, Rex qoudem, Rexque futurus.*" Here lies Arthur, Once and Future King!

Early Celtic Christians saw in these ancient tales reflections of their own beliefs, and in the promise of the return of Arthur they saw the Second Coming. And this is not surprising because the roots of the new religion also grew out of the Pagan past.

The historic facts—whether Arthur actually was King, or if he really existed—are irrelevant. What is important is that here we have a tale that has been told and re-told. Bards have sung it, poets have put pen to it, and Hollywood has put it on videotape. It is the tale of a child born at the New Year. He becomes King and weds the Queen in May. He reigns and the land flourishes; then his reign declines , and on the eve of the New Year he is killed by his sister's son.

A Sun Wheel on a Solar Disk

To look at a legend for its historical truth is to look through the wrong end of the telescope. The Legend of King Arthur—Once and Future King—is not the story of a king who died, but of a God reborn, and the promise of life renewing itself.

The warm, dry afternoon of June invites walks in quest of magickal herbs, along sunny country lanes, past fields of new moan hay drying in the sun, and in the shaded forest where lady's slipper orchids and faery candles grow. Mentally, we mark the location of the herbs that on Midsummer's Eve will be ritually gathered, to be offered on the Sabbat fire or hung as amulets for protection. As the lengthening days of June darken into honeysuckle-scented nights that twinkle with fireflies, we begin to prepare for the Sabbat rites.

Of all the solar Sabbats, this is the one that marks the greater glory of the Sun, and so it is appropriate to have a Sun symbol as a focal point within the Midsummer Circle. In ancient times, the Sun was portrayed in various ways by different cultures. The ancient Egyptians depicted it as a great gold disc carried on its daily voyage by a celestial boat. To the ancient Greeks, it was drawn in the solar chariot, and later personified as Helios, the God of the Day, as Sol, and eventually as Apollo, God of the Sun and brother to the Moon Goddess Artemis. By Northern Europeans, the Sun was visualized as a great golden disc carried on the back of horses, and later came to be personified as Balder. But one of the most powerful and universal Sun symbols of all is the solar cross contained within a circle, or Solar Wheel. This Solar Disc or Sun Wheel can be made out of a variety of materials. One of the simplest is made of grape vine. Vine that has been pruned in March is still flexible enough to be bent into a tight circle, wound around two or three times with the ends tucked around to the back. Once the circle has been formed, two short lengths of vine, a little longer than the circle is wide, can be used to form the cross. Place one length horizontally across the back of the wheel. Then, place the vertical length behind that one so that the lower end is in front of the circle, and bend it gently forward so that the upper end is also in front of the circle, locking everything in place.

This Sun Wheel can then be adorned with streamers of yellow ribbon, bright yellow flowers, or symbols of the four elements: e.g., bird feathers for air, a stone for earth, sea shells for water, and Yule log ash for fire. It has become our tradition here at Flying Witch Farm to hang the Solar Disc in a Rowan tree over the altar of stone in the woodland wildflower garden after the Midsummer rites, and to burn the old one on the Midsummer fire.

This is the time of year when birds that have built their nests and laid their eggs begin to molt their feathers. Since ancient times, feathers have been collected for magickal uses, and one of the most famous charms using feathers is the Witch's Ladder.

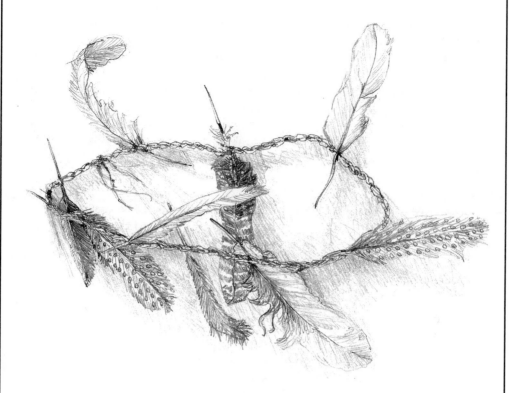

The Witch's Ladder

To make a Witch's Ladder, first braid together three different colored yarns three feet long, the colors depending on the type of magick you wish to work. Enchant the cord as you braid it with words like:

> *Yarn of red, black and white*
> *Work your magick spell this night*

Then take nine feathers, all different, or all the same, or a combination, again depending upon the type of magick. One at a time, tie each feather onto the cord with a knot, saying words like:

> *With this feather and this string,*
> *Protection to my home I bring.*

When all nine feathers have been tied onto the cord, tie the ends of the cord together to make a circle, consecrate it, and hang it high in your home or Wish Tree.

In ancient times, livestock was driven through the embers of the purifying Midsummer fire after the flames had died down. Today some traditions are reviving this ancient ritual. One safe way to do this is to build a second fire from the first one, leaving a safe path between the two, to walk or drive livestock through. An even safer method is to gather some of the ashes after they are cool and rub them on the animals, making the sign of the Solar Cross.

If this sounds like a Yule log tradition, remember that the Midsummer fire of June and the Yule log of December stand across the Wheel of the Year from one another, one marking the moment of the Sun's greatest power just before it begins to wane, the other marking the moment when the Sun ceases waning and begins to grow in strength and power—and the Solar Year, the Divine Child, is born anew.

Whether you are planning to drive a herd of cattle through the Sabbat fire, or just a beloved pet and familiar, it is traditional to kindle the Midsummer fire with two kinds of wood, oak and fir. Originally, this Sabbat fire was lit by the friction of these two woods. This combination of woods can be interpreted as representing the God and the Goddess, the oak being the Sun King and the fir the Moon Goddess, united in the element of Fire. Even if the Sabbat rites are held indoors, and the fire is kindled in a cauldron, these two kinds of wood should be present to lend their special magick to the celebration of the season.

About this time of year, the warm, dry hay scented breezes of early June become the hot, oppressive stillness of high Summer. The buzz of insects and the roll of distant thunder are all that break the quiet of the afternoon hours, and many of us seek the cool of the mountain forests or the refreshing ocean breezes. As we plan our summer trips it is a time to remember that the traditional magick of Midsummer places an emphasis on the protection of animals, not only of beloved pets and faithful livestock, but of those wild creatures who are likely to cross our path when we venture out in our cars and RVs. So this is a perfect time to cast a spell of protection around your vehicle so that it will not become a vehicle of harm to any living creature.

Obviously, this ritual will have to be performed in your driveway, so it might be wise to make it appear to be part of a traditional Saturday afternoon car washing ritual. Suds and hose the car if necessary, then asperge it with salted water walking sunwise around the car, all the while imagining any negativity being washed away. You might say words like:

> *I purify you with this water*
> *So that you will not be a weapon of harm.*

Use the car's name if it has one, most of our vehicles do. Then when the car is dry, anoint the headlights, front bumper, front fenders, grill, hood, tires, any part of the vehicle you can imagine colliding with an animal, with a protection oil (pure olive oil in which herbs of protection, such as those mentioned earlier in this chapter, have soaked). Finally, anoint the hood ornament, or whatever passes for one on your car (these serve the same function as figure heads on ancient ships, to look out ahead of the vessel) saying words like:

Lord Faunas, I ask for your protection
God of the wild creatures
Let not this car of mine
Be a weapon for destruction,
As I will, So Mote It Be!

When the magickal herbs have been gathered, the Witch's Ladders have been hung, and the Midsummer fire has died to ashes, the warmth and joy of the Solstice Sabbat will linger until Lammas. Meanwhile, as the light of the Sun wanes its heat intensifies, ripening the first sweet strawberries, then fragrant raspberries. The white, round heads of cabbages swell, and the strangely scented vines of the tomatoes begin to set fruit. The hazy heat of the summer afternoons drive sheep and dairy cows alike to seek the shade of trees, and other creatures more secretive only venture out at night. By day the toad is hidden from the sun, and snails and slugs leave only silver trails to be found in the light of day. And all the while the grain, still green, ripens in the fields in preparation for the sacrifice of the harvest.

Chapter Five
LAMMAS

LAMMAS

The rooster's call pierces the early morning haze that promises another day of heat and humidity, and in the distance gathering crows call to one another while silently the corn ripens.

As the summer sun climbs higher in the sky, we are driven indoors to the coolness of the old stone farmhouse. Baskets of freshly picked tomatoes fill the kitchen with a strange pungent smell of the vine blended with the sweet herby fragrance of basil, and a frosty pitcher of iced tea flavored with fresh spearmint soothes and cools us.

In the dark coolness of the cellar, the empty mason jars, whose contents were consumed last winter, once again glisten in neat rows, filled with colorful fruits and vegetables—bright red tomatoes, soft green string beans, brilliant orange peach preserves and ruby red raspberry jam.

As the summer day draws to a close, the sun bathes the neighbor's horses in golden light and casts long purple shadows across the meadow grass, just before it slips behind the hill. Then the meadow grass is atwinkle with fireflies, and on a certain night the sky beyond the surrounding hills bursts with brilliant sparkles of light, as surrounding towns and villages celebrate the 4th of July.

Around the time of the 4th of July and other national holidays, we of the Old Faith are confronted with the symbolism used by our American forefathers in their struggle for independence, and we are often struck by the Pagan meanings of many of them.

Our first national flag, affectionately known as the "Betsy Ross," features a circle of thirteen white five-pointed stars (pentagrams) on a field of blue, and thirteen red and white stripes. Both the stars and the stripes, of course, symbolize the thirteen original colonies; but to a Witch, thirteen stars in a circle also represents the thirteen lunar months in the Wheel of the Year, and the thirteen members of a coven. The red and white stripes are actually strips of cloth that are remarkably like the red and white streamers of the traditional May Pole, and the similarity is all the more striking when one considers the natural position of the flag, atop a flag pole.

Some of the earlier flags of the colonies are of even greater interest. One, for example, shows a snake cut into thirteen segments, each one

Harvest Time

named for one of the colonies, and above them the slogan, "Join or Die." This symbolism recalls the myth of Isis and Osiris, in which the body of the murdered Osiris was cut into fourteen pieces by his brother, Set. Isis roamed the world in search of the pieces and found thirteen of them, which with the help of Anubis were reunited, and Osiris resurrected.

A later version of the serpent flag shows the snake intact and coiled into a perfect spiral, above which is the slogan, "Don't Tread On Me." The spiral, of course, is one of the most ancient symbols of the Goddess, and the serpent is a symbol of the male principle, as well as a symbol of Paganism.

Another colonial flag simply had the white crescent of the waxing moon in the upper left hand corner of an entirely blue flag, and between the horns of the moon the word "Liberty." This flag might seem to many of us just as appropriate today as it did over two hundred years ago.

There has been already much said about the appearance of the number thirteen in the great seal of the United States, but these explanations tend only to see thirteen as representing the number of colonies. But I find it interesting that the original colonies just happen to be thirteen in number. I am not suggesting that the delegates from these colonies, who sat in that stuffy room in Philadelphia in 1776, drafting the Declaration of Independence and the Bill of Rights, were a Coven of Witches, but rather that our ancient Gods move in strange and mysterious ways to protect their hidden children.

So it seems natural that the United States, founded for the purpose of religious freedom, should be the scene of the greatest Wiccan revival—although it is also happening everywhere on the planet. It is possible that in the not too distant future that the Constitution of the United States, and especially those who have sworn to uphold it, will be tested as never before; and we will keep in mind the other meanings of the Stars and Stripes, the serpents and the crescents.

Like American architecture and American cuisine, American Witchcraft is something completely unique. In what other country could a Witch cast the circle in a Celtic tradition, then call upon a Greek Goddess and God, and then perform an Anglo-Saxon ritual to a tape of Native American drums? Of course, this sort of "melting pot magick" might be frowned upon by some purists on a specific path, but in truth, the more we learn about the various Wiccan and Pagan paths, the more we are struck not by the differences, but by the similarities; and the differences that there are, are differences of culture, not religion. As American Witches, we have all of the best of the traditions of the Old World to draw from. There are some who are fortunate enough to have been born into one of those pockets of hereditary traditions that seem to be scattered about the Old World like pieces of a jigsaw puzzle from a passing cloud. As American Witches, we may not feel that as individuals we hold an original piece of the puzzle, but we do seem to have glimpsed the cover of the box.

The heat and the humidity of summer days have inherent in them the possibility of afternoon and evening thundershowers. It is not just an invention by Hollywood that causes so many films about the so called "supernatural" to be set in haunted houses and castles on stormy nights, but an instinct that is part of all of us. There is something very real that seems to be a connection between severe electrical storms and the spirit world. Dan and I have observed on several occasions when working the wine glass (a simple device that works much like a Ouija Board) while a storm is approaching that there is often static. And several times there have been abrupt changes in the communicating entity or the message being given, as if someone had turned a dial to change a station on the radio. Also, on two or three occasions, our young dog Samhaintha (pronounced "Samantha") had gone outside only to come slinking back into the house terrified, hours before a particularly severe thunderstorm had struck. Apparently there is some connection between thunderstorms and the earth's electromagnetic field, and the electromagnetic field with psi and the spirit worlds.

Thunderstorms have the power to stimulate or enhance psychic activity, and this magickal power of the thunderstorm is contained in the rainwater from it. This water must be collected in glass or glazed earthenware containers, which insulate it. It can then be used to enhance the power of amulets and such objects as crystal balls, the wine glass, or the Ouija Board. An especially powerful way to do this is to place a few dried leaves of mugwort—an herb that also has the power to enhance psychic energy, in a glass container and pour some storm water over them. Allow them to stand in the moonlight for the three nights prior to the Full Moon. Then, on the night that the Moon is full, cast your Circle according to your ways, and have on your altar all of the objects and amulets you wish to charge.

At the appropriate point in the esbat ritual, dip your fingers in this highly charged potion and anoint each of the objects liberally with it, saying words like:

> *Thunder and Lightning*
> *Mugwort and Moon*
> *Your powers will be*
> *This amulet's soon.*

Then leave all of the objects you have anointed, where they will be in the moonlight until morning; but do put them away before sunrise.

Two objects that really should be charged this way are the wand and the athame.

Storms, on the other hand, can be destructive. Peony has long been used as an herb of protection against the dangers of storms. House-leek, called in Dutch, "donderbloem," or thunder-flower, was at one time planted on roof tops as protection against lightning strikes. Of course, a prerequisite for this is a sod or thatch roof, but to plant them near the house affords some protection.

Pysanky too are amulets of protection against lightning.

When the summer storm has passed, it is often followed by clear blue skies and hot dry breezes. This is just the time of day to go to the beach, that magickal strip between land and sea where so many an ancient God and Goddess first drifted ashore.

Among these was the ancient Greek Goddess of Love and Beauty, Aphrodite, whose name means "Foam-born." Aphrodite was not only beautiful, she also admired beauty in others, and granted the gifts of beauty and charm. A visit to the shore is a perfect time to pay homage to the Goddess in her aspect of Goddess of Love and Beauty. Myrtle, apple, rose and poppy are all sacred to Aphrodite; sea shells, especially those of the genus Cypraea, popularly called cowries, were left as offerings at her temple on the island of Cyprus, for which the genus is named. As Goddess of the sea, swans and dolphins are also sacred to her. So if you are at the edge of the sea and wish to honor Aphrodite, cast a circle in the sand when the Moon is new. Strew rose petals about the Circle, face the ocean and gaze at it for a while. Then hold high a sea shell you wish to make an offering of. Let it be the loveliest and most perfect you can find. Speak words such as:

> *Aphrodite, born of the sea*
> *I offer this shell onto thee.*
> *Its perfect beauty, like your own,*
> *Gracious Goddess, born of foam,*
> *It's all I have to give to thee,*
> *Grant that I may blessed be.*

Then place the shell on a stone altar in the center of the Circle, or on the sand where the sea might take it and let the rose petals be claimed by the incoming tide.

To the ancient Romans, July was the time to celebrate the Neptunalia, the festival of Neptune, God of the Seas and the Roman counterpart of Poseidon, the Greek God of the Sea. Neptune was also the creator of the first horse, which later became a symbol of the Goddess. It is Neptune who presides over all of the creatures of the sea, as well as the sea itself. His symbol is the trident and dolphins; black and white bulls, as well as horses are sacred to him. A visit to the sea, especially during the month of July, is an appropriate time to do honor to this sea deity, and to ask for protection when traveling by the sea, or from drowning. Go to the edge of the sea and cast a Circle in the sand. Mark the four directions by placing a horseshoe, or drawing a horse's hoof print in the sand with your finger, at each of the four compass points. At the center of the Circle, place a trident or symbol of one. A pickle fork is perfect because of its shape and its association with brine. Or draw a trident in the sand. Then hold a cup of white wine or ale aloft, saying words like:

> *Neptune (or Poseidon), Lord of the Ocean*
> *Who dwells beneath the sea,*
> *Accept this offering I pour*
> *Where your domain meets the shore.*
> *Grant that I will always be*
> *Safe from the dangers of the sea.*

Then collect the horseshoes and trident, and leave the offering to mingle with the waves.

A similar ritual might be performed in honor of Ler, the Celtic God of the Sea.

But these domains of the Sea Gods, like the rain forest, are threatened, and with them so is all life on earth. While it is necessary to dance in the Magick Circle cast beside the sea to show our love for these ancient deities, it is equally important to take physical action and support legislation to protect the world's oceans—and especially groups like Greenpeace, whose members have risked their lives to protect such creatures as dolphins, sacred to the ancient God and Goddess of the Sea.

While at the shore, there is a really fun project that can be tried right there at the beach; or sand can be collected for experimentation later at home: Candles cast in sand are fun to make, are very attractive, and make excellent candles for marking the four corners of the Circle because they are quite safe (they do not fall over easily, and there is no glass to break). Dan and I made many of them in the late sixties and they came to be called "hippie Witch candles." All that is needed are wet sand, wax, wick, and a double boiler (to melt the wax in).

A double boiler can be a coffee tin in a pot of water. Colors and scents are optional, but can be purchased at some arts and crafts supply store. Crushed crayons can also be used for colors and essential oils or extracts for scents. If the candles are to be cast at the beach, then work where the sand is already wet. (But if collecting sand for later use, use dry sand from the upper beach. This should be put in a cardboard carton eight inches deep and about two feet by two feet square, and then moistened with a hose later on.)

To begin making the candles, while the wax is melting in the double boiler, scoop out a hollow about the size of half a grape fruit in the wet sand using a tablespoon. This basic shape can be ornamented in several ways: "hobnails" can be made by poking the sides of the hollow with a

Sand Candles

pencil eraser or fluted edge can be produced by pressing thumb prints around the rim, and a nice "pre-Columbian" look can be achieved by just making three indentations evenly spaced around the rim. But our favorite is the cauldron shape, which comes in somewhat at the neck before flaring out again at the rim, and which has three legs made by poking a pencil into the sand at the bottom of the hollow. When the shape is pleasing, hold a length of wick over the approximate center and gently pour the colored wax, being sure that the legs of any legged ones are filled. Allow the wax to set, which can take quite a long time. Gently test the wax, and when it is ready, slip your fingers into the sand under the candle and gently lift it out. Brush off any excess sand. No matter how perfectly symmetrical you may think you made the shape, there are always surprises, which is part of the charm of sand candles. Any that are too round bottomed or uneven legged to stand can be leveled by being stood in a hot frying pan.

As the month of July nears its end, there is much to be harvested. Tomatoes come in by the bushel now, to be cut and packed into hot sterilized jars and canned.

A simple ritual to ensure that the jars will seal is to first wipe the top rim of the jar with a hot, clean sponge before placing the lid in position and screwing down the rim. Then with the tip of your finger, inscribe a pentagram on the lid, saying words like:

Lid seal—protect this meal!

The practice of hermetically sealing jars, which is what canning is, actually began as a magickal process. It is attributed to Hermes Trismegistus, the Greek name for the Egyptian God Thoth (who is reputed to be the founder of alchemy and other occult sciences). In the seventeenth century, or even earlier, the white wine of the Rhine Valley of Germany was placed in stonewear vessels called bellarmines. While bellarmines were presumably named for an early bishop of the new religion, they were typically ornamented with the visage of the God Baal or Bel—or sometimes the foliate mask of a vegetation god—in order to protect and preserve its contents. For this reason, such bottles were frequently used as Witch's bottles—charms of protection which contained the urine and sometimes the blood of the practitioner, and also might include symbolic protective weapons such as pins, thorns, rusty nails, and broken glass. These bottles were then buried upside down in the earth, and their protection would last as long as the bottle and its contents did. Such charms are fairly common archaeological finds in Europe, and one such bottle was discovered in the United States, on Tinnicum Island in the Delaware River just below Philadelphia. (However, this particular charm was contained in a green glass bottle, and not a bellarmine.)

A Bellarmine

Even today, the glass jars we use to preserve our harvest of tomatoes and peaches are blatantly adorned with the magickal symbols of Freemasonry, such as the pentagram, because they are, after all, Mason jars. For this reason they make excellent containers for contemporary Witch bottles, and it really doesn't matter if they spell Baal "Ball"!

As the harvest progresses, there are many things that can be done to prepare for the Lammas celebration. Sweet corn is becoming available and it can be used in many ways. I have found that one of the best ways to get in touch with the spirit of the season, any season, is to adorn one's surroundings with the natural objects of the season. One of the easiest ways to do this is to obtain an ear of fresh sweet corn, the larger and tougher the kernels the better (but not dried completely). Break the ear in half after the husk has been removed and then begin popping off the kernels, beginning at the broken end of each half and going around and around. Try not to break the kernels in half, but to leave the white points on them. Then, with about two or three feet of heavy thread on a large needle, begin stringing the kernels by putting the needle through the very center of each one. When the strand is long enough to make a necklace, and one ear is usually more than enough, tie the ends of the thread together and hang the necklace in a warm, dry place for a few weeks. The kernels will dry, shrivel and shrink, and it may be necessary to tighten the knot. Beautiful variations of this necklace can be made using Indian

A Necklace for Lammas

corn that has not been field dried. You might grow your own or ask at a local farm stand if you can buy ears of Indian corn that are still tender. If you don't wish to make a necklace of corn kernels every year, but instead want to use the same necklaces for Lammas year after year, spray them with polyurethane or varnish to protect them from becoming infested with moths.

The idea of wearing a necklace of corn kernels to celebrate the grain harvest sounds simple enough, but in fact, carrying this idea of costuming in imitation of the Spirits of Nature a few steps further can be a very powerful link to the Spirits of the Grain.

Another idea along these lines is to braid the long leaves from corn stalks together to form a crown or head band. This can be further adorned with the tassels from the tops of corn stalks. There are many ways of making adornments with corn husks. Field dried ears of corn cut into slices can make beautiful rosettes that can be worn in many different ways. All that is necessary is a supply of corn, corn husks, and an active imagination.

Around the home too—and especially the area where the Lammas rites will be celebrated—it is appropriate to decorate with bowls of fruit and baskets of vegetables and all the signs and symbols of the season.

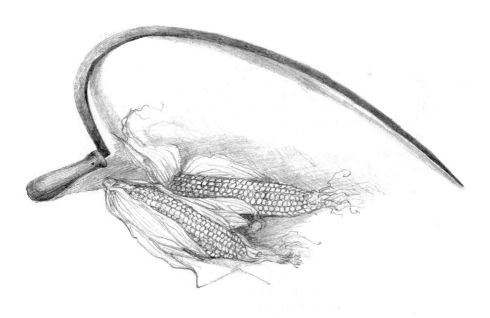

A Reaping Hook

Among these are the tools of the harvest. Eventually, the Lammas Circle might be adorned not only with the fruits of the harvest, but the tools as well, especially those associated with the grain harvest. The reaping hook and sickle are both sacred to the Goddess, not only because of their association with the sacred grain, but also because their shape resembles the crescent moon. Pitch forks or hay forks are not only harvesting tools, but their tines resemble the horns or antlers of the Horned One. The scythe is also called the Tooth of Saturn. Saturn is an ancient God of Death who was also the father of Zeus. The scythe is also carried by "Father Time" as a symbol of the passing of the old year at New Year's Eve. It is also carried by the more somber figure known as the Grim Reaper, which is the non-Pagan view of the Lord of Death, but who still shows his association with the grain god of death and resurrection. The flail too is associated with the grain harvest and was also a symbol of the pharaohs of Egypt. Along with the flail, the winnowing basket is also a symbol of the harvest.

The grain itself is an especially powerful symbol. Bundles of corn stalks or sheaves of harvested wheat or other grain might flank the altar area, or on a smaller scale vases of wheat, oats or barley might adorn the mantle or table that will be the altar when the Sabbat night arrives.

In ancient times, the gathering of these bundles of grain were accompanied by much ritual and tradition. It was believed that the spirit that dwelled in all of the field of grain retreated as it was cut, into the grain still standing. For this reason, no one wanted to be the one to cut the last sheaf of grain. Instead, the harvesters took turns throwing their sickles at it until it was finally cut.

The bundle was probably believed to still contain the spirit of the grain. It was ritually gathered up and tied to resemble the form of a woman, and was called the Corn Mother, or variations on this name such as the Old Corn Woman, Rye Mother, Barley Mother or Wheat Mother, Old Woman or Harvest Mother, depending on locality and the kind of grain that was grown there. The Corn Mother was then dressed in women's clothing, or adorned with cloth or ribbon. She might then be mounted on a post and ceremoniously carried back to the village or farmhouse in a joyful procession of carts and wagons that contained the entire grain harvest. The Corn Mother would then have been mounted up in the barn above the threshing floor while the grain harvest was being threshed, and then kept in the farmhouse until the following Spring.

In Germanic countries and those of Eastern Europe, she is the Corn Mother and her counterpart is the Corn Maiden. In Celtic countries she is called the Cailliach and her other half in Spring is the great Goddess Bride herself; and in ancient Greece, she is Demeter and her counterpart is her daughter Persephone; to the Romans, Ceres and Proserpina. Together they are simply called, "the Two Goddesses."

MAKING THE CORN MOTHER

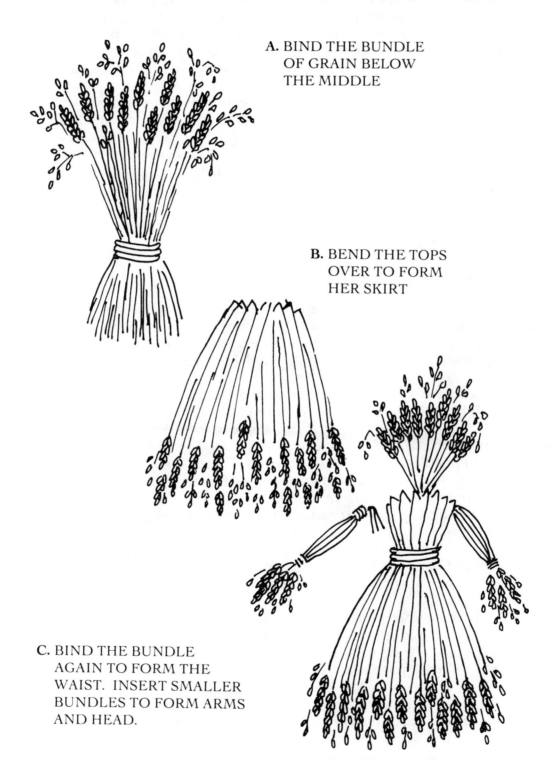

A. BIND THE BUNDLE
OF GRAIN BELOW
THE MIDDLE

B. BEND THE TOPS
OVER TO FORM
HER SKIRT

C. BIND THE BUNDLE
AGAIN TO FORM THE
WAIST. INSERT SMALLER
BUNDLES TO FORM ARMS
AND HEAD.

The Corn Mother was, and still should be, a central part of the Lammas Rites. Making one can be as simple, or as complex, as the imagination dictates. The first part of the process is to obtain the grain. Small bunches of wheat are available from florists or from craft suppliers. This is convenient because in other times, where the Old Religion lingered on, the Corn Mother was sometimes made up of twelve or thirteen smaller sheaves of grain.

If you live in the country near where grain is grown, you might, with the farmer's permission, gather the grain yourself. Ideally, you might arrange with the farmer that he leave a small portion of a row or corner of a field standing for you after he has harvested the rest; or you might find some grain still standing after a field has been harvested.

In any case, this grain should be harvested with a bronze sickle or white-handled knife, saying words like:

> *Mother of Corn*
> *I harvest Thee.*
> *In Spring Thou wilt*
> *A Maiden be!*

In ancient times and in certain traditions, a few of the straws with the heads of grain still attached were plucked from the Corn Mother and set aside for weaving into the magickal amulets known as corn dollies, or for wreaths to be worn by young girls celebrating in the harvest procession.

To form the Corn Mother, tie the bundle of grain about the middle or a little lower, being sure to reserve some for the arms and the head. Then bend the tops down all around the bundle to form the skirt out of the grain heads and bind the bundle once again to form the waist. Tie two smaller bundles at both ends (rubber bands can be used here) and insert them in the upper part of the bundle to form the arms. And finally, insert a fine bundle of grain to form the head.

This figure may then be adorned as desired. A cloth skirt or apron is traditional. Corn necklaces or bracelets, ribbons, and flowers are all appropriate. When the Corn Mother is complete, she might be mounted on a post and carried in procession around the Circle, and finally stood up in the East or South of the Circle, where she may witness the rights held in her honor.

In order to appreciate the Lammas festival fully, it must be understood that just as Beltane is the opposite of Samhain, and Midsummer is the opposite of Yule, so is Lammas the opposite of Imbolc, and this is directly reflected in the relationship of the Corn Mother at Lammas with the Corn Maiden at Imbolc. They are two aspects of the same Goddess— the one the Calliach or Crone, after her days of growth and fertility have ended and her grain has been harvested; and the other the Maiden again

The Lammas Altar

after she has renewed herself through the death-sleep of Winter, and is about to be impregnated once again.

There can be little doubt that sacred seeds of grain contained in the bundle of harvested grain called the Corn Mother were originally kept as the seed for the next year's crop, and treated with much magick and ritual to insure another successful harvest.

If these ancient traditions of Lammas are seen only as quaint remnants of a religion from a time when human survival depended on a good local harvest, there can be little in them that a contemporary Pagan living in a time of industrial farms and chemical fertilizers and insecticides can appreciate; but if we can see in these ancient rituals the symbolic essence of the rhythms of all of Nature, upon which all of our lives are dependent, we can once again celebrate the ancient ways and draw upon their potent powers for our own well being and that of the planet.

As in all things, Lammas is not only a celebration of the Goddess but the God as well. It is very likely that in the earliest phases of the old religion there were actually two religions that existed side by side and worked in tandem for the benefit of the whole community. One was practiced by women and dealt with child birth, time keeping, agriculture, tribal history and medicine. The other was practiced mainly by men and dealt with rituals to appease the spirits of hunted animals, and with communication with the tribal ancestors. The latter is what is popularly called Shamanism, and the former came to be known as Witchcraft. Certainly, the lines between the two were not clearly drawn, areas overlapped, and priests and priestesses worked together and exchanged information for the benefit of all. Yet independently the priests served the Horned God of Death and Resurrection, and priestesses served the Goddess of Fertility, the Earth Mother. Perhaps during the season of fertility and abundance the Goddess was seen to dominate, while ever in the background lurked the Lord of Death. And in the Winter months, the Horned God was seen to dominate, and yet it was known that the Goddess would reawaken and return from the Underworld. No doubt priests and priestesses at the great Sabbats performed rites that expressed the interaction of the Goddess and the God. It is this combination of practices that we, as contemporary Pagans and Witches have inherited, and we must be ever mindful to maintain the balance.

As Lammas is the celebration of the harvest and the Corn Mother, so it is the celebration of the Grain God whose life is sacrificed at the harvest. Some of the most ancient Gods, Tammuz, Adonis, Attis, and later Dionysus, were vegetation and grain Gods. As the Goddess is eternal, ripening and aging and sleeping through the Winter to be renewed and become the Maiden once again, or descending into the Underworld alive to find her beloved consort who has died, so the God must die in order to be born again.

This theme is told and retold, in the battles between the Oak King and the Holly King, the myths of Adonis, Tammuz and Balder and the tales of Gawain and the Green Knight, and Taliesin and Cerridwen. The Gods of these tales and legends are either the Sun or the Grain God, but it is not important which, since the two are ultimately one God. This God has spent the Winter months in the Underworld of the Dead, returns in Spring at the Vernal Equinox, grows to maturity through Midsummer and is cut down in the prime of his life at Lammas or dies at the Autumn Equinox or Yule.

Most Sun Gods have two things in common, the fact that they die annually and are resurrected; and that they have a radiant head of golden hair. These two aspects describe both the sun and ripening heads of grain perfectly.

Another name for Lammas is Lugnassad, named for the ancient Celtic Sun God Lugh, whom these rights honored. It was not his life being celebrated, however, but his death being mourned that these rites commemorated. Lammas follows Midsummer when the Sun is at its height of power, and marks the time when the darkness begins to wax as the light of the Sun wanes.

It is quite obvious that in all cultures, the God in his aspect as the Sun God, whose return in Spring brought light and warmth and resurrection of Nature, was recognized and honored long before his aspect as the God of Grain and Agriculture. When his aspect as the Grain God was recognized, he was often perceived as the son of the Sun God. In this aspect he is far more clearly a God of Death and Resurrection. In many mythologies, he combines the elements of the new Grain God with the older Sun God. One such myth is that of Llew Llaw Gyffs.

LlewLlaw Gyffs came into being as an emanation from the body of the Goddess of Death, Arianrhod. The emanation was captured by the God Gwydion before anyone could see what it was. The spark of life brought forth from the Goddess of Death grew rapidly into a young man with radiant golden hair. It is this rapid growth and blond hair that identifies him as a God of Grain, but the radiant head of hair also identifies him as a Sun God. Furthermore, his name Llew Llaw Gyffs is usually translated as meaning "the lion with the steady hand"—and a lion is an animal frequently associated with the Sun. (The sign Leo, for instance, is ruled by the Sun.) And finally, when Llew Llaw Gyffs is tricked into revealing the only way in which he can be killed, he is shot in the leg and turns into an eagle, another animal that is a symbol of the Sun.

The similarities between the Celtic Llew Llaw Gyffs and the Teutonic Sun God Balder are stunning. Balder, the beautiful and beloved God who was called "The Shining One" could only be killed by one creature, the Mistletoe. So invulnerable was he, like Llew Llaw, that the

Gods used to take turns throwing weapons at him, until the secret of his destruction was revealed and the God of Winter was tricked into throwing a shaft of mistletoe at him. Mistletoe grows on the tops of sacred oaks, which is where Llew Llaw sought refuge after he was fatally wounded. The idea that the myth of Llew Llaw Gyffs is telling us of an annual event is expressed in the fact that the only weapon that could harm him had to take a year and a day to be forged.

The fact, in the myth of Balder, that the Gods took turns throwing their weapons at the god certainly resembles the old Pagan tradition of reapers taking turns throwing their sickles at the last standing sheaf of grain until it is finally struck down.

In order to represent the God at the Lammas Sabbat, we have found that a Sun Wheel made of eight ears of miniature or "squaw" corn, serves as a very powerful symbol. To make this Sun Wheel, all that is needed is some coat hanger wire, a wooden or heavy cardboard disc about three inches in diameter, carpenter's glue, floral wire or twist-ties, and eight ears of squaw corn that are fairly equal in length. Bend the coat hanger wire into a circle about ten or twelve inches in diameter—wide enough that two ears of corn will fit across it with their tips touching in the center, and the point where the husk grows out of the cob resting on the wire. With the wire circle lying flat on the table, arrange the ears of corn in a radiating design. Then using floral wire or twist-ties, wire each ear to the circle of coat hanger wire (or use hot glue). Then, lifting the tips of the ears in the center of the circle slip the wooden disc under them where all eight ears meet. Finally, lifting the tip one ear at a time, drop a large amount of the carpenter's glue or hot glue under each one and allow the Sun Wheel to dry overnight.

The following day some of the husk of each ear of corn can be wound around the coat hanger wire to hide it, and held in place with a drop of glue. The Corn/Sun Wheel will, of necessity, be made from ears of corn obtained the previous Fall.

As a part of the Lammas Sabbat, both the Corn Sun Wheel and the Corn Mother might be carried in procession into and around the Circle, as part of the ritual, and then set up: the Corn Sun Wheel in the West or North, the Corn Mother in the East or South.

Following the Sabbat rites, the two powerful ritual objects can be displayed until the Autumn Equinox, and then stored away, separately, in a place where they can rest throughout the dark half of the Wheel of the Year, safe from moths and mice. This Corn Mother is the same one that will be honored again at Imbolc. The Corn Sun Wheel would not be used again until Lammas, and if it has been made to be kept permanently, it will become an even more powerful ritual object that will gather magickal energy to itself with each Lammas Sabbat.

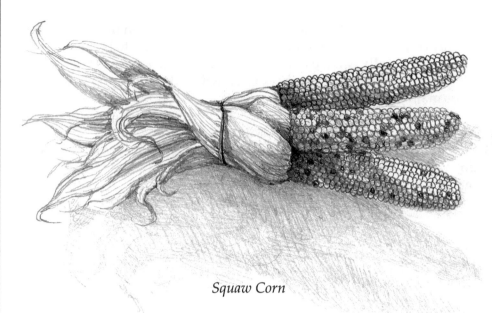

Squaw Corn

When the Grain has been harvested, it is then threshed and win-nowed. The process of threshing breaks the grain from the straw and also releases it from the chaff, the hard shell that surrounds each grain. This is accomplished by pounding the bundles of grain which are laid out on the threshing floor with a wooden tool called a flail. So sacred was this process and the grain it liberated, that the ancient pharaohs of Egypt were depicted holding a flail in one hand (and a crook in the other). And when King David entered Judea, he purchased a threshing floor upon which he built a temple. The threshing floor had such a powerful link to fertility that even today, of the myriad of rites and rituals that accompany a modern wedding, one is that the groom must carry the bride across the threshold on their wedding night. It is apparent from its name that at one time a threshold was a board nailed down to the threshing floor to prevent any of the precious grain from spilling out. In the Celtic myth of Cerridwen and Tailiesin, the boy named Gwion Bach, through magick gained by receiving a drop of brew from Cerridwen's cauldron, turns himself into a grain of wheat on a threshing floor. In the form of a black hen, Cerridwen eats the grain of wheat, and later in her own form she gives birth to the wizard Tailiesin.

Once the grain is threshed, it is then winnowed. This was done by tossing the threshed grain into the air with a basket or rake, and allowing the breezes to separate the wheat from the chaff.

The next process is to grind the wheat or other grain into flour. This was done, at one time, with a small hand quern and later with huge millstones. If the harvested grain is the body of the sacrificed Grain God, then the millstone might be the Silver Wheel—the Death Goddess Arrianrhod, herself.

When the grain has been ground to flour, it is then moistened (and usually combined with other ingredients) and baked into bread. It is this loaf that is ritually eaten as the central point of the Lammas Feast.

Here are two recipes for bread that will make appropriate and delicious main dishes for the Lammas Feast:

The first is a corn bread recipe which is especially appropriate for American Pagans, since the predominant grain grown in this country for thousands of years has been corn. It does not require yeast and rising time, and it can be especially beautiful if it is baked in a corn bread mold that produces little loaves shaped like ears of corn.

Corn Bread

Pre-heat the oven to 425°. Then sift together:

> 1 cup all-purpose flour
> 1/4 cup of sugar
> 3/4 teaspoon salt
> 2 teaspoons baking powder

Then blend in:

> 2 eggs
> 1 cup milk
> 1/4 cup soft shortening

Beat the batter only until it is smooth, but do not over beat it. Pour it into well greased corn molds, muffin tins, or a 9x9x2" pan and bake for 20 to 25 minutes.

The corn bread is best when it is served still warm, with lots of sweet butter.

As the harvesting, winnowing and grinding of the grain represents the death of the Grain God, then to eat the sacred loaves is to partake of his body—and in so doing, to gain a tiny portion of his divine essence. For this reason, in many an ancient tradition loaves of bread were baked in the shape of a corpse, not human form, but mummi-form.

The following recipe for whole grain bread is one that is easily sculpted in the final moments of the last rising.

Whole Grain Bread

In a large mixing bowl combine:

> 2 cups milk (warm to the touch)
> 2 packages of dry baking yeast
> 1 teaspoon salt
> 1/2 cup honey
> 1/4 cup dark brown sugar

Cover this mixture and set it aside in a warm place until it has doubled (about half an hour). Add to this mixture:

    3 tablespoons softened butter
    2 eggs
    1 cup of unbleached white flour

Stir until bubbly. Now mix in:

    1/2 cup wheat germ
    1/2 cup of rolled oats
    2 cups stone ground wheat flour
    2 tablespoons sesame seed

With floured hands, turn this dough out onto a floured board and gradually knead in more unbleached white flour until the dough is smooth and elastic and no longer sticks to your fingers. Place this dough in a greased bowl, turning it so that the dough is greased. Then cover it with a clean cloth and keep it in a warm place to rise until it is doubled (about an hour). Then punch it down and divide it into two or more elongated loaves, roughly sculpted into mummiform shapes, and placed on greased cookie sheets. Cover these and return them to a warm place until they double again. Bake the loaves in a pre-heated oven at 350° for about an hour, or until they are done and sound hollow when tapped.

Corn Bread Sticks for the Lammas Feast

If the harvesting of the grain is the death of the Grain God, then the sprouting of grain is his rebirth. In some Mediterranean countries women would sprout grains of wheat in clay dishes or bowls. These bowls of sprouted grain were called "Gardens of Adonis," and were offered to the ancient God by being thrown into streams, rivers, or the sea. (In later times, they were offered to the Old God by being left in the churches of the new one.)

As a preparation for the Lammas rites you might wish to sprout some grains of wheat to be baked into the Lammas loaf as a symbol of rebirth, and also to use as offerings during the Lammas rites.

The best type of container to sprout anything in, I have found, is the unglazed terra cotta dishes exactly like the ones used under flower pots. Two of these about eight inches in diameter will be needed. Then soak about half a cup of wheat grains (available at a health food store) in a cup of cold water over night. The following morning, rinse them in a bowl of cold water and reject any that float. Then place them in one of the terra cotta dishes and cover them with the other. Leave the covered grain in a dark, quiet place where it will begin to grow and stir as if in the womb of the Earth herself. On the following day, rinse the wheat again in cold water and return it to its covered dish and dark, quiet place. Rinse the sprouts each day, and then on Lammas Eve (or whenever the Lammas loaves are to be baked) remove about half of the sprouts and stir them into the bread dough at the appropriate time. (Sprouts may be substituted for the rolled oats and sesame seeds in the recipe given above.) Rinse the other half one more time and allow them to stand in direct sunlight. This will bring green chlorophyll into any of the leaves that might have formed.

These are the sprouts that will be offered on Lammas Day. When the right stream or river has been found, lower the dish of sprouts into the water and gently allow them to float away, with words like:

> *God of Grain*
> *Lord of Rebirth*
> *Return in Spring*
> *Renew the Earth*

Lammas Day in Europe was traditionally a day to pick berries, particularly bilberries. Picking and eating bilberries was once a sacred act. At Lammas in our part of the country there are no berries to be picked. Strawberries, raspberries and blueberries all have passed, and there won't be another crop of raspberries until October. But these berries were picked and preserved earlier in the year, and the jam from them is delicious on corn bread or whole grain bread, especially when it is warm from the oven. And even more especially when it is served along with sweet butter.

Bread spread thick with butter is an especially appropriate Lammas meal, because butter is sacred to Bride who is another aspect of the Corn Mother.

Liquor made from grain, such as ale, beer or whiskey, is as much a part of the Lammas Feast as bread. In this aspect, the God of Grain is known affectionately as John Barley corn. Because these liquors have the power to alter consciousness as well as give good cheer they were held in the same regard as certain herbs and mushrooms by the ancient people. To the followers of the cult of Dionysus, wine was sacred for the same reason and the drinking of it was considered a sacred ritual. Dionysus is a vegetation God identified with the vine, but, like other grain and vegetation Gods, he is primarily a God of Death and Resurrection. Dionysus apparently evolved directly from an earlier shamanic god of animals, who presided over the spirits of animals slain in the hunt and who brought about their rebirth in order that they might be hunted again. The priests of Dionysus, the Lupercei, still wore the goatskin costumes of their shamanic predecessors; while the God himself was a God not only of the Wild Hunt and the Vine, but of the Death and Resurrection of humans as well.

Dionysus came to be considered the male counterpart of the Grain Goddess Demeter, who established the center of her worship at Elusis, where she was once treated with much kindness. Here the Elusian mysteries were annually performed, but little is known about them because those that participated in these rites were sworn to secrecy. Only one small portion of the rites is known, that is that participants were shown a single ear of corn and told, "Behold the ear of corn, reaped in silence."

Like the followers of the Cults of Attis, and of Dionysus, the worshippers of Demeter and Persephone were granted victory over death and life everlasting.

As the Wort Moon wanes and the Barley Moon waxes, the afternoons of August buzz with the sound of insects. High in the trees cicadas call, while in the fields and meadows crickets chirp and the sounds of insects are louder than the songs of birds. In the pear tree the bird house hangs empty now, where a month or so ago busy wrens fed their hungry brood.

Where men once walked with sickles and scythes gathering the golden harvest by hand, now mechanized monsters mow the sacred grain. Yet here and there in secret silence, small groups gather to honor the Grain God and the Corn Mother, to share the sacred loaf and sip the ancient brew, and by these ancient ways retrieved from the past, ensure a future for the Old Gods and their hidden children.

Amid the abundance of August, we sense an urgency to prepare for the leaner days that lie ahead. Now braids of onions with crisp amber skins hang from the rafters of the wood shed, drying in the summer breezes. In another month they will be brought to the root cellar where they will be kept for winter meals. Red tomatoes ripening now will soon be crushed and simmered and canned for winters ahead, and the crock of sauerkraut that has undergone a transformation in a quiet corner of the cellar, too, will be packed into bright shiny glass jars.

In the vineyard, the broad leaves of the grape vines bask in the sun, producing sugar for the clusters of grapes that hang, still green, from the vines; but as September approaches, and roadsides and hedgerows are splashed with the yellow of goldenrod and the red of sumach, so will the grapes blush to purple and black. But for now we must wait and look forward to Autumn days.

Chapter Six
AUTUMNAL EQUINOX

AUTUMNAL EQUINOX

The clear white light of a September morning slants through the wavy glass of old window panes, casting shadows on the bedroom wall and highlighting the faded stitches of a sampler wrought by someone long forgotten. Across the valley a neighbor's rooster crows to answer ours, and in the garden pumpkins ripen in the waning sun.

By midday the chill is gone, and the warmer air is scented by the sweet smell of the first fallen leaves on the damp earth. The herb garden has been cut back, most of the herbs having been gathered when the Wort Moon was full, and now the rest pruned back before a killing frost. In the vegetable garden, tomatoes still ripen on the dying vines and huge yellow blossoms of squash and gourds open in profusion. On the hillside, the sheep with fleece growing thick grazes closer now, seeming to sense that our afternoons in the sun together will soon be coming to an end.

As white "rooster-tail" clouds streak across the clear blue sky, promising a change in weather, we gather the green tomatoes that would be damaged by the frost. Later, as the shadows gather before the setting sun, the kitchen is filled with the smell of green tomatoes or peppers, onions, corn or pears, all simmering with brown sugar, vinegar and spices, to become an assortment of pickles, relishes and chutneys which will enhance the winter meals that lie ahead, and will add excitement to the holidays just around the corner.

One morning in the month we awaken to discover that the sunlight flooding the room is not white but golden, due to its being filtered through the yellow leaves of the maple tree that embraces the corner of our bedroom. Here, where only a few months ago doves built their shallow nest, now seeds ripen as the sap runs down again into the earth, reminding us that the balance is about to shift as we turn from the lightness into the dark.

All around us, trees are changing their colors, each according to its own schedule, and reminding us once again of their magickal importance and significance.

The rowan tree at this time of year does not display the most vividly colored leaves; rather, its leaves fade to a yellow and brown, and fall unnoticed. The berries, however, turn to brilliant clusters of red-orange.

Rock Art for a Sanctuary Garden

Rowan is a tree of protection. Its branches and twigs are made into amulets of protection, and the tree itself is planted outside cottage doors and farm buildings to protect both family and flock from lightening and harmful magick. It is a tree associated with Faery-magick, and its leaves are usually divided into the magical number of thirteen leaflets. Its bright red berries, like other red fruits (including tomatoes, woody nightshade and amonita mushrooms), were up until recent times considered foods fit only for the Gods. But red is life-giving, like the color of blood, and so a necklace of rowan berries gives life and energy to its wearer—just as red thread gives life to the amulet of rowan twigs.

In orchards, hedgerows and forest edges, the woody rosettes of hazel ripen and burst open, revealing the little nuts inside as the foliage of the tree turns a deep copper brown. Hazel trees and hazel nuts have had close association with magick and Witchcraft since ancient times. The leaves, twigs and bark may be brewed into a healing liquid that soothes a wide variety of physical ailments, and the very straight year-old growth of the branches are excellent as wands for general, but powerful magick. While older, forked branches are the typical diving rod or dowser of the water-witch. For this reason, a single hazel nut on a string makes an excellent pendulum for dowsing. The twisted spiraled branches of the contorted filbert, another member of the hazel family, also makes an attractive and popular wand, and may be the perfect wand for certain types of magick. But generally speaking, the straighter the wand the better because the purpose of the wand is to direct magickal power. The shorter the distance the energy has to travel, the stronger it is when it reaches the object at which it is directed. On the other hand, a naturally spiralled hazel rod may act like the spiraled groove in a rifle barrel, enabling the power to travel a greater distance in a straighter line.

The nuts of the hazel tree are associated with wisdom, and particularly with occult and ancient wisdom. Amulets of hazel nuts strung together on a red thread are protective against harmful magick, and necklaces of hazel nuts might be worn when seeking occult wisdom or learning magick.

The tiny, heart-shaped leaves of birch turn yellow and dance on swaying black branches above the papery white bark of the flexible trunk. The delicate branches of birch have long been popular Yuletide decorations, even among followers of the new religion (who seem to be unaware of their Pagan significance). At Yule in many countries throughout Europe, bundles of birch twigs were used to drive out the gold-crested wren, the symbol of the Sun God of the waning year, in order that it may be replaced by the robin, symbol of the waxing sun of the new born year—the Divine Child. For this reason, too, birch is a popular wood for the Yule log, its white bark showing off well the other sacred greens with which it may be adorned.

MAGICK OF DECIDUOUS TREES

TREE	LEAVES	MAGICK
ROWAN		PROTECTION FAERIES
HAZEL		WISDOM WANDS DIVINING
BIRCH		SACRED TO THE GODDESS BESOM YULE LOG
MAPLE		BEAUTIES OF LIFE PEACE
SASSAFRAS		MEDICINAL THE MOON
HAWTHORN		FAERIES PROTECTION PURIFICATION WISHING
WILLOW		BESOM SACRED TO HECATE
ASH		BESOM WORLD TREE RUNES
OAK		MALE FERTILITY THE SUN SACRED TO THE GOD

Birch is also a symbol of the Goddess of Spring, and its budding in some countries signifies the beginning of the agricultural year. It is also one of the three woods used for the traditional broom or Witch's besom. Because of its white bark, graceful beauty and early spring budding, it is associated with the Maiden aspect of the Goddess. When used as Yuletide decorations, whether as bare branches or painted white to resemble frost and snow, or adorned with sacred greens and burned as a Yule log, birch in the house signifies abundance in the coming year.

As Autumn progresses, one of the most spectacular displays of color is to be seen among the maple trees which may turn yellow, orange or red, depending on the species. Little is written in books of magick of the esoteric significance of maple trees, which are found throughout Europe and North America. But the Pennsylvania German tradition tells us that the maple symbolizes the beauties of life. When studied closely, the five-pointed leaves of most maples resemble the splayed fingers of the human hand, and these five points also represent the five senses.

The maple tree more than any other appeals to the majority of the senses: its dense foliage in the summer provides cooling shade, while its hardwood burns in the winter fire to produce ample heat, satisfying our sense of feeling all year round. Its sap may be boiled down into sweet syrup or sugar to please our sense of taste. Its wood, often figured in variations such as "tiger" or "bird's eye," may be turned or carved into beautiful shapes, and the splendor of its colors in Autumn are a delight to our sense of visual beauty. In the late 1960s, the Canadian maple leaf also became a symbol of peace and love, appealing not only to our five physical senses, but to our higher, more spiritual senses as well.

An ancient tradition was to plant a pair of maple trees at the south side of a house when it was being built. Since houses in ancient times were almost always built facing south in order to take advantage of the Sun's warmth, the trees were planted in the front of the home.

In summer, the trees provided shade from the sun. These trees came to be called Bride and Groom, because a house was usually built when a couple got married; but it is likely that in earlier times these trees that provided protection year round were called Goddess and God trees.

In Autumn it is an instinct, almost a tradition to some, to gather some of the beautiful fallen leaves in order to press them between the pages of books and preserve their fleeting beauty. Among these leaves, some of the loveliest will be maple leaves. To carry such a leaf as an amulet can help to open the senses and expand our awareness of the joys of life and the beauties of nature that surround us.

Along the roadsides and hedgerows of early fall, the sassafras turns a brilliant orange. Its twigs have a rootbear flavor and its roots can be brewed into delicious and medicinal beverages or tonics. But it is the leaves of the sassafras that are most unusual. The typical sassafras leaf has three rounded lobes, reminding us at once of the Triple Goddess. But the sassafras is unusual in that one branch may have as many as four different kinds of leaves on it: the three-lobed leaves already mentioned, a single-lobed leaf, and double-lobed leaves that might form both left and right handed "mittens." As the three-lobed leaf reminds us of the Triple Goddess of the Moon, so the single leaf suggests the Maiden of the New Moon, and the left and right mittens the waxing and waning of the Moon. For these reasons, the creative Witch will certainly find uses for sassafras leaves in Moon magick, and especially the branches bearing all four kinds.

Later in Autumn, another tree of magickal significance, the hawthorn, will turn a deep bronze or burgundy, as its rose-hip like fruits ripen to dark red. Its fruits are not especially important food for birds, but its thorns provide protection for smaller birds to nest among. It is the thorns too that are most important in magick. Thorns may be used wherever pins are used in magick, for instance, in a Witch's Bottle. Thorns can be used to inscribe magickal symbols on candles, or to actually pierce a candle (as is done in certain charms and spells). Hawthorn is one of the trees favored by Faeries, and may be planted near a house to attract Faery-folk and the good fortune they might bring with them. It is also planted for protection. Strips of colored cloth might be tied onto the branch of hawthorn, or fastened onto a thorn to make a wish, i.e., the color expressing the nature of the wish. The white blossoms of this tree are sacred to the Goddess in her aspect as the Maiden, and are used to adorn the altar at Beltane (but according to ancient tradition, it is unlucky to pick the flowers or to bring them into the house before the first of May).

The ash is one of the first trees to loose its leaves, which are actually fronds of leaflets. The ash in Norse mythology is the World Tree, the Ygdrasill, whose trunk unites the branches of the upper world with the lower world, which are its roots. To every shaman, regardless of the culture, one piece of equipment is believed to be made from the offshoot of the World Tree—usually his staff, or the wooden hoop of his drum. It is this piece of the World Tree that enables him to travel to the upper world of Nature Spirits, or to the lower world of Shades, in order to gain information vital to his community. For this same reason, the handle of the besom—the traditional Witch's broomstick—is also of ash. It was beneath the spreading branches of the ash that the Triple Goddess of the Norse myth, the Norns, decided the fate of men. Odin (or Woden or Woton) hung crucified by his ashen spear on the World Tree for nine days and nights in a shamanic vision quest, during which he received the sacred Runes. For this reason, ash is the ideal wood to use if you plan to make your own set of Runestaves. Finally, to the ancient Greeks, ash was considered to be sacred to Poseidon, so the wood of ash is carried as protection against drowning.

While other trees change color in brilliant displays, the grey-green leaves of willow remain unchanged as they sway gracefully from trailing branches. The willow has long been associated with magick and Witchcraft, and it is the third wood used to make the Witch's besom. The weeping willow is also associated with death, and was often embroidered on mourning samplers of the 18th and 19th century. The birch, on the other hand, represents the Maiden aspect of the Goddess and forms the brush part of the besom. The ash, or Tree of Life, represents the Mother aspect and forms the handle, while the willow and its associations with death represent the Crone aspect of the Goddess. But the willow is also sacred to Hecate, the Goddess of the dark mysteries, and so if the ash handle of the besom represents life and the birch brush represents the Maiden or rebirth, then the willow used to bind the one to the other represents not only physical death, but the death of true spiritual initiation that leads to the rebirth of the self.

So close is the association between the willow and Witchcraft that it is likely that the root of the word Wicca, meaning wise, and the root of the word wicker, meaning flexible or pliant (such as the branches of willow) have a common origin. The word wicker cannot be mentioned in connection with Paganism without bringing to mind the image of the Wicker Man—a huge wicker work figure in which the ancient Pagans of Britain were said to make both human and animal sacrifices. But it must be remembered that the famous engraving of the Wicker Man was done in 1669 by a minister of the Reformation, an arch-enemy of the Old Religion during the height of its persecution. His rendition was based on a single line from Julius Caesar, whose main purpose in writing was to prove "what savages" he was attempting to civilize.

Finally, like other trees associated with death, willow is also associated with love magick. A simple age-old charm to attract a lover is to take a single whip of willow and by the light of the waxing moon, tie a knot in it, saying words like:

> *I tie this knot*
> *That I may meet*
> *The one who will*
> *My true love be (or lover, if a shorter term*
> *   relationship is desired).*

Then hide the charm in a secret place. If the relationship should become unpleasant, simply untie the knot by the waning moon to banish the love with no hurt feelings.

The pussy willow, a relative of the weeping willow, is also sacred to the Moon Goddess, and is also useful in love charms.

Among the most sacred of all trees, the oak is one of the last to lose its leaves. Whether they turn scarlet, copper or pale brown, the oak will

Herb Closet

retain some of its leaves all winter, only to have them displaced by new leaves in the spring. In fact, some oaks in warmer climates are evergreen, and it is possible that the original sacred oaks were of an evergreen variety. To the Romans, the oak was sacred to Jupiter, or Jove, the supreme God, and to the Greeks it was sacred to Zeus, father of the Gods. To the Norse, the oak was sacred to Thor, a sky and storm God who shares with Zeus an affinity for thunderbolts. To the priests of the Celtic people, the Druids, the oak was a sacred tree, associated with the sun at the Summer Solstice, and it is upon the oak that the sacred mistletoe grows. The pre-Celtic people of Northern Europe buried their honored dead in hollow trunks of oak, and according to one version of the Arthur myth, the Druid Merlin was sealed in a trunk of hollow oak.

As the birch and willow, graceful and delicate trees, both are sacred to the Goddess, so is the oak, tall and strong, sacred to the God—especially in his aspect as Lord of the Dead. Because of the very obvious growth rings in the wood of the oak, it is also sacred to Saturn, a God of the Dead, whose Roman festival, the Saturnalia, was held about the time of the Winter Solstice. Saturn is the father of Zeus/Jupiter, father of the Gods.

Since oak is sacred to the God in both his aspects of the Dying God at the Summer Solstice, and the Divine Child at Yule, it is the very essence of masculinity. For this reason, the traditional wand of male fertility, the phallic or priapic wand, is of the oak and tipped with an acorn. For this reason, too, many Witches wear necklaces of acorns, or of a single acorn—male Witches as amulets of fertility as well as a symbol of the God, and female Witches to honor the God as well as his masculine traits in ourselves.

In stark contrast to the colorful splendor of the deciduous trees with leaves of orange, red, gold, copper and bronze, the evergreens distinguish themselves: the cool green beauty of holly, pine and yew will last throughout winter, when the beauty of autumn is passed.

The waxy, dark green leaves of holly conceal the still green berries, which now like beads of precious jade will, in another month, begin to blush and by Yule be the brightest red. Holly is the symbol of the Sun God in his waning, from Midsummer to Yule, at which time he is replaced by the oak, the Sun God of the waxing year. The thorny crown of the ancient Holly King is still to be seen as the sprig of holly in the hat of many traditional Santa Claus figures.

The holly, along with the oak, was sacred to the Druids. Its Celtic name "tinne," meaning sacred tree, is probably related to the German word "tannenbaum," a sacred evergreen. But tannen, or tannin, is a word associated with oaks. In Mediterranean countries, the sacred holly is actually an evergreen oak. It is this holly that in ancient times decked the halls of Rome during the Saturnalia.

In the legends of the vampire (a product of the Christian Era), the figure of the cross (a solar symbol) affords protection from the undead—but it is a stake of holly that will finally stop their evil. Ancient tradition tells us that a holly tree planted near the house protects against evil influences—but in the case of English or American Holly, it is necessary to plant a pair of trees, one male and one female. This is because it is necessary for the female tree to be pollinated by the male in order to bear berries, and it is considered unlucky to have a holly tree that does not bear berries. English and American hollies, then, planted as a pair, not only protect the home from unfriendly influences, but also represent the Goddess and the God.

The pine or the fir tree is sacred to the Moon Goddess, just as the oak and holly are sacred to the Sun God. It is one of these trees that will be entwined with ribbons as the May Pole at Beltane, and adorned with fruits, nuts or ornaments at Yule. The earliest account of a fir tree so adorned is in the myth of the great Goddess Cybele, who gathered violets and decorated a fir tree with them in honor of her beloved Attis. To decorate a fir tree with fruits, nuts or berries, or ornaments that represent them, is of course, an example of fertility magick. The Moon Goddess to whom the fir tree is sacred also presides over childbirth; and so as the acorn-tipped wand of oak is used in rituals of masculine fertility, so is a pinecone tipped wand of fir useful in rituals of feminine fertility and in child birth and in Moon magick.

The dark leathery needles of the yew are toxic, but the fleshy red berries are edible. In Norse myth, the yew as often as the ash is considered to be the Tree of Life or the World Tree; but in other mythologies, possibly due to its toxic nature, it is considered a tree of death. As both the World Tree and the Tree of Death, its trunk is seen as a two-way channel to the world of the spirits, through which we can travel to the spiritual planes or spirits can travel to the physical planes. Because of this strong shamanic association, yew is another excellent and traditional wood for the making of Runestaves.

As the days of September slip by, it is not only the trees that will undergo transformation, but the wild herbs of the fields as well. Along fencerows, foxtail grass turns a pale amber and the leaves of sumach change to brilliant orange and red. Even the poison ivy is beautiful this time of year.

The milkweed which has hosted the caterpillars of the monarch butterfly most of the summer, as well as the beautiful red milkweed beetle, now changes to a bright yellow, giving a clue to the color of the dye it will yield. As the color of its foliage changes, the seed pods begin to split, releasing the seeds which drift on silken parachutes to be dispersed by the breezes. Milkweed is favored by the Faeries, especially the pods and the silky seeds, so to aid in rituals to attract the Faery-folk gather the stalks and the bursting pods to adorn the Circle with; collect some pods to combine with rose petals to form a ring in which the Faeries might be invited to appear. A pod may be carried along with other herbs as an amulet when you wish to see the Faeries.

The bright fuchsia stems of the pokeberry plant and the evenly spaced rows of plump black berries are positive keys to its identification. The berries yield a deep pink to purple dye, but the color will quickly fade to grey. The juice of the berries, when boiled with vinegar, can also produce a deep rust dye or ink whose color is quite long lasting. It is a fine natural ink for inscribing Runes or other signs or symbols, wherever the color is appropriate. The deep, blood-like color is "life-giving," and is a traditional color for tinting Runes after they have been incised.

Another natural dye or ink that is available in abundance at this time of year is from the outer hulls of black walnut—but care is needed in collecting them because they seem to be able to almost permanently dye fingernails a deep brown. A plastic bag filled with the nuts or broken fresh hulls will begin to fill with deep sepia liquid. Be sure to place the bag somewhere where it will not stain anything important because the dye can seep through some plastic. Pour off some of the pure liquid into a bottle and add vinegar as a preservative. Black walnut dye is also a beautiful natural stain for wood and handmade baskets. (Do not dispose of the hulls in your compost. Black walnut is a soil toxin, and very few plants can grow in its shade.)

Gourds in every shape and color are ripening in the Autumn sun, and anyone who does not grow their own just needs to take a short ride in the country to find a wonderful selection. Aside from being some of the loveliest of the natural seasonal decorations with which to adorn the Sabbat altar or Circle, some gourds can also make useful magickal tools.

Gourds

Coyote melons, when ripe, are about the size and shape of tennis balls and are banded dark green. As they dry out, the stripes fade and the gourd becomes an overall straw color. Coyote melons are native to the American Southwest. And unlike other gourds or squash, they usually dry out without spoiling. For this reason they make excellent natural rattles—musical instruments almost anyone can play—especially appropriate for anyone on the shamanic path. When the coyote melon is completely dried out, perhaps a year after it was picked, drill a small half-inch hole in the opposite end from the stem. Using a strong pair of tweezers, such as those used in a biology lab, pull out the fibrous filling and the seeds. When the shell of the gourd is quite empty, add something to make the rattle sound. Small pebbles or beans are perfect. Only a few are necessary, and the number of them should be significant. For instance, the rattle pictured on the title page of this chapter was made to be used around the Circle and is decorated with designs symbolizing the four directions. It contains four white navy beans. (Beans are also sacred to the Goddess.) Then using a length of wood in a pleasing proportion to the gourd, and whose diameter is a bit larger than the hole in the gourd, glue the wooden handle to the gourd so that it seals the opening completely, using carpenter's wood glue. When the glue is dry, the rattle can be decorated with artist's oil paints or oil based house paints, and adorned with feathers or beaded cords.

Gourd Dippers

Another useful magickal object that can be made from a gourd is a dipper. To make a magickal dipper, select three or four gourds when they are just about to begin drying out. These are the gourds that have bulbous or egg shaped bases and long, thin, sometimes curved necks. The reason for using so many gourds is that not all of them will dry out perfectly, so by using several a few perfect ones will be ensured. Using a sharp knife, slice off one side of the bulbous base and scoop out the seeds and meat, going as far into the neck as possible. Then hang the gourds in a dry airy place for a couple of months. It is unfortunate that during this time, the beautiful brilliant orange, yellow and green will fade to a straw color, leaving no hint of the gourd's original beauty; but that can be replaced by designs or the inscription of magickal Runes and symbols. These dippers made of natural gourds are excellent for using to add powdered incense or herbs to charcoal or fire, for ritually sifting herbs into water or air, or for pouring libations of wine onto the earth. However, if the gourd is to be used for liquids, it must be sealed with polyurethane or shellac first. This will also keep it from becoming mildewed in hot and humid weather.

Just as the leaves of the trees are beginning to change from green to copper, bronze to gold, and the gourds and pumpkins on the vine are turning from green to orange, so too are the deer changing colors, from the bright orange of summer coats to the drab brown of winter camouflage. This is appropriate, because now begins the hunting season.

It is probable that early man did not differentiate himself from other living creatures, let alone see himself as being above them. He did, however, know himself to be a spiritual being, as evidenced by ritual burials and grave offerings, and almost certainly he understood all life to be spiritual by nature. For this reason, it is highly likely that some of the first magickal rituals ever performed were not for hunting magick (as is often suggested), but to appease the spirits of animals that had to be hunted for food. In the words of one Eskimo shaman, "All of the creatures we have to kill to eat, all those we have to strike down and destroy to make cloths for ourselves, have souls as we have."

It is out of these ancient and shamanic roots that Wicca and the other Pagan religions grew. And it is from these first hunter gatherers that eventually civilization and agriculture grew. But the ancient traditions continued, and when their original meanings were forgotten, the rituals degenerated into such blood sports as hunting, bullfighting, animal and eventually human sacrifice.

As Wiccans, we (Dan and I) believe that "If it harm none, do as ye will." We also honor the words of the Goddess as expressed in The Charge, "Nor do I demand sacrifice; for behold I am the Mother of all living."

Because of our strong feelings for the sanctity of all life here at Flying Witch Farm, Dan and I have set aside an area that we call the Grove of Faunas. It began twelve years ago as a one acre wood lot of renewable hybrid poplar trees, planted appropriately enough, on a site that according to old maps was once an Indian hunting camp. Before they were planted, the trees, one hundred of them in all, fit in the bottom shelf of the refrigerator; but today they are a forest of trees, fifty feet tall. "New Forest," as we called it in the beginning, soon became a refuge for deer, red fox, raccoon and dozens of varieties of birds. It is the only forested area in the midst of hundreds of acres of farmers' fields, where hunted animals can find a sheltered hiding place to raise their young in safety, die in peace, and be reborn in the shade of the trees. I guess it was the morning that we saw the two newborn fawns, all rusty orange with rows of white dots, tip-toe out of the sumach and honeysuckle thickets of New Forest, to explore the world, that we decided never to cut the trees.

Instead we set aside the area to those other children of the Horned God and Mother Goddess. We chose the day of the first New Moon of the year to dedicate this acre of forest to the Horned God in his aspect as Faunas, Lord of the Animals, who presides over their cycles of life, death and rebirth.

Here is the ritual that we used, which can be adapted to fit any area of any size. Dan prepared the ritual by placing large stones as markers on the center of each side of the square acre. On the southern side of the forest, facing North, Nature had already provided a flat stone that protrudes from the slope of the hill. Then, beginning at the southern point (which is the only practical way to enter New Forest), Dan defined the boundaries of the grove with the tip of his athame. When he had returned to the stone at the southern point, we made an offering of Yule log ashes and addressed the Guardians of the South, with words like:

> *O Spirits of the South*
> *Whose Element is Fire,*
> *We ask that You protect this Grove*
> *And those that dwell within it.*
> *Let it be a Sanctuary of Safety*
> *For the Wild Children of the Mighty Gods.*

At the stone in the West, we made an offering of a vial of herb-scented water, and Dan repeated the enchantment, addressing the "Spirits of the West, whose Element is Water."

At the stone in the North, we left an offering of a semi-precious stone, and Dan addressed the "Spirits of the North, whose Element is Earth."

At the stone marker in the East, we made an offering of stick incense (which we lit only because there was an inch or two of snow on the ground) and Dan spoke the same enchantment, addressing the "Spirits of the East, whose Element is Air."

Two steps past the stone in the East, Dan found exactly what we had been looking for, a small menhir or standing stone, about three feet in height. We had planned to find a stone of exactly those proportions to place just behind the flat stone in the South. So to complete the ritual, Dan carried the menhir back to the point in the South, where he stood it in the spot that the Gods had given it to us for, and here he completed the enchantment of the grove with the words:

> *O Lord Faunas*
> *Horned God of the Hunted*
> *We Your Servants*
> *Ask that You accept this Grove*
> *That we dedicate to Your Honor.*
> *Let it be a Sanctuary of Safety*
> *For the Wild Creatures of Your Domain.*
> *So Mote It Be!*

The following day, which also happened to be my birthday, we were given a sign that the wild creatures of the Grove of Faunas were aware of the magickal ritual we had performed for their well-being. When Dan went out to feed the chickens and collect the eggs, there was a beautiful Bob-white quail at the gate of the chicken pen, begging for some feed! This has never happened before, or since.

As the Moon waxed to full, Dan and I completed our plans for the Grove of Faunas. On the menhir, which was already the perfect shape—a tall, narrow phallic shape symbolic of regeneration—we painted a copy of "The Sorcerer," from the Cave of the Three Brothers in Ariage, France. This paleolithic painting of a shaman expresses perfectly the fertility magick of birth and rebirth with which we empowered the Grove of Faunas. Now this painted menhir stands above the flat stone that had marked the Southern point of the Grove, and on which we leave our offerings.

The use of stones to mark the boundaries of sacred places is certainly not new. Stonehenge is probably the first example that comes to everyone's mind. But other than these huge, ancient temples, there are some simple stone monuments that can be reproduced on a much smaller scale.

One of these, of course, is the menhir, or single standing stone. The word "menhir" comes from Breton, "men" meaning stone, and "hir" meaning "high" or long. Menhirs are usually unhewn, or in their natural shape, and may be ornamented with painted symbols or with symbols and signs carved into stone. Because of their tall phallic shape, they may be considered as being appropriate monuments to the God or male principle.

Petroglyphs on a Stone Wall in the Woodland Wildflower Garden

Another type of stone monument is the "dolmen" or "cromlech." "Dolmen," a Breton word meaning "table stone," is applied to a single stone which may be anything from a flat slab to a huge boulder, placed on top of three or more upright stones. Most dolmens or cromleches were originally tombs, and most were covered with mounds of earth or were originally partially underground. Small or miniature versions of the dolmen make excellent outdoor altars and offering tables.

The interior structure of burial mounds such as the one at New Grange (Co. Meath, Ireland) are in some senses actually Cromleches. Passage tombs such as the one at New Grange are especially complex, having a long passageway that is aligned with the rising sun at Midwinter so that its rays illuminate a chamber at the rear of the tomb. There can be little doubt about the symbolism intended here: the rays of the Sun God/Sky Father penetrate the tomb/womb of the Earth Mother in a symbolic union of the God and the Goddess in the hope of bringing about the rebirth of those buried within. Chambers on either side of the passageway give the floor plan of the tomb a cruciform design. Interestingly, a similar floor plan appears in Wiltshire, Britain, in a temple dedicated to the Orphic mysteries. Orpheus himself was a priest of the Sun God, Apollo-Helios. If there is a connection between the cruciform floor plan of the tomb at New Grange and the Orphic temple at Littlecote, and the solar alignment of the New Grange tomb with the solar divinity served by Orpheus, it is a connection that spans several thousand years, and links pre-historic Ireland with the Pagan revival in Christian Rome. One of the basic beliefs of the Orphic Mysteries was that if one could live three consecutive lifetimes of purity, one could be released from the cycle of birth, death, and rebirth, and enter Elysium, the paradise of the Greeks.

Whether an earthen mound enclosed a simple cairn, the grave of an individual, or an elaborate passage tomb designed to hold the remains of many members of a clan, the loose earth itself was sometimes held in place by a ring of curb stones or dolmens. As the thousands of years passed and wind and rain eroded away the mounds of earth, the curb stones, dolmens and menhirs were left to stand free once again, to become the small stone circles and cromleches that dot much of Northern Europe. Such stone circles and monuments on a smaller scale can be constructed almost anywhere—even indoors—and for almost any purpose.

As already mentioned, menhirs are symbolic of the God. They have been placed singly, or in avenues of pairs of dolmens, or in great numbers of parallel rows, such as those at Carnac in France. Smaller menhirs may be placed here or there in a garden as a focal point in planting, and to honor some particular aspect of the God. Indoors, a standing stone in honor of the God will not look out of place among potted plants, nor on a window sill where rays of the rising sun—perhaps at Midsummer or Yule—will cause its shadow to caress a figure of the Goddess.

Some circles, like the Magick Circle, the necklace of the Goddess, and the Wheel of the Year, are symbolic of the Goddess, and might be erected in her honor. Stone circles, like other Magick Circles, were probable constructed to contain magickal energy, and over the years the stones themselves absorbed a great deal of magickal power. Smaller versions of stone circles need not be permanent, as long as the stones are treated with honor and respect afterward. Ideally, stones for an indoor Circle would be used again and again, gathering power with each usage. Stones weighing only a few pounds may be collected and stored at the Covenstead between rituals. Each stone should be carefully selected, and might even be the object of a quest.

The number of stones might vary according to the purpose of the Circle: eight for Solar Sabbats, thirteen for the number of the lunar months, or twenty-eight, the number of days in the lunar month for a lunar esbat. But whatever the number, the minimum should be four to mark the four directions and their corresponding elements. The stones might be gathered at one time, and all from the same place; or sought individually. For example, a stone for the North of the Circle which corresponds to the element of Earth might come from a cave, or deep within the earth. This need not be as difficult as it sounds. Just look for a plowed field or an excavation, preferably north of the Covenstead. A stone for the South and the element of Fire should come from that direction, and perhaps be of volcanic origin. For the East, a stone from a high windy hill might be appropriate, and for the West, a stone from a river bed or the edge of the sea. As each stone is obtained, it should be consecrated to the Spirit and the Element of its own direction, buried in the earth, bathed in water, scented with incense or rubbed with ashes before being placed around the Circle. Stones to be placed in between these stones might be gathered in the appropriate season: the south-east during May, the south-west during August, and so-forth. When the Circle is complete, it need only be consecrated in the way of your tradition. Each time the Circle is cast, the stones will gain in power.

Stones for the lunar esbat Circle might be gathered one at a time as well, one during each lunar month, and consecrated on the night when the Moon is Full. Here again, each consecration might be different: the stone gathered during the Barley Moon might be heaped with barley and left in the moonlight on that night. A stone gathered during the Wine Moon could be anointed with wine, and a stone gathered on the Blood Moon anointed with (one's own) blood. Some Moons present more of a challenge. It might not storm on the night that the Storm Moon is full, but the stone could be anointed with storm water gathered at another time. Likewise, the stone for the Snow Moon. The Wolf Moon would also present a problem if it weren't for the wolf's domesticated kin, the dog. A dog might be coaxed to lick the stone or sleep with it on the night the Wolf Moon is full.

Cornstalks

Stones for Magick Circles might also be collected from special places, or taken to special places to absorb their power.

No matter what kind of stone structure is being created, whether a single menhir or a full solar circle within a lunar one, it might be desirable to mark or inscribe the stones in order that they further express the purpose of the stones—or in the case of an impermanent stone Circle, to identify them.

For simple identification, labeling, or even numbering is sufficient, but not very magickal. One of the primary requirements of any magickal object is that it stimulates our own magickal excitement. With this in mind, then, labeling might be done in Runes if your tradition is somewhat Nordic; or in one of the many magickal alphabets such as Ogam or Theban, or drawn in pictographs for those on a more shamanic path.

Other stones may simply be decorated with powerful magickal symbols such as the Sun Wheel, spirals, triple spirals, pictographs, and single Runes; or elaborately painted according to one's skill.

When the warm days of September darken into the frosty nights, the Wine Moon waxes to full. This is the time of the grape harvest and the bunches hang dark and heavy on the vine, awaiting the harvesters, the crush, the fermentation, the initiation-like transformation that will take place in the darkness of the oaken barrel, changing ordinary grape juice into wine. In rituals of the new religion, bread is equated with the body of Jesus while wine is equated with his blood. But in earlier Pagan religions, wine because of its ability to induce an altered state of consciousness is equated with Spirit, while bread because it is the staff of life, is equated with Matter. Wine therefore is associated with the God and bread with the Goddess.

In the Pagan cult of Dionysus, which reached its height in about the eighth century B.C.E., wine and the grapevine were sacred because of their associations with this God of Resurrection; while in other countries where the grapevine does not grow, ivy or bramble berries are sacred. In ancient Egypt, ivy was sacred to Osiris, also a God of Resurrection.

A remarkable artifact dating from the second half of the fourth century B.C.E., known as the Derveni Krater, seems to suggest a link between the religion of the followers of Dionysus and a far earlier, more primitive belief system. This Greek mixing vessel, or wine crater, was discovered in a tomb and contained the ashes of a man who had been cremated. It seems appropriate that an object portraying a God of Resurrection and used for mixing water and wine should also be used as a funereal container; but unlike the sophisticated myth of Dionysus, the crater contains scenes of something more ancient.

On one side of the bronze vessel is the Silenus, part man and part beast. He has the ears and tail of an animal and has an erect penis. He seems to be conducting the dance of two ecstatic women, while a third is trying to hold them back. Other women on the vessel are carrying a fawn which, according to ancient myth, the Maenads, legendary followers of Dionysus, would tear apart in a frenzied ritual of sacrifice. Still another woman carries an infant over her back, suggesting human sacrifice as well. The two women dancing under the direction of the Silenus, who holds a hunting club behind his back, have bared their breasts—recalling another fragment of the ancient myth—that the Maenads also suckled and nurtured newborn wild animals. The vessel seems to be portraying an earlier shamanistic ritual of death and rebirth, presided over by the Silenus who in some ways resembles the ancient painting of a priest known as "The Sorcerer" mentioned above. The fact that the scene was embossed on a vessel that held the cremated remains of a man (and was probably commissioned for that purpose), seems to suggest that this is the Greek version of the Cauldron of rebirth.

There is yet another myth of Dionysus that would associate the Derveni Krater with the mythical cauldron of Cerridwen. In the Turkish myth of Zagreus-Dionysus, the God referred to by this name was being pursued by the Titans, a race of evil giants who were the forerunners of the human race. In order to escape, he changed his appearance, first into that of a goat, then a stag, then a serpent, and finally a bull—but it was no use: in spite of his magick, he was captured by the Titans and sacrificed. Only his heart was left, and this was taken by Zeus and from it he created Dionysus, who is also called "The Reborn."

This sounds remarkably like the story of Tailiesin, who, as Gwion Bach, was asked by Cerridwen to stir a potion brewing in her magickal cauldron for a year and a day. At the instant the potion was ready, a drop of the fluid splashed out of the cauldron, anointing Gwion Bach rather than Cerridwen's son, for whom it was intended. Cerridwen was furious. She reached out for Gwion, but he changed his shape into that of a fish, a hare, a swift, and finally into a grain of wheat; and he hid himself among the thousands of other grains on the threshing floor. But Cerridwen shifted her shape into a black hen and she devoured him. Eventually, Cerridwen gave birth to him and he was reborn as the beautiful bard and master of magick, Taliesin.

These two ancient myths from such distant lands have several elements in common: the hero's ability to shapeshift into four different kinds of animals; the hero's being reduced to a single, seed-like object; and the hero's being reborn as an immortal.

One last figure on the frieze of the Derveni Krater is an armed hunter wearing only one shoe. It has been suggested that this device symbolizes that the individual so depicted has been consecrated, or dedicated, to a particular God. In this case, it is Dionysus who is shown reclining at the top of the crater, serene and detached from the scene below. While the semi-shod figure may represent the mythical Pentheus, it almost certainly represents the man whose remains are contained within the crater, and who was, no doubt, consecrated to the God Dionysus.

Of all the many myths of Dionysus, the one that associates him the most closely with wine is the tale of his voyage to Naxos on a pirate ship. One day at sea, Dionysus was seated on the deck of the ship, drinking a cup of wine, when he fell asleep. The pirates, who had planned to sell him into slavery in Asia, tied him to the mast. When Dionysus awoke and realized the pirates' plans, he flew into a rage and caused the mast of the ship to sprout into a grapevine. He flung his wine cup into the sea and turned the water into wine. He changed himself into a great panther, and when the pirates saw his magickal powers, they jumped into the sea whereupon they were turned into dolphins—all except for one sailor, who had tried to protect Dionysus from the other pirates.

Though Dionysus is a God of Wine, his festival is not celebrated in September during the Wine Moon, but rather in Spring during the season of resurrection. At this time in ages past in the city of Athens, the Sacred Marriage of Dionysus was performed as an annual ritual. Whether the roles of the God and the Goddess were played by human performers or by statues is not known, but these rituals are almost certainly the forerunners of the Bride and Groom of the May customs, usually performed at Beltane throughout most of Western Europe.

The consort of Dionysus, and his bride in these rituals, is Ariadne (who is probably Arianrhod), but in actual practice of the ancient Pagan religions of Greece, he is so closely linked to Demeter that she is often taken to be his consort. Actually, the two are counterparts, and express perfectly the God/Goddess balanced polarity. Dionysus personifies the ancient and primitive Sky Father, and Demeter the Earth Mother. Their mysteries both were celebrated at Elusis, where centuries later, the Orphic mysteries evolved the concept of a single, abstract divinity of which every God and every Goddess was an aspect.

As we approach the night of the Autumn Equinox, we are standing at a threshold: we are about to leave the Summer months of light and abundance, and step into the Winter months of darkness and spirit. To our ancient Pagan ancestors of hunter gatherer times, this surely meant that the time of physical abundance of fruits and vegetables, grains and berries, was coming to an end, and the time when animals would have to be hunted to supplement the food supply was about to begin. This night when the hours of light and the hours of darkness are equal is a night to honor the balance of the Goddess and the God and the balance of matter and spirit because the Pagan religions celebrate not only spiritual life of the next world, but also the physical life of this world. There can be no better way to do this than by ritual feasting upon fruits and berries, and especially bread baked of grain given by the Goddess at Lammas during the Barley Moon, and with wine symbolic of the spirit, given by the God during the Wine Moon.

The Altar Prepared for the Autumn Equinox

The Goddess is associated with the Earth itself and the grain and other fruits that sprout from it to give us physical life. In fact, the word "mother" comes from the Latin word "mater," which is also the root of the word "material." The God is associated with the spirit, that invisible essence that animates the physical body during its lifetime, and re-animates it when it is reborn. It is very likely that this is the reason for the abundance of Paleolithic "Goddess figures," in contrast to the almost total absence of figures of the God. It is perfectly natural to sculpt a figure of the Earth Mother out of clay or stone, which is, after all, Her own body. But how does one sculpt a figure of spirit, and of what?

One of the most frequently occurring themes in the mythologies of Demeter and Dionysus is the rewarding of mortals who showed kindness to them, and the punishment of those who either were evil, or who refused to acknowledge their Godhood. Dionysus punished the pirates who would have sold him into slavery by turning them into dolphins. He punished Pentheus for not honoring him by driving the women of his house mad. Pentheus wore a single shoe ever after to symbolize the lesson he had learned. Demeter established the center of her worship at Elusis and taught the secrets of agriculture there where she had been treated with an act of kindness. As Pagans we do not worship vengeful Gods, nor do we believe in sin and retribution. The ancient myths were not intended to emphasize fear and punishment, but rather they are telling us to honor the God and the Goddess in every man and in every woman, within ourselves and without.

And so as we eat the consecrated bread of the Autumn Sabbat and sip the sacred wine, honoring in perfect balance of the Goddess and the God, we are then compelled to bid farewell to the Lady of the Summer and to welcome the Lord of the Spirit.

As September draws to a close and the purple shadows fall across hills and meadows now more gold than green, the scent of woodsmoke drifts across the valley from fires kindled to ward off the chill of a frosty night, and quilts folded at the foot of the bed exude the familiar fragrance of cedar and camphor. The hens seek the shelter of the coop as soon as the sun sets, and the sheep's fleece is growing thicker.

Chapter Seven
SAMHAIN

SAMHAIN

The golden days and frosty nights of October fill us with anticipation for the holiday season that is about to begin, and all around us are the signs of its coming. By the front porch the apricot buds of chrysanthemums have opened into golden blossoms that spill out across the grass like so many buckets of gold, while pumpkins decorate the doorstep. On the back porch, squashes—flesh colored butternut—green zucchini, and colorful Turks hats mingle with baskets of tangy apples. In the kitchen on the long pine dinner table, a hand hewn trencher overflows with colorful gourds and squaw corn; while shelves of early slipware in the cupboard are adorned with miniature pumpkins.

On the well-worn hearthstone, a basket of hazelnuts still in the hulls are drying. Some wintery evening in the weeks ahead will be spent hulling them, and another cracking the hard shells. Eventually they will be baked into crescent cookies for the Yule Sabbat. But for now they must just cure and dry by the kitchen fire as we prepare for the Sabbat night that is closer at hand.

Since Halloween, or Samhain, is one of the most important days of the Wiccan calendar, naturally Dan and I are interested in anything pertaining to it, so over the years we have accumulated a rather nice collection of antique Halloween party favors and decorations. In recent years, we have begun the practice, soon to be a tradition, of decorating our summer kitchen with all of these delightful bits of paper nostalgia from long ago. Here an iron cauldron hangs over glowing coals of the old fireplace, while on the pine tavern table that stands before it Witches, bats and wide-eyed owls fly across orange cardboard nut cups, place cards, and tiny lampshades.

Paper dolls cut out of an October 1917 issue of *Ladies Home Journal* attend Betty Bonnet's Halloween party dressed in costumes that look far more like apparel of Nature Spirits than those worn by the children of today. One wears an inflated orange suit with green stockings, collar and cap, and carries an orange paper lantern. He is the essence of Jack-O-Lantern. Another wears a skirt of brown leaves adorned with bunches of grapes and a headdress to match. She is the Spirit of the Grapevine.

In stark contrast to the dark old red paint of the pewter cupboard, a greenish white cardboard skeleton dances an eternal jig while he stares, grinning, at the cardboard cat with its back arched in terror. Oaktag Witches with flowing capes fly across eighteenth century pewter plates

Telling the Future at Samhain

that seem to symbolize the Moon; and candlelight shines through the wicked tissue-paper eyes and grin of a cardboard pumpkin head. Party whistles that uncoil, tissue paper party hats, crepe paper candy baskets, and Jack-O-Lanterns of every description clutter the table and cupboard in a riot of black and orange designs. Among these pieces of paper and cardboard treasured for generations are objects with meanings and symbolism older and far deeper than these turn-of-the-century party favors would, at first glance, suggest.

One of the most recent additions to our collection is a tambourine: it is of fine leather stretched over the rim of maple wood. Silver lamé streamers trail from the openings in the rim, where tiny symbols are attached. On the skin are painted the dancing figures of a Witch, a ghost, and a Spanish lady. Beneath them is the poem, "Ghosts and goblins and Witches lean, all proclaim this Halloween." On the inside of the tambourine is pasted a newspaper clipping browned with age. It was cut from the society pages of a Philadelphia newspaper and it describes a Halloween party of the 1920s, the decorations and the names of every guest who attended. Each of the guests had been given a tambourine with their name on it. But this is not the only tambourine in our collection of party favors. There are others, with parchment for the head and rims of tin decorated with bats and cats and haunted houses. But why tambourines?

In the last century, tambourines were one of the standard tools of the Victorian seance room. Apparently, this is because it was an instrument that could be easily made to sound, even by the most non-material of entities. The slightest touch could cause the tiny symbols on the rim to jingle. Along with the trumpet, the tambourine was standard equipment of the 19th century medium.

But elements of the tambourine go back much further than the Victorian seance parlor. According to some accounts, the Maenads, played symbols and tambourines as they danced their ecstatic dances in the forests and in the wild places of ancient Eastern Europe. The little cymbals on the rim of the tambourine seem to have descended directly from one of the most ancient instruments, the sistrum, which is associated with Isis.

Still, the association of the tambourine with the spirit world goes back even further, further than we can know, to the earliest instrument of all: the shaman's drum. A tambourine is simply a drum with symbols attached to its rim. It is a small, hand held drum, just like those used by shamans throughout the world in order to induce an altered state of consciousness. This altered state enables the shaman's spirit to leave his body to travel to the spirit realms in order to gain important knowledge for the future of his tribe. These two elements, contact with the spirit world, and divining the future, are as much a part of Halloween

Antique Party Favors

celebrations today as they were during the earliest shamanic beginnings of the Pagan religion.

Tambourines are not the only musical instruments among the collection of party favors. There are whistles that uncoil into long lengths of orange tissue paper decorated with black cats and bats, a cardboard horn with a smiling pumpkin face surrounded by crepe-paper sunflower petals, and most unusual of all, an embossed tin "clicker" in the shape of a frog, painted the brightest red orange and dotted with black cats. A frog is certainly not the first thing that flashes to mind when one thinks of Halloween, but its link to Witchcraft and the Samhain Sabbat soon become apparent. Folk and Faery tales abound with stories of princes turned into frogs or toads by irritated practitioners of the Craft. There are also numerous references to the use of spittle or ashes of toads in magickal brews. During the persecution, the presence of a frog or toad in a person's home was considered evidence that the person served Satan, because frogs were considered to be a Witch's familiar. Such evidence often sent a person to the gallows. Also given as evidence during the trials were long lists of ingredients for the famous Witch's flying ointment. One of the basic ingredients is soot. Many of the ingredients are probably fictitious (since they were often extracted under torture), some not understood today, but many are some of the most poisonous herbs known: hemlock, hellebore, aconite, digitalis, and amanita. Frogs and toads produce a poisonous substance on their skin. (Those of North America and Europe do not produce a deadly poison, but the beautiful orange, blue, green or yellow and black frogs of Central and South America can be fatal even to the touch.) In ancient Mexico, the priests of Tezcatlipoca, in order to overcome fear, would rub themselves with an ointment, the basic ingredients of which were the ashes of poisonous reptiles and insects, and soot. In all probability, tree frogs were among the "reptiles" used. It is just possible that one of the ingredients in flying ointment was the ashes or skin secretions of frogs and toads.

Other animals that seem to be part of the traditional decorations for Halloween are cats, bats, and owls. Paper napkins, paper plates and cups, tin toads and tambourines, all were spotted or splashed with the images of these animals, and most particularly, the black cat. With its arched back, claws extended, and eyes staring in terror, whether it is perched on a picket fence or hitching a ride on the broomstick of the Crone, the cardboard "scardy-cat" almost as much as the Crone herself has come to symbolize Halloween. Not just any cat, but a black cat, and one that is absolutely terrified.

The dog was probably the first animal to be domesticated, but eventually cats worked humans into their plans. The Egyptians were probably the first to keep cats as pets, and Bast, the Egyptian cat-headed Mother Goddess became the patron of the happy home. Like Isis, she too is depicted holding a sistrum. According to Plutarch, the sistrum of Isis was inscribed with a cat as the symbol of the Moon. The Greek and Roman Moon Goddess, Artemis and Diana, sometimes took the form of a cat; and the Teutonic fertility Goddess Freya was often pictured as riding a cart drawn by cats.

Because of their nocturnal habits, cats became associated with Witchcraft and cats along with frogs and toads were considered to be Witches' familiars. Witches were believed to assume the form of a cat almost as frequently as that of a hare, and it was believed they were able to do so only nine times in their lifetime (nine being the number of a cycle completed). At some period of time, hares and cats were probably considered as interchangeable symbols of fertility, Moon magick and women's mysteries; but eventually rabbits and hares, because of their wild behavior during the Spring mating season, became associated with the Vernal Equinox and Beltane, and the fertility rites of Spring; while the cat, with its uncanny ability to sense the presence of the deceased, became associated with Samhain and the season of the Spirit. This is especially true of black cats, whose color is the symbol of the Crone, the aspect of the Goddess honored at this time of year. Because of their association with Witchcraft during the persecutions, these lovable and loyal pets were often tortured and burned, or otherwise killed, along with their human companions. So we hang the cut-out cardboard cats at Halloween, let their staring eyes remind us to open up our own intuitive eyes to the spirits of those that gather around us on this night; and let them be a symbol, too, of "never again the burning."

The other two animals that are popular as decorations at this time are owls and bats, animals which are also nocturnal. This also associates them with the Moon, and therefore magick and Witchcraft. Owls are also associated with the Greek Goddess Athena, the Goddess of Wisdom, but also a Goddess of War. For this reason, the likeness of an owl was embossed on the coins of the ancient city of Athens, of which Athena was patroness. As a Goddess of War, she was also a Goddess of Peace and in this aspect she cultivated the olive tree. As a Goddess of Wisdom, she was also the inventor of the spindle and distaff. (In most traditions, the Goddesses of the Moon are also spinners, and this is another indication that she is the Moon Goddess.)

There is a myth of Athena that explains a magickal practice that is practically universal today: from Kazak weavers of the intricate and breathtakingly beautiful oriental rugs of the Near East, to the Amish quilt makers of Pennsylvania, it is unthinkable to weave or stitch a piece without including some imperfection in the geometric design. In the myth of Athena (Minerva to the Romans) and Arachne, Arachne was a daughter of a dyer of purple cloth who challenged the Goddess to a weaving competition and produced a beautiful and perfect piece. Already insulted by the idea of competing with a mortal, Athena examined the piece, and when she could find no imperfection she flew into a rage and punished Arachne by turning her into a spider, who weaves her web throughout eternity. And ever after, no oriental rug is without its imperfection, no Pennsylvania German quilt without its "Amish mistake"—because only the Gods can create perfection, and to be so unwise as to try to violate that law is to invite the "evil eye."

Athena is an aspect of the Triple Goddess and her symbol, constant companion, and one might say her familiar, is an owl. Owls have been considered symbols of wisdom ever since. They have also been considered messengers from the spirit world, and Witches' familiars. For this reason, an owl's wing feather makes a perfect quill pen, especially for keeping a book of shadows. Instructions for making such a pen are given in my book, *Wheel of the Year*. An owl's flight feathers are easily recognized by the fringed edges that gives these night hunting birds their silent flight. They are also excellent additions to the Witch's Ladder charm if the acquisition of wisdom is desired.

Of all the antique party decorations, the object that appears most often is the Jack-O-Lantern. There are embossed cardboard pumpkin faces to hang in windows and large cardboard ones to tie over lamps with glowing tissue-paper eyes and leering tissue-paper grins. There are cut out cardboard pumpkin heads to be worn as masks, and even some to be used as icecream decorations. Everywhere throughout the month of October, pumpkins are lined up at roadside stands, sold by the pound at supermarkets, piled up in huge pyramids at pumpkin farms, and form a pattern of orange polka-dots on a distant hillside pumpkin patch. There can be little doubt that there is a very close tie with the Jack-O-Lantern pumpkins and the Samhain Sabbat. It has been said that in Europe, candles were traditionally placed inside of turnips and other vegetables to keep them from blowing out. Naturally, these vegetables had to have openings cut into them to let out the light, and this eventually evolved into the stylized human face of the Jack-O-Lantern. But this axplanation does not provide a link between this practice and Halloween. Although the type of vegetable that is used is probably of no great importance, the pumpkin, an American vegetable, certainly symbolizes the season; but it is the candle inside the pumpkin that is of magickal importance. The candle flame represents not only the element of Fire, but also the white light of pure spirit. Spirits, ghosts, and Faeries often appear to us as sparks of white light. Many and elf from Tinkerbel to the Ghost of Christmas Past has either been, or has been associated with, brilliant light.

In Japan, on a day equivalent to our Halloween, paper lanterns are hung at garden gates to welcome home the spirits of the deceased. In Egypt, candles are lit in cemeteries to guide the spirits of the dead back from the City of Osiris, and in Ireland candles are lit in cottage windows to welcome home the ghosts of the dead.

It has become traditional among many Pagans to mark the four quarters of the Samhain Circle with Jack-O-Lanterns, but it might also be

Jack-O-Lanterns

in keeping with the season to light one white candle in a Jack-O-Lantern placed in a window or on a front porch as a beacon to the spirits. The candle might be anointed with patchouli oil (patchouli is sometimes called "graveyard dust"), and enchanted as it is being lit with words like:

> *With this candle*
> *And by its light*
> *I welcome ye Spirits*
> *This Halloween night.*

Since pumpkins seem to have become a symbol of Samhaintide, it seems natural that they should also become a major part of the Sabbat feast. Two of the most popular ways of serving pumpkin are as a pie or as bread. Here is one recipe for pumpkin bread:

Pumpkin Bread
2 cups pumpkin (cooked or canned)
1 cup of corn oil
3/4 cup water
4 eggs (beaten)
3 2/3 cups of unbleached flour
1 1/2 teaspoons salt
1 teaspoon nutmeg
2 teaspoons cinnamon
2 teaspoons baking soda
2 1/4 cups of sugar
1 cup white raisins/1 cup walnuts (chopped)

Mix corn oil, eggs, water and pumpkin until smooth. Add flour, salt, nutmeg, cinnamon, baking soda, and sugar. Then combine to this mixture raisins and nuts. Bake for about one hour at 350° in loaf pans that have been greased and floured.

Pumpkin bread is wonderful served with cream cheese and can be decorated with little pumpkin-shaped candies. In fact, recently for our Halloween festivities, I baked a sheet cake (it may have been banana bread or spice cake, or possibly pumpkin bread, I don't remember) and iced it with a cream cheese icing. Then I dotted it with candy pumpkins and went over the whole cake with green icing to form pumpkin vines with lots of spiral tendrils and green leaves. It really was lovely.

If you cut several Jack-O-Lanterns for your Samhain Sabbat, here are two more ideas:

After scooping out all of the seeds, separate as many as possible from the stringy flesh and rinse them under cool running water. You may wish to set aside a few at this point to bless at the Vernal Equinox and to plant in your garden later; or to scatter on a sunny roadside or waste place. Then lightly salt the rest of the seeds and mix them well. Spread them out on a cookie sheet or two and place them in a very low oven, 200-250°, with the door open a crack, turning the seeds occasionally until they are thoroughly dry. Then store them in a tightly closed jar for a healthy winter snack.

Jack-O-Lanterns that have stood on the window sill or porch even for just a night or two are usually pretty moldy and ready for the compost heap, but the fleshy pieces that have been removed from the eyes, nose and grin can add up. For a wonderful and unusual soup, peel the outer skin from the pieces of pumpkin and boil them in water until very tender (about 20-30 min.). Then mash them with a potato masher (or run them through a food processor). Meanwhile, in a pot of an appropriate size, melt some butter and saute one chopped onion per cup of pumpkin. When the onions are ready, add the mashed pumpkin for each cup, and add 1 1/2 cups of milk, 1/2 teaspoon of salt, a dash of pepper, and 1/4 teaspoon of curry powder (more or less according to taste). Bowls of the hot soup can be garnished with a dash of cinnamon just before serving.

Now that the pumpkins have been picked and the gourds have been gathered, we are reminded that Halloween is the celebration of the final harvest. It is the third harvest, the first being Lammas, the barley or grain harvest, and the second being the Autumn Equinox, the grape harvest with its wine festivals. Now when the October sun has set and the moonlight bathes the corn fields, the cornstalks bleached bone white dance their final dances; and in the orchard, ancient trees, gnarled and twisted, are about to be relieved of the burden they've born since the summer.

The final harvest is the harvest of fruit and nuts. This corresponds to the Roman festival of Pomona, Goddess of Fruit Trees, whose symbol is the pruning sheers. Some writers say that Pomona did not have any festival celebrated in her honor; but in all likelihood the harvest was the festival, and it celebrated the supply of fruits and nuts stored for the winter. What is also of interest about Pomona is that her consort is Vertumnus, God of the Changing Seasons. Since Pomona is the Goddess of all fruit trees and all fruit-bearing shrubs, she seems to be a late Roman version of an earlier fruitful Earth Mother Goddess—not of grain and agriculture, but perhaps dating back to a more primitive Earth Mother of hunter gatherer times; while her consort, Vertumnus, is obviously the Sun God, or Sky Father. Although Pomona is the Goddess of all fruit trees, she is most commonly associated with the apple, and in her honor the fruit is named in Latin "pomum."

Apples are associated with both love and death, as are willows and myrtle. Apple blossoms, like hawthorn blossoms, are associated with Beltane, which is when they bloom in temperate climates, and therefore are associated with the sacred marriage. Because of this, it was sometimes used to divine the identity of one's future mate. One method of doing this was to cut an apple into nine equal parts, eat eight of the parts and throw the ninth over the left shoulder, and then turn quickly and catch a glimpse of your future mate.

Apples, apple wood and apple blossoms are sometimes used in love charms and spells.

Apples are also used in healing, possibly because of their association with death (i.e., "What can kill can cure" so "an apple a day keeps the doctor away."). When an apple is cut horizontally, it reveals within its core a five-pointed star. One method for healing warts was to cut the apple in this manner, rub the wart with both halves, put the apple halves back together and bury it. As the apple decomposed, the warts disappeared.

It cannot be overlooked that the word "core," for the heart of the apple, is almost the same as Kore, the Greek name for the Goddess in her aspect of the Virgin.

As the apple tree blossoms at Beltane, and is therefore associated with the Sacred Marriage, so does its fruit ripen and await the harvest at Samhain; and so is also associated with death and the realm of spirits. In Celtic myth, the land of Avalon, where the spirits of the dead dwell while they are rested and rejuvenated, is a fair island to the West where lovely apple trees grow and bear fruit year round. It is here that the Triple Goddess Herself brought King Arthur. Apples sweeter than honey also grow on the beautiful Tir-Nan-Oge, island home of Mananann Mac Lir, who is really more of a Lord of the Dead than a God of the Sea.

Hera, Greek Queen of the Gods, had a magickal apple orchard, and apples were also sacred to Hel, the Norse God of the Underworld. It was believed that apples were the fruit of immortality and resurrection. In the story of Persephone and Hades, when it came time for Persephone to leave the Underworld and be reunited with her mother Demeter, Hades made her eat the seed of a pomegranate to ensure that she would return to him. The pomegranate is an oriental fruit that looks very much like an apple, and the first syllable of its name suggests that there is a link between the two. Had Persephone eaten the seed of a pomegranate, she would have ingested her minimum daily requirement of vitamin C. However, it is likely that it was originally the seed of an apple she ate, because apple seeds contain the deadly poison cyanide—cyanide (one would need to eat many apple seeds) would have certainly ensured Persephone's return to the Land of the Dead.

The ancient custom of wassailing the apple trees was performed to magickally ensure that the trees bore fruit abundantly in the coming year. Today, what is left of the ancient custom of wassailing, usually just drinking a toast with hot apple cider, with or without alcohol, is performed during Yuletide. But it was probably originally done at Samhain when the apples are harvested. To the Celts, Samhain marked the end of the old agricultural year and the beginning of the new, and the custom of wassailing was probably moved to New Year's Eve when the calendar was changed.

Today apples and apple games are still very much a part of the traditional Halloween celebrations, even if the majority of people are completely unaware of their magickal and Pagan significances.

An apple dangles from a string while children, hands clasped behind their backs, take turns trying to get a hold of it with their teeth. Elsewhere, apples bob like corks in a tub of water as once again children try to take one out of the water with their teeth; and all the while, by the flickering light of the Jack-O-Lantern's glow, candy apples glisten, awaiting the cry of "trick or treat!"

Another part of the final harvest is the nut harvest. Nuts, as every squirrel knows, store well for the winter and for that reason alone they are a popular Yuletide treat. From the Brazil nuts in Ben and Jerry's Rain Forest Crunch to the hazelnut crescents of the Yuletide Sabbat, nuts also have magickal significance.

In countries around the Mediterranean, almonds were sacred to the God in his aspect as Attis, the Fertility God of Death and Resurrection. Attis was conceived when his mother placed an almond on her lap so that she might enjoy the perfection of its symmetry. It vanished and eventually the young God of Fertility was born. This is no doubt the reason that almonds encased in a white sugar shell are a traditional part of Italian wedding ceremonies.

Nuts, including acorns, symbolize the male principle of resurrection and rebirth. They are also symbols of masculine virility. For this reason, they are particularly appropriate decorations for the Samhain season and the Sabbat Circle, especially acorns.

Acorns are used in charms for male potency and also for such traditionally masculine qualities as strength and courage. To acquire these qualities, acorns can be inscribed with Runes such as $\uparrow$ and added to the amulet bag along with herbs and stones like hematite, the feathers on a rooster, and so on. Because of their association with the masculine principle of death and resurrection, acorns are also appropriate to wear as necklaces at this time, either a single acorn or as a string of them. Acorns come in a variety of sizes and shapes. In this part of the country they are the small, sometimes striped, acorns of the black oak with its smaller, delicately pointed leaves; or the larger, inch and a half high acorns of the white oak, with its rounded lobes. The larger ones are better for altar and Circle decorations, but both are fine charms for amulets and for seasonal adornment. If you collect acorns fresh, you may find that the caps fall off as they dry. But the cap is a necessary part of the acorn, if it is to be used for magickal purposes. One way to remedy this is to line up the acorns in some place to dry, in such a way that when the caps do fall off, you will know which cap belongs to which one. While the caps are off is the easiest time to drill the acorns for stringing. The caps can then be permanently attached with wood glue.

Of all nuts, though, probably the one most closely associated with Halloween, Witchcraft and magick, is the hazel. In fact, the association between Witchcraft and the hazel is so close, that a popular Witch name is Hazel. (Another is Samantha, probably derived from Samhain.) The most popular wood for an all purpose magick wand is hazel, and so potent is the magick of the wood that the staffs of the early Celtic bishops were of Hazel. The wood is also used for the traditional divining rod used for locating underground water and other minerals. Another name for this is dowsing, or "water witching." The hazel nut symbolizes wisdom and especially occult wisdom. It is the tree for which the ninth month of the Celtic tree calendar is named, and so the number nine is closely linked in magick to the hazel nut. The number nine is also the number of the Crone (3 the Virgin, 6 the Mother) who grants the kind of wisdom gained through the initiation processes of many incarnations.

The property of protection is also attributed to the hazel nut, especially protection from harmful magick. "Rosaries," or strings of hazel nuts, may be hung in the home as an amulet of protection. Also, because of the nut's association with wisdom, occult knowledge and dowsing, it

Using a Pendulum

makes a particularly good pendulum for gaining knowledge. Simply suspend a hazel nut from a string made of natural fiber. In a method similar to a Ouija board, this pendulum can be held over a board containing the letters of the alphabet and used to receive messages from non-physical entities. The same pendulum can be used for dowsing, either water witching, which is done on the site where the source of water of other mineral is to be located; or map dowsing, which can be done anywhere, even miles from the site. The map need not be an actual map either. Dan has successfully dowsed a map that was merely a couple of hand-drawn lines on a blank sheet of paper. Using this method, he was able to find the exact location of Indian artifacts on a farm he'd never seen.

The pendulum comes in really handy for locating lost articles. All that is needed is a rough sketch of the area where the object is believed to have been lost, a quick floor plan or diagram. All of these methods can be done using almost anything for a pendulum—a crystal, a shell or bead—but the hazel nut's association with the Crone, occult knowledge, and with dowsing, make it one of the most natural tools for any of these methods.

Because Halloween is the celebration of the final harvest it was considered unwise in ancient times to eat any fruit or grain that had been left unharvested after Halloween.

As Halloween is the celebration of the final harvest of fruits and nuts for winter storage, it is also the harvest of the flesh. At this time for our hunter gatherer ancestors, who laid down the foundation of our great religion, it surely was a time when tribal activity abruptly shifted from the Goddess-dominated gathering of the fruits of the earth, to the hunting of animals who's spirits were presided over by the Horned God. It was a time when the spirits of animals that had been killed had to be honored, and appeased, in order that the cycle of birth, death, and rebirth could continue.

At this time, as the Blood Moon waxes and then wanes, we feel all around us the spirits that have been recently released from the physical body, human or animal, horned or fanged. At this time of the year, the veil between the worlds of the living and the dead is very thin. As the old Pagan year draws to a close, it is time to receive messages from those who had gone before, and there are a number of ways to facilitate this.

Necromancy is technically the raising of the dead for the purpose of learning the future from them. Spirits can contact us directly, conveying messages to us telepathically, or in rare cases, controlling the physical body and the vocal cords. This type of mediumship is the focus of Spiritualism, and is believed to come from the deceased. But any message from the spirits is welcomed.

Today another type of mediumship called "channeling" is popular. One of the main differences between the two is that while mediums receive messages from spirits of the dead, channelers receive them from highly evolved or ascended entities. In either case, to make decisions based on the advise of unseen entities (who may or may not be who they say they are) is like letting an anonymous phone caller tell us how to run our lives. I cannot think too highly of an entity who would possess another (that's really what it is); nor does being in the spirit make one all knowing and wise. Still, there are many good reasons for wanting to contact the spirit world, not the least of which is affirmation of its existence. And there is much wisdom to be gained from contact with spirits.

There are a number of devices that might be used for the purpose of contacting spiritual entities, such as the Ouija board with its unnecessarily grim reputation, and the pendulum and the alphabet board which was discussed a few pages back. Our personal preference is the wine glass, which, like the Ouija board, can be worked by quite a number of people at one time, thereby making self-delusion a bit more difficult; but it can also be highly personalized by a hand drawn alphabet or a one-of-a-kind antique wine glass. This will make it a somewhat more effective tool than one that is commercially produced. The wine glass is worked by each person's placing a fingertip on the up-turned base of the inverted glass, which will then move from one letter of the alphabet (i.e., placed in a circle around it) to another, much like the Ouija board. The pendulum on the other hand, can only be worked more conveniently if the alphabet is placed in a semi-circle. If a wine glass is chosen, it should be used for this purpose and no other.

When you have found the glass that you feel is right for you, wash it first with soap and water to cleanse it in the mundane world, and then bathe it with a tea of mugwort to intensify its occult powers. If, however, the glass is not new, purify it first in the smoke of wormwood. The same is true for the Ouija board. Then consecrate the wine glass or Ouija to its specific purpose within the Circle, the Samhain Circle being ideal.

Whether you are working with the wine glass, Ouija or pendulum, if you expect to receive messages that will be spelled out one letter at a time, use a tape recorder. The spirits often give messages that go in very unexpected directions, and they use some surprisingly long words. So do not try to remember the words in sequence because they may not make any sense at the time, and the confusion might lead to forgetting the sequence. It is also not a good idea for one of the participants to try to write with one hand while working with the wine glass or Ouija; this reduces the energy of the group and what the spirits need from us in order to communicate is energy. Of course, one person could write the message while others work the glass or Ouija, and they can clarify messages which sometimes make more sense on paper but they would not be participating in the seance then. As much as I personally dislike anything invented after 1840, especially when magick is concerned, there are still some "modern conveniences" I'd prefer not to do without, and a tape recorder is one of them. (I am also still enough of a textbook Aquarius to enjoy spinning fleece on an eighteenth century spinning wheel while watching old episodes of *Star Trek* on the V.C.R., a plastic model of the Starship Enterprise docked atop the T.V. set.) Once the messages have been recorded they can be stored that way or transferred to paper. In either case, the date and names of all of the participants should be included, and any unusual occurrences noted. Messages that make no sense at all may make a great deal of sense in the future.

Once the tool for receiving messages has been chosen and there is a blank cassette in the tape recorder, it might be helpful to decide what type of entities we hope to contact. It can then be useful to have some object to form a link with them—for instance, a photo album containing pictures of your grandparents or great grandparents could form a link not only with a beloved grandparent who has left the physical plane, but also with a long line of ancestors stretching back through time. Wearing a piece of jewelry given by a loved one can also form a link. If you wish to contact a Native American shaman because you are on that particular path, and wish to gain some knowledge, make an offering of sweet grass, sage , tobacco, or corn meal within the Circle.

To form a general link with the spirit world, it is traditional to wear some amulet symbolic of death, such as the Egyptian charm of Anubis, Lord of the Underworld. For this purpose I have a necklace that contains several beads carved into tiny human skulls. They are from Tibet, and are said to be made of human bone. (Many years ago Dan and I saw a spectacular antique necklace of ivory skulls and huge amber beads, but we could not afford it at the time. Years later I met the antique dealer who had it, and she told me that she sold it to a "good" Witch.)

For many of us on the Wiccan path, it would be desirable to contact any of those sisters and brothers who stood in the Circle of the Wise in ages past, and who may have lost their lives due to their beliefs—although something tells me that the majority of them are presently incarnate. This idea raises a question: How many of the millions executed for Witchcraft were actually Witches? The answers found in books on Witchcraft vary from, "None, they were probably all good Christians," to "A few misguided individuals who 'thought' they were Witches." It is my opinion, after reading much of the testimony given at the trials, not by the tortured victims but by witnesses, that the majority were indeed practicing some form of the Craft, since the accused clung to it reverently, costing them their lives.

I have recently completed a cross-stitch sampler that contains the names of nine women accused of Witchcraft during the three hundred years of the persecution. In order to form a strong link, the names were worked in counted thread cross-stitches on an ancient piece of homespun that Dan and I found in the back of a framed eighteenth century sampler purchased some years ago. The first of the nine names is Alice Kytler, one of the first people ever to be accused of Witchcraft in England. The rest are women whom I believe were Witches. Their stories are written on a piece of paper attached to the back of the sampler. Here are a few:

Agnes Marshall, a midwife accused of incantations.

Isabel Mure, was seen placing burning straws in running water and chanting, "I see fire burn and water run and grass grow and the sea flow."

Elizabeth Fotman, accused of healing a horse by drawing crosses on its belly with a stick and reciting a charm; the horse got back on its feet and was healed.

Agnes Robson, accused of healing piglets by reciting a charm.

Anne Whittle, who used a charm to help the brewing of ale that had been bewitched.

The sampler is decorated with cross-stitch designs typical of the late 1600s, and across the bottom are the words, "Each name on this sampler represents one million men, women and children, tortured and killed for Witchcraft" (although this number is disputed).

Witch Sampler

The sampler will hang over the altar at all of our future Samhain Sabbats, because it is the hope of many living Witches to make contact with the spirits of Witches on the other side—not for the purpose of learning about the future, but about the past and perhaps to glean a bit of ancient wisdom from a kindred spirit.

It is important to remember that most Pagans consider the disturbance of the dead immoral, and at Samhain only voluntary communications are expected and hoped for. The departed are never harassed, and their presence is never commanded. The spirits of the dead are, however, ritually invited to attend the Sabbat and to be present within the Samhain Circle. This is often done by a spiral dance or procession, beginning at the western point on the Circle, where a doorway has been left open for the dead to enter; and then spiraling "widdershins," or anti-sunwise, into the center of the Circle. In ancient times this was known as the Troy dance. Before the rites are ended, the spiral is turned back upon itself and danced or walked "deosil'" or sunwise, as the spirits are escorted back to the doorway. Naturally, messages received during these rites by wine glass or Ouija, pendulum or personal contact, can be very profound and filled with personal meaning. These are experiences to be treasured. Some may also find that "power shared is power lost," that is, that the power of the experience seems to be diminished with each retelling in the mundane world. This applies to many things that happen within the Circle. For this reason, most Wiccans and Pagans keep their experiences to themselves, and also because each person must learn for himself the magick of the Circle.

Although most Wiccans and Pagans invite the spirits to join the Samhain Circle, it is usually for the purpose of feeling their presence near us for a while, rather than for the purpose of necromancy (commanding the spirits of the dead to reveal secrets about the future). Instead, we enjoy contact with the spiritual realms and there are many other methods of glimpsing the future.

Divination was so closely related to Witchcraft that the early Church, in an attempt to eradicate the Old Religion, forbade "soothsaying" in many variations. In England, such prohibitions can be seen in laws as early as the Anglo-Saxon period. Later they are evident in such laws as the Homilies of Wielfstan and Aelfric, the Cannons of Edgar, and the Laws of the Northumbrian priests (ca. 1028), up to the Norman Conquest, long before the Witchcraft Acts of Henry VIII (ca. 1542), and Elizabeth I (ca. 1563). These laws certainly reflected similar laws on the continent. By the time of the persecutions, after James I ascended the throne in 1604, the charges of Necromancy and Divination were frequently among the accusations made against Witches that almost inevitably led to their execution.

One of the terms often appeared in the testimony was the Charge of "Sortilege," or of "casting of Lots." A lot might be any object that could be drawn from the hand, such as straws or cards, or put into a container and tossed, like dice. Runes and Tarot cards are also forms of sortilege, because the cards or symbols are chosen by random chance. Tarot cards, Runes and similar methods of divination require the knowledge of a system of symbols and their meanings, often both on a mundane divinatory level, and a more esoteric level.

Still, there are other methods of divination by random chance that are quite simple. One method used by young women to learn the identity of their future husband was to name a hazel nut for each boy they knew and then roast them all together on an open fire. The name of the first hazel nut to jump or pop was the name of the boy she would marry. Should a nut burst open in the fire, it predicted infidelity; but if a nut glowed among the coals, it was a sure sign of true love.

In more recent times, a variety of games and objects for predicting the future on Halloween night have been developed and mass produced. These include a "wheel of fortune" type game that select a number by random chance and give a set of predictions which correspond to the numbers. There have been little charms that could be baked into cakes which would be later sliced and served at random. No doubt many a child swallowed his fortune by this method, which originated with the Irish custom of Colcannon, a part of the traditional Samhain feast. Colcannon was made of mashed potatoes, parsnips and chopped onions, and baked into it an assortment of tiny objects. Each object had a prophetic meaning which predicted the future for the person who received it in his portion of colcannon. Some of the typical objects are: a ring for marriage, a tiny doll for birth, a coin for wealth, and so on.

Along with divination and sortilege, the Synod of Exeter in 1287 condemned conjuration "by means of sword and basin" as being "dishonorable to God." "By sword and basin" (or "blade and bowl," as it was also called) refers to scrying, or mirror magick, and is of special importance to people on the Wiccan path for several reasons. One of these reasons is that the blade and bowl are the athame and the cup of traditional Wicca; the other reason is that scrying, or mirror gazing, has a special association with the Goddess. A set of traditional symbols is the mirror and the comb. She is sometimes portrayed as gazing into a mirror while stroking her hair with a comb. There is a clue in this for those who would scry. To gaze into the mirror is one thing, but to comb or brush one's hair at the same time accomplishes two things: one is that combing one's hair can be very soothing, and relaxing, and helps to achieve a slightly altered state of consciousness. The other is that the act also generates static electricity, and electricity (like that released in a thunder storm) seems to have the ability to increase psychic energy. Static electricity is also generated when cat's fur, or the fur of certain dogs, is stroked. This might explain why cats have a reputation for being so psychic and are so popular as Witch's familiars.

To the people who have developed the ability to scry, images of the future might appear in a mirror, a bowl of water, a crystal ball, or the polished blade of a sword. In order to scry, it is necessary to free the mind of hopes, fears, delusions, and pre-conceived ideas. For this reason, wizards and magicians sometimes used a young child to do their scrying for them. Regardless of who did the scrying, there are several objects that have been traditionally used for the purpose.

The earliest mirrors were discs of copper and bronze, but an ordinary "looking glass" will do just nicely. The mirror can be either a hand held one or a wall mirror. To gaze into a mirror is to gaze into one's own reflection, and for this reason subdued lighting is required. Candlelight is ideal, but be sure to place the candles where they will be an aid and not a visual distraction. Repeating a chant can also help to stop the constant stream of thoughts that flow one into another and away from the task at hand. Chanting words like:

> *Mirror, Mirror, to me show*
> *What it is that I should know.*

This helps to drown out the stream of consciousness while you're gazing steadily and deeply into your own reflection.

Whether a hand mirror or a wall mirror is used, a mirror used for scrying is never used for anything else. Large wall mirrors are usually kept draped while the small hand mirrors can be hidden away, or simply kept face down.

Probably the most popular object for scrying with among Wiccans today is the cauldron, another symbol of the Goddess. The traditional cauldron is a three-legged, black iron vessel with a neck narrower than its widest part. The method of scrying with it is simply to fill the cauldron with water and gaze into it. As the looking glass is a symbol of the Goddess in her aspect as the maiden, Goddess of Love and Beauty, the cauldron is a symbol of the Goddess in her aspect as Mother, and it is associated with the Full Moon. So often was the cauldron used for scrying that a reflection of the Full Moon was caught in its water's depths. If it was not possible to capture the Full Moon's reflection, a coin silver and round might be dropped into the cauldron instead.

Another early method that recreates the seemingly boundless depths of the water-filled cauldron is the "black mirror," or Witch's mirror. This is made by holding a small earthenware bowl inverted over the flame of a candle until the interior of the bowl is entirely covered with black soot. Then the bowl is gently filled with pure and fresh water. Throughout Europe, there are numerous sacred springs and wells, and

A Crystal Ball

many of these are associated with prophecy. Water from such a spring would be ideal for filling the cauldron or the Witch's mirror.

This method was known to the ancient Greeks, who would foretell the future of anyone whose reflection was caste into the water's surface. It may also be the origin of the superstition which states that a broken mirror brings seven years bad luck. The Greeks who practiced this form of divination believed that if the scrying bowl were dropped or broken it would be an ill omen.

The crystal ball of the Gypsy Witch is still another tool used for scrying. It is usually used by gazing into it while it is cradled in both hands in a piece of black cloth or other non-reflective fabric.

Several early methods of learning the identity of one's future mate or partner involves scrying. One method was to go to a well at midnight on Halloween with a candle and gaze into the water, in an attempt to catch a glimpse of his face. Another was to gaze into a mirror by candle light while peeling an apple, and a variation on this was then to toss the apple peel over the left shoulder. The peel would form the initial of the future mate as it landed on the floor. The significance of the apple peel becomes apparent when it is realized that the peel of the apple can form quite a long and perfect spiral if it is peeled carefully. And of course, the spiral, like the apple itself, is sacred to the Goddess. It is also apparent that any of these methods can be applied to other questions besides the identity of one's mate.

The key word in all forms of scrying is "gaze." This means to throw the eyes slightly out of focus, to look through or beyond the object gazed into. This unfocused gaze, combined with the proper meditative state of mind, can allow pictures to form, either within the object being scryed or in the inner vision of the third eye.

The psychic energy of any of these objects is enhanced by an occasional bath with mugwort, and this will be all the more effective if it is done on the night of the Full Moon. Then leave the crystal, bowl, or mirror in the moonlight overnight, but be sure to remove it by sunrise. The Moon itself is a mirror in the sense that it reflects sunlight, and by reflecting one mirror into another can theoretically see into infinity in both directions. This is probably one reason that the looking glass is also sometimes used to look into previous lives.

During the Witch Trials, Witches, especially male Witches, were sometimes accused of gazing into the polished blade of a sword or a knife to predict the future, and it is important to remember that at that time sword blades, mirrors, and even cauldrons, were made of the same kinds of metal. "Sword and basin" is a very interesting choice of words, and very meaningful to contemporary Pagans, expressing as it does the union of opposites, life and death, male and female, God and Goddess.

As the night of the Great Sabbat approaches, we prepare not only for the more solemn rites of Samhain but for the neighborhood children, who will be shuffling through the sweetly scented fallen leaves to our front door to beg "trick or treat." Here they will be greeted by a glistening array—deep red candy apples and gleaming golden lollipops made in the shape of flying Witches, owls and frightened cats flavored with butterscotch or pineapple; here too on the old pine table adorned with gourds and oak leaves and Indian corn, a cauldron overflows with popcorn; and a spider, an early frying pan with three tall legs, is heaped with bright orange candy corn, while a tray of cookies, orange flavored pumpkin heads and chocolate scardy cat forms the center piece.

Samhain is the dark counterpart of Beltane, and trick or treat type door to door begging is a part of both Sabbat traditions. In earlier times the treats would have been the fruits of the season instead of pre-packaged candies, and in some cases—like candy apples—they still are.

A major part of trick or treat is costuming, and a good costume begins with a good mask. The purpose of wearing a mask in most primitive religious traditions is to make a spiritual connection with the deity or the Nature Spirit represented by the mask. The making of such a mask would have been accompanied by ritual every step of the way, from the planning stages to the gathering of materials and so on to the completion of it. The mask would then have a spirit, or magickal power of its own, and each time a shaman wore the mask he would contact the power of it. It seems like the most natural thing, to use masking as a part of the Samhain Sabbat.

The first stage in making a mask is deciding what the mask should be of—an aspect of the Goddess or the God, a particular Nature Spirit, or, for those in the shamanic tradition, a totem animal.

Then there are a wide variety of materials to choose from. Probably the most widely used material for the basic form of the mask has been wood, but not everyone is a wood carver and there are many other materials to work with. Papier-mache is also popular and can later be painted and lacquered to be quite permanent. I have seen very powerful masks

A Feathered Mask—Crone Aspect

woven of basket splint and bark, but unless you have some particular skill that lends itself to mask-making, probably the simplest way to begin is with the Lone Ranger type of masks sold by the hundreds around Halloween. These masks come in a wide variety of colors, and that might be the first part of the symbolism of the mask. For example, a mask of white or silver for the Maiden aspect of the Goddess, red for the Mother, black for the Crone; Gold for the God in his aspect as the Oak King of the waxing year, green for the Holly King, and so on. These might further be adorned in all manner of ways. Here are just a few ideas:

For a mask of the Maiden, begin with a white or silver mask. A long veil of sheer white might be added for mystery and the mask might be adorned with white silk blossoms on silver or pearly white sequin crescent moons.

A red mask for the Mother can be decorated with corn husks, possibly braided to form a crown, and sprays of wheat ears, or just decorated with a mosaic of interesting and colorful seeds to express her abundance and fertility.

For the Crone aspect of the Goddess, a black mask might be embellished with peacock feathers as an expression of her mysteries, as well as a black veil, black feathers, or black crescent moon sequins.

A gold mask for the Oak King can obviously be decorated with acorns and oak leaves. Natural ones can be sprayed with lacquer to be made more permanent.

A Holly King might be painted with the designs of holly and embellished with fresh holly when it is to be worn, There is also a wonderful type of artificial holly of glazed paper that is made today much as it was at the turn of the century. I have no objection to this type of artificial holly at all, because what is imitative magick, after all, but the use of one thing to represent something else?

Of course, a mask representing the Lord in his aspect of the Horned One would need only be of black, embellished with horns of some kind, and whatever other symbols or objects that seem right.

For masks representing Nature Spirits, there is obviously a wide range of materials to work with; textiles and fibers, feathers, leaves, silk flowers, sea shells and sequins, all of these and much more. Once you have decided to make a mask, let the entire process be a ritual. Ask the spirit or deity that the mask will represent for guidance in design and materials. Let the search for the materials be a quest, and as the materials have been acquired, gather them within a Magick Circle and consecrate them. As you work on the mask, enchant it, inviting the deity or spirit to enter it, and when it is finally finished, consecrate it to the one that it represents. Then ever afterward treat it as a representative of that deity or spirit.

Masks in shamanic times were probably of the heads of animals. One reason for this is that, as in some traditions today, the head was probably believed to be the part of the body wherein it resided. These heads, and possibly other parts of the body, skins, tails, genitals, etc., were worn in ritual dance, as suggested by the painting known as "The Sorcerer." It is likely that the dances were like those performed by some contemporary Pagans today, first spiraling widdershins, inward toward the center of the Circle, then deosil and outward from the center, representing what they still do today—the eternal cycle of birth, death and rebirth. That such dances were performed well into the current era is attested by such statements as that of the Archbishop of Canterbury (ca. 668), "anyone who goes about as a stag or bull . . . Putting on the heads of beasts, etc. . [must do] penance for one year." The existence of such objects as the horned mask known as Dorset Oaser, which only disappeared early in this century, proves that in spite of the Church's attempts to stamp out this as well as any other part of the Old Religion, they do survive. That the practice of masked dancing is still today associated with Samhain, the time when the veil between the living and the spirits of the dead is very thin, suggests that in some way the masked dancers were trying to contact the spirits of the slain and hunted animals. That the dance associated with Samhain is often a spiral dance suggests that the magick performed had to do with death and rebirth. And this is not surprising, because Samhain is not only the hunting season, it is also the beginning of the rutting season of the deer and many other wild animals. In all likelihood, these magick and masked dances were an invitation to the spirits of the hunted animals to enter into the new animal bodies now being formed.

Though much of this has been lost or temporarily forgotten, there is still much about the traditional costumes worn by children today that tells us Halloween is a celebration of the spirits. There are glow-in-the-dark skeletons, the ghosts in bed sheets, and the truly creative mummy wrapped entirely in toilet tissue. And among the little goblins and ballerinas, the clowns and the corpses, there is the inevitable Halloween Witch. Her much maligned figure is linked to the earliest aspects of religion, and almost every aspect of her costume has symbolic meaning.

Beginning with her hat, the traditional Witch's hat is a tall, pointed cone with a flaring brim. It is usually stated that Witches were only later depicted wearing this type of hat, which was in vogue during medieval times, in order to portray them as being out dated and out of fashion. It has also been told that in the Middle Ages there was a monk named Dunce who discovered that a tall, cone-shaped hat like that worn by Wizards increased mental activity—and so the dunce cap was invented not to humiliate children but to help them. The Witch was wise enough to use this design to strengthen her own energies, and added the flared brim as a means of sending out the energy to do her will in any direction. The traditional Witch's hat, stereotypical as it might be, also symbolizes the Cone of Power raised within the Magick Circle.

Beneath the brim of the hat, there usually protrudes a long and warted nose. It is believed that the earlobes and the tip of the nose continue to grow throughout life, and so a long nose symbolizes great age and the wisdom that comes with it—just as the elongated ears of the Buddha do. Wisdom and age are attributes of the Crone, the aspect of the Goddess that is honored this time of year.

As for the warts on her nose, they are a reminder that the wise old women known as Witches were also healers, and one of the things they seemed to have been most adept at healing was warts. Still today in remote areas, even in this country, there are women who possess the secret of wart healing. These methods are many and various, and include "buying" the warts for a half penny apiece; or "throwing them away" in the form of a small bag of pebbles or stones. More elaborate rituals cutting a notch in an elder stick for each wart, rubbing the warts with a stick, then burying the stick; or holding a bit of fleece from a white sheep on a thorn from a black thorn tree, dipping it in milk from a red cow, and anointing the warts with this milk. The latter ritual includes using objects related to the three symbolic colors of the Triple Goddess. The warts might be rubbed with a slice of apple or bacon rind, either of which would then be buried; or they may be cured by the Witch's simply saying, "They'll go." If any of these methods seem silly, or the idea of curing warts at all seems trivial, it is important to remember that some warts are cancerous.

The black clothing of the Halloween Witch represents not "the powers of darkness," as followers of the new religion would have people believe, but that great luminary of the night, the Moon, in its waning phase. The waning phase of the Moon, of course, represents the Crone aspect of the Triple Goddess. This Triple Goddess that influences the destinies of mankind is sometimes referred to as the Fates. To the ancient Greeks, they were the Moirae: Clothe the Spinner, Lachesis the Weaver, and Atropos, who cut the thread of life at death. To the Romans they were the Parcae: Nona, Decima, and Morta. And to the Old Norse, they were the Norns: Urdr, Verdande and Skuld. These three Goddesses preside over life, at the end of which each individual spirit bids farewell to the realm of the Goddess and crosses the threshold into the realm of the Horned God of Death and that which comes thereafter. Samhain represents this threshold separating the dark half of the Wheel of the Year, presided over by the Horned One, from the light half presided over by the Goddess. It is the counterpart to the threshold crossed at Beltane by those re-entering the realm of the Goddess in her Maiden aspect.

Along with the pointed hat, warted nose and black robes, another object that is likely to be seen as a part of the costume of the Halloween Witch is, of course, the cauldron. The Norns of the Old Norse, the Parcae of the Romans, and the Moirae of the Greeks, all dwell in a dark cave which has in it a pool or a well, but the Wyrd, the Anglo-Saxon version of the Triple Goddess, dwells in a cave with a cauldron. This cauldron which appears in Celtic myth as the Cauldron of Cerridwen, the Grail of Arthurian Legend, and as one of the four Magickal Treasures of Ireland, the Cauldron of Plenty (the others being the Stone of Destiny, the Spear of Victory, and the Sword of Light, in other words, the four elements) is also the Cauldron of the Goddess and represents the eternal cycle of Birth, Death and Rebirth. It is the Samhain counterpart of the Sacred Wells that are such an important part of many Beltain Sabbats.

But the most important symbolic object carried by the Halloween Witch is the besom, or broomstick. In the past they have been made of windle straw, bean stalks, bullrush, thorn branches, mullein stalks or ragweed (mugwort or wormwood); but the most traditional Witch's besom is a brush of birch bound by willow to a shaft of ash.

In Ireland, the besom was sometimes called a "Faery's horse." Today, "jumping the broom" has become a traditional part of the Wiccan Hand-fastings, symbolizing the transition from the Maiden phase of life to the Mother. Among descendents of the old Europeans there was a lovely custom: the bride prior to her church wedding was given a wreath-like crown made of eggs. Then old folk songs were sung to her by the elder women of her clan. In more recent times, the songs would

The Witch's Besom

would tell of the trials and the tribulations of being a woman; but there can be little doubt that in earlier times, the songs revealed the wonders of "women's mysteries," and undoubtedly much ancient magick. Then when the songs had all been sung, the crown of eggs was removed from the bride's head and she was handed that sacred symbol of womanhood, the broom. To those not of the Craft, it might be seen as a symbol of drudgery, but for those to whom the ancient mysteries had truly been revealed, it is one of the most potent magickal symbols of all.

Shamanism, as it is still practised in remote areas of the world, holds certain beliefs in common. One of them is that through chanting, or dancing, or drumming, or ingesting trance-inducing herbs, the shaman is able to leave his body and travel to the spirit realms to accomplish whatever his purpose might be for the benefit of the community. Whether the shaman is practising on the plains of Mongolia, the frozen tundra of North America, of jungles of Guatemala, he will have one tool that is universal. In one tradition it will be a pole, a tree trunk with its branches removed and propped up to the smoke hole of his tent; such tree trunks, which might have been May Poles, have been found in sacred wells in Britain, and one is shown on the Gunderstrup Cauldron (second century B.C.E.) from Denmark. In another culture, it might be a drum of skin stretched over a wooden hoop, and in another it might be a staff of wood. But in all cases it is considered to be an offshoot of the World Tree. In the latter case, it is sometimes called the "Shaman's Horse," upon which his spirit rides, up through the smoke hole of his tent, to the world of spirits.

The World Tree, which connects the world of the living with the various realms of spirits, can be identified with Yggdrasil of Norse Mythology, the Sacred Ash upon which Odin hung crucified for nine days and nine nights before receiving the sacred Runes. It can also be recognized as the May Pole entwined with ribbons in Spring, and it is the Witch's Broomstick at Halloween. Using this broomstick, or Faery's Horse with its shaft of ash, the Witch traditionally rides up the chimney of her hut and over the Moon to the spirit realms on Halloween night.

Shaman is a Siberian word meaning "one who knows." Samhain is the Celtic name of Halloween. It is just possible that these two words, so similar in spelling and meaning, yet from vastly different places, have a common root somewhere in Old Europe.

As Halloween represents the threshold between the world of the living and the realm of the spirits, and it is a time when the veil between the worlds is very thin. It is a time when special preparations can be made to show our love and our remembrance for those close to us who have crossed the threshold.

What has been called the "Feast of the Dead" or the "Dumb Supper," can be an important part of the Samhain preparations; it is the

A Besom and Cauldron by the kitchen fireplace at Flying Witch Farm.
(photo courtesy of *Fate* magazine)

tradition of leaving offerings of food and drink for the deceased practised in many parts of the world. In ancient Egypt, funerary temples to receive these offerings were built adjacent to tombs, and in Japan, entire families have picnics at the graves of their ancestors. But for most Europeans, the offerings are simpler and made in the home. In Celtic traditions, the offerings were left for the "Pookas." For many, a portion of the cakes and the wine blessed during the Sabbat rites is left for the spirits. But for those who have recently passed on, or were very close to us, something more personal might be appropriate, e.g., a glass of a favorite kind of wine or a piece of favorite cake. A small ritual of personal invitation might be performed during the Sabbat rites such as the following:

For each beloved spirit, prepare a small plate with a piece of a favorite food and a cup of favorite beverage. Then at an appropriate time during the ritual, lift each plate, one at a time, and speak the invitation using words like:

Grandfather, here we do invite you
To return home this night
To share with us once again
The food you loved in life
May these tokens of our love
Renew and refresh you,
And merry may we meet again.

When the Sabbat rites have ended, and the Circle has been cleared, leave this plate on the table with a chair. It was traditional in the earlier times to leave the offering by the glowing embers of the hearth, but most homes are without fireplaces now. Instead, leave it at the person's usual place at the dinner table; or, if you live somewhere that the person never visited in his life, leave it by the place usually given to a guest of honor.

On the following morning, dispose of the food and drink in an appropriate manner. Dan and I have an altar stone in the Faery garden where we leave such offerings until Nature does what She will with them, their essence having already been assimilated by those to whom they were offered.

When the Sabbat fire has flickered and died to embers, and the wind sighs down the chimney in the wake of the Crone, and as the Moon climbs high shedding Her silver light on the rooftops, we bank the fire and bid goodnight to the silent spirits who are gathered all about us. Warmed by the love they had for us in life, and the knowledge that they are not really gone, we bid farewell to the season that has ended.

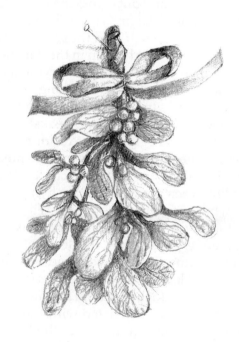

Chapter Eight
YULE

YULE

From Samhain to Yule, the days grow shorter and the nights grow longer. This is the darkest time of the year. But the dark nights of December are illuminated by candles flickering in the windows, and fir trees dotted with rainbows of colored lights. The cold of December's nights is warmed by logs crackling and popping in the fireplace, as the smoke drifts silently up the chimney and out across the valley to mingle with the chimney smoke of neighbors. The fire's glow is reflected in the soft grey gleam of pewter on the mantle shelf, and the red berries of the holly that adorn it. A spray of mistletoe, half hidden in the dancing shadows of the smokey beams, hangs among the other herbs drying there. The warm air is scented with the sweet smell of cookies baking, of vanilla and melted chocolate, of hazel nuts and almonds; while outside quietly the snow falls, filling in the hollows and drifting into peaks.

The dark half of the year begins at the Autumnal Equinox and ends at the Vernal Equinox. The darkest time is from Samhain to Imbolc. To Pagans, this symbolizes the time of spirit activity. Yule is the darkest night of all. The veil between the world of the living and the dead is the thinnest at Samhain, but not on that night only. The dark nights of Winter, from Samhain to Yule, are filled with spirit activity. For this reason there are many Yuletide ghosts, not the least of which are Charles Dicken's Ghosts of Christmas Past, Present and Future.

As suggested by the last of these three spirits, Yuletide, like Samhain, was a time for looking into the future, There are a number of ways of doing this that are traditionally associated with Yuletide. One was to sit on a bull's hide at a cross roads on the eve of the New Year, in a sort of vision quest. The significance of the bull's hide is interesting, because such hides were often associated with the mound burials of pre-Celtic Europe. The location of a cross roads for the exercise is also interesting because Magick Circles were traditionally cast at cross roads. The resulting symbol of the Circle with the North to South, East to West, intersection at its center was of course, the solar wheel.

A simpler method of Yuletide divination was to toss a shoe over your left shoulder. If it landed upright, the prediction for the coming year was favorable.

Lighting the Yule Log

But of all the methods of divining the future, and of all the devices created for the purpose, perhaps the most natural method is learning to read the signs and omens provided by Nature. In order to be able to recognize the signs and omens that occur, it is first necessary to become intimately familiar with the local species and ecosystems. That is because natural omens are commonly given by the unusual behavior of plants and animals, and it is first necessary to know what behavior is usual. In order to recognize the rare or unusual species in your area, you must first be aware of what species are indigenous. To understand natural omens and signs, it is of vital importance to become aware of your environment.

Natural signs and omens can fall into two categories: the normal and the paranormal. The first group is concerned with such things as weather predictions; for instance, "rooster tail" clouds foretell a change in the weather, often an approaching storm. While a "mackerel sky" out of the northwest usually predicts a nice day. A misty morning is a sign of a sunny afternoon. Sea gulls inland are a sure sign of a storm at sea, while an absence of gulls at the shore is usually a warning to head inland. Other signs in this category predict seasonal trends. For instance, the higher squirrels build their nests, the more severe the Winter. I have noticed this to be true, too, of the white dots on the winter plumage of starlings. The more pronounced the dots, the more severe the winter.

It is when we enter the realm of paranormal portents and omens, i.e., those that foretell not the weather or the season, but our personal futures, that things are not so simple, and the signs and symbols can be infinite. Now it becomes not only necessary to know the species of native wildlife and their normal behavior, but it is also helpful to know what those plants and animals represent in traditional folklore and occult literature; and also to understand how they fit into the context of the present situation.

A few years ago, I tripped in the herb garden and severely fractured my femur. The result was five months in a cast and a wheel chair. One afternoon during the first month, I was sitting in the wheel chair near the front door, reading a book on shamanism, when something outside caught my eye. I looked out at what first glance seemed to be a dog, but then I recognized it for what it really was—a coyote! There was a wild coyote walking right up the middle of the road, in northern New Jersey; and just in case there was any doubt that this sign was meant for me, the coyote paused right in front of our front door so that I could get an unhurried look at him. A further indication that this sign was for me was that this beautiful animal was favoring his right leg, as if it had been injured—the same leg that I had just broken! I knew that this was an important sign and that it had been given to me, but what did it mean? I happened to be holding part of the answer in my hand—the book that I was reading at the moment, on shamanism. Many of those on the shamanic path place

SOME NATIVE ANIMALS
AND THEIR POSSIBLE MEANINGS AS OMENS

BEAR	POWER, PROTECTION
BIRDS ESPECIALLY WHITE	DEATH OMENS ESPECIALLY INDOORS
BISON	THE HORNED GOD
BUTTERFLY	THE SPIRIT TRANSFORMED
COYOTE	THE TRICKSTER, SURVIVAL SHAMANISM
CROW	DEPENDS ON THE NUMBER
DEER	THE HORNED ONE, SACRIFICE THE HUNTED
EAGLE HAWK	THE SUN GOD THE SPIRIT, VISION
FOX	CUNNING, CLEVERNESS
FROG TOAD	MAGICK, WITCHCRAFT
HERON CRANE	A MESSAGE FROM GODS OR SPIRITS THE WRITTEN WORD
LION (MTN.) BOBCAT	STRENGTH, COURAGE, PROTECTION
OWL	WISDOM, SPIRITS
SALAMANDER	TRANSFORMATION, ADAPTATION
SQUIRREL	PREPARE FOR THE FUTURE ASSOCIATED WITH THE OAK
TURTLE TORTOISE	STEADFASTNESS SELF-PROTECTION

great emphasis on the identification of their totem animal. One of the animals in the Native American spectrum of totem animals is, of course, the coyote, and he is not necessarily one of the most positive. In most shamanic traditions, he is the one known as "The Trickster," a mischief maker. But in some ways the shaman himself is a trickster, fooling, if necessary, the spirits into doing his will. Still the name "coyote" according to some, means "little brother," and in the language of my maternal grandfather, Ukrainian, an affectionate name for a stray dog or mutt is "kyudle" (excuse the phonetic spelling, I have no idea where to look up Ukrainian slang). Above all, the coyote is a survivor. In spite of attempts to eradicate it, the coyote has flourished, and extended its boundaries. If it cannot find rodents, it will eat insects or fruit. And finally I understood the sign I had received: if I cannot stand at an easel and paint, I could still sit and write. But I would survive the months ahead, and when they finally had ended, and I was on my feet again, *Wheel of the Year* had been written.

If I ever choose to follow the path of the shaman more closely, I already know that one of my totem animals would certainly be the coyote, and another for both Dan and me is the heron, which brings with it all of the magickal symbolism that is associated with this beautiful bird. One of our first encounters with the heron was most eerie. As Dan and I crossed the bridge over the Delaware River in an early morning mist, two great shapes emerged from the fog, crossed in front of us, and silently vanished back into the mist. With long pointed bills, serpentine necks tucked tight into S-curves, huge wings flapping in utter silence, and long stilted legs trailing behind, these apparitions were the very color of the fog. Here in this Otherworld in the center of the bridge, our path and that of the herons crossed for one brief instant.

Since the misty dawn of pre-history, the heron, the crane, the ibis, and the stork have been symbols of divinity and messengers from the spirit realms.

The Indo-European word "kern" probably originally applied to all long-legged, long billed, long necked marsh birds. First pronounced with the guttural "ch" sound formed at the back of the throat, the word was eventually differentiated, along with the two species of birds as "heron" and "crane." A similar differentiation probably took place between the names of the Horned God, "Herne" the Hunter, and "Cernunos" the Horned One.

Herons, cranes and similar birds are of magickal importance and spiritual significance in various cultures throughout the world. Cranes were believed by the Chinese to live for 1,000 years, and so are symbols of longevity in that country where children would give their elderly parents gifts of robes embroidered with the magickally potent symbol of the crane. Their supposed longevity (cranes actually live about 30 years) also

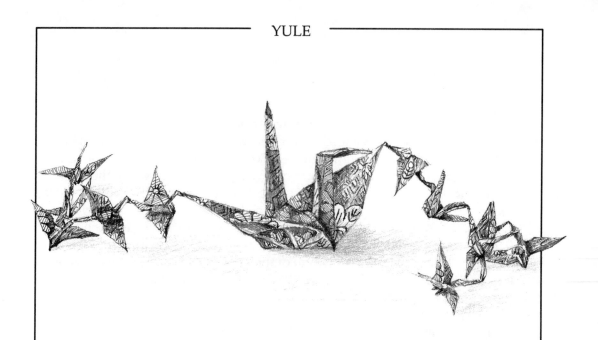

One Thousand Cranes—Symbols of Peace

make them symbols of good health, and so in Japan, crane amulets are made using the art of paper folding known as origami. These paper crane amulets are used as protection against illness. Because cranes mate for life, they also symbolize marital fidelity and happiness, and so their images are used on many Japanese wedding items, including the bride's gown, in order to impart their magick.

In certain Native American traditions, the heron is a totem animal representing intuition. In China, the spirits of warriors slain in battle were believed to be carried on the backs of cranes. And in Russian folk–lore, soldiers killed in battle were believed to be transformed into cranes. In Germanic countries, the Valkeries (the 13 maids of Odin who chose half the warriors slain in battle to take to Valhalla) took the form of swans. Swans share the same habitat, migratory habits and the V–shaped flight pattern of the cranes, but not the long bill and long legs.

The earliest images of herons or cranes in Europe appeared in the Eastern European countries of northern Greece, Bulgaria, Czechoslova- kia, Rumania, the Ukraine, etc., now known in archaeological terms as "Old Europe." Here, clay figures, ca. 5000–7000 B.C.E., part woman and part marsh bird, are sometimes engraved with the meander design, which usually symbolizes water. This marsh bird Goddess is associated with, or interchangeable with, a snake Goddesss. Both Goddesses seem to be associated with sacred bread baking and with rain. They are also de- picted with hands to their breasts, suggesting a connection between life– giving rain and the milk of the Goddess.

Some of these figures and the miniature shrines associated with them are incised with V or chevron patterns, suggesting the migratory flight patterns of cranes.

The cranes of Europe are migratory birds which winter in southernmost Europe (where they feed on the acorns of the evergreen oak, originally the sacred tree of the ancient Celts) or in northern Africa. According to the Koran, the cranes are "good birds" that go to Mecca when they disappear to fly north. The migratory habits of the crane certainly made them harbingers of Spring to the Northern Europeans, as well as foretellers of Winter, To these people, they were known as "messengers from beyond the North Wind"—a euphemism for the spirit world which lies to the frozen North. The arrival of their chevron flight formations announced the return of Spring, and their departure in Autumn signaled the beginning of the dark half of the year. Storks, which resemble cranes and herons, and which at one time, no doubt, were considered the same bird, also migrate. A popular folk tale is that storks bring babies. This probably comes out of an ancient belief that they brought the spirits of the newborn. This might be the result of the stork's association with the rebirth of Nature in the Spring, and also its habit of nesting in chimney tops—in shamanistic cultures often the exit and re-entry point for the spirit.

Migrating cranes often fly at night by the light of the Full Moon, which associates them with the Moon Goddess Artemis who also presides over childbirth.

The crane is mentioned in several creation myths such as "The long-legged strider of the Marsh." In Ireland, it is the crane that has existed from the start of creation—the solitary crane of Iniskea. In ancient Egypt, every temple had a "lake of creation" which represented the waters of chaos at the dawn of creation. It was believed by the Egyptians that the world began when a water bird laid the first egg which contained the atmosphere and the bird that made the first sound. Every morning a symbolic ritual, the release of the water bird onto the lake was performed by the priests of the temple.

The crane is sacred to Apollo, the Sun God who once took the form of a crane. As God of the Sun, Apollo not only brought the season of rebirth in the spring, he also taught mankind music and poetry, and granted the gift of prophesy.

Hermes, the Greek messenger of the Gods, was inspired to invent writing by watching the flight patterns of cranes. Thoth, the Egyptian counterpart of Hermes, is the sacred scribe, the God of Writing, and is depicted with the head of an ibis.

In Celtic myth, the Sea God Mannanan dwells on an island where the sweetest apples grow. This is certainly Avalon, and Mannanan then is Lord of the Underworld. This corresponds to the British Arawn, King of

Annwyn, who lived in a castle on Mannanan's island, and who had three cranes at his gate to frighten away passersby. Mannanan possessed a "crane bag," usually interpreted as a bag made from the skin of a crane, and which was said to contain the secrets of the sea. It held every precious thing that Mannanan possessed: his shirt, his knife, the shoulder strap of the smith, the shears of the King of Alba, and the helmet of Lochlann. The crane bag is somehow associated with the Moon, for when the tide was in, all the treasures were visible; but when the tide was out, the crane bag was empty.

Druids and magicians carried bags called in Gaelic "bhuily chraobhaich," which is usually translated as a bag with a branching pattern; it might also be translated as "a bag containing little branches" or twigs. This might be, as some believe, a bag containing little branches upon which Ogam was inscribed and used for divinatory purposes. This connects the crane bag of Mannanan to the "glory twigs" or Runes of Odin. It is highly probable that the hieroglyphics invented by Thoth and the alphabet of Hermes were originally used for sacred purposes, such as receiving messages from the Gods; or for divinatory purposes, like the Runes and Ogam or the oracles of Apollo; or else for the storage of sacred knowledge. And so the crane bag may not have been a bag made from the skin of a crane at all, but simply a bag containing some magickal device used to receive messages from the spirit realms or from the Gods themselves.

In the Celtic tree alphabet, the heron and the cranes are associated with the hazel tree, the tree of wisdom. This does not mean knowledge in the sense of the accumulation of mundane facts, but rather the awareness of the fundamental truths underlying these facts.

Cranes dance by leaping, bowing and skipping. Courting is always accompanied by dancing, but dancing can take place anytime and often does. To the Ainu people of Northern Japan, the Crane is the God of the Marsh, and a dance imitating its movements is performed to weave a spell of protection because the crane is noted for its fierce defense of its nest. The Australian Aborigines perform a dance that imitates the dancing of the crane as part of their cycle of seasonal celebration. There was also a crane dance performed in ancient Greece, attributed to Theseus, the hero of the myth of the Minotaur and the Labyrinth. This dance was supposedly performed around a horned altar (symbolizing the horns of the minotaur), and represented the inward and outward spiral of the Labyrinth from which Theseus escaped (not without Ariadne's help). Said to be nine steps and a leap (Polwart in 1605 said, "The crane must eye—Take nine steps ere she fly."), this dance would be familiar to most Pagans as the widdershins and the deosil spiral dance.

But this dancing bird of happiness, messenger from the spirit world, sacred to the Moon Goddess and the Sun God, is in danger of becoming extinct. Of the fourteen species of cranes in the world, six are vulnerable or endangered. The last breeding crane was shot in Britain in 1908. Still there is hope. Due to the efforts of a few determined people, the remaining breeding and feeding habitats are beginning to be preserved, and obstacles in their flight paths are being marked or removed. In Japan, the 25 white-naped cranes known to exist in 1945 have become about 1,000; and the few hundred hooded cranes there have become about 6,000. And in the United States, the 21 whooping cranes that faced extinction in the 1940s had become 130 birds by 1988.

As we watched the two great birds vanish into the morning mist, on the bridge suspended between sky and river, we felt we had met them half way, these messengers from beyond the north wind and that we had just begun to unravel the mystery of their message.

Not all of the signs and omens given in Nature originate in the animal or vegetable kingdoms. Some are signs formed by fractures in stones or in snow or ice. These are sometimes visible only when the sunlight strikes them from a particular angle. Timing, then, as well as your own vantage point, are what makes these signs personal.

One day, Dan and I went to shop at a small local mall and we found a parking spot in the back of the parking lot, with a view of a landscaped lawn that featured an enormous group of boulders. As we gazed at the contemporary "henge" adorning the side of the adjacent professional building, I began to recognize several Runes naturally formed in one of the limestone boulders. The Runes ᛉ and ᛦ occurred several times at that particular time, and I interpreted them as a need for protection and constraint; or that "the Gods are with us, but proceed with caution anyway," which we did. The ride home and the rest of the day were uneventful, but perhaps they would not have been if we had not been extra cautious. It is always better to heed a negative prophecy than to fulfill it.

As a sign that this is so, when we went back to the parking lot to photograph the Rune stone for this chapter, we entered the parking lot from another direction, only to discover another "henge," and this one featuring a huge holey stone. Holey stones are stones with naturally formed holes in them, and they are sacred to the Goddess, and are considered to be signs of good fortune. And judging from its size, this was the Queen-Mother of all holey stones!

Not all such signs have to be naturally made. A few years ago, on what was probably the hottest day of the year, our fairly new car broke down on a major highway. A very nice man in a pick-up truck behind us at the toll booth offered to push us to the next exit where we could get help. When Dan managed to get the car going again, he drove us to a nearby shopping center. When Dan parked the car it quit again and would not start, so we called AAA. As we were waiting around I noticed a set of initials on a post left by a graffiti artist. The initials were SB, but

A Rune Stone. Natural markings on the stone form several runes.
ᛉ and ᛦ appear a few times.

A Holey Stone

drawn like the Runes ᛋ ᛒ. These are two of the most positive signs in any Rune row. ᛋ is a Sun symbol, a sign of the Sun God, and means life force and vital energy. ᛒ is a sign for the Goddess in her aspect as the fertility Goddess of Spring. The two symbols together could not have been more affirmative, and I knew everything would be alright. It took a couple of hours, but we got home just fine.

Some omens are of supernatural origin. My maternal grandmother was skilled at reading omens (and also at having them occur). One of the first she ever saw happened when she was still a child in Europe. She awoke one morning before the dawn and went outside to use the outhouse. Her family was poor, so when she saw a bed sheet lying in the road (where it had probably fallen out of someone's wagon), she went to get it. As she put her hand out to pick it up, what had looked like a bed sheet got up off the ground and divided itself in two. One half went up the road, and the other half went down the road. Later that day, my grandmother's family received word that two of their neighbors had died, one living up the road and the other down it; one elderly, and the other a child.

There are several standard types of death omens. One of these is a ball or spot of light that seems to hover in the darkness with a life of its own. It might seem to be trying to get the attention of one particular person. Such lights are sometimes called "fetch lights," and usually appear to a relative or close friend of someone who is about to die.

Other death omens are a knock at a door when no one is there, a phone ringing when no one is on the other end, or the stopping of a clock. For my family and those close to us, it is sometimes a loud sound, like an explosion, that tells us that the spirit of a loved one is about to leave.

Probably the most common of all death omens is a bird. It might be any kind of bird; but the idea probably originated in the belief that the spirits of the deceased, or those about to be born, were transported to and from the spirit world by means of cranes or storks. For many, the death omen is a bird entering the house. For many others, it is specifically a white bird, usually a dove or a pigeon, either inside of the house or anywhere near it, that foretells the death of someone living in that house. I had a pet dove for many years without losing a single family member, but I took him to visit someone once and a neighbor stopped in to visit at the same time. When the elderly woman saw the white dove she began screaming that it was a death omen. She died two days later. Some believe so strongly in this omen that even feathers are considered unlucky. This belief is especially common among people from Mediterranean countries of Europe. To give such a person a peacock feather, which is a feather plus the evil eye, would be considered the same as cursing them.

While for some cultures birds and feathers are considered ill omens, for the Egyptians and other cultures it is a symbol of truth. This is especially interesting since it was some time later that the quill became an instrument of writing, bringing with it the responsibility suggested by its earlier meaning.

As birds, especially white ones, are sometimes omens of death, crows can be omens of many things, depending on their number. According to an old nursery rhyme:

> *One crow for sorrow, two for mirth*
> *Three for a wedding, four for birth*
> *Five for silver and six for gold*
> *Seven for a secret that's never been told.*

Birds are not the only signs that might appear in the sky. There are shooting stars, upon which wishes are made; one might also wish upon "the first star I see tonight." The first star light, star bright, one is likely to see is the evening star, or the North Star, which in ancient times was associated with the Goddess Ishtar and her Roman counterpart Venus, So to make a wish upon the evening star is to ask the Goddess for a favor. To the Greeks the morning star, actually the planet Venus, was Lucifer, the light bringer, son of Eos (Goddess of the Sunrise).

Another light that appears in the sky is the Aurora Borealis, or Northern Lights. But North is the dwelling place of the spirits, and these beautiful rainbow lights are associated by some with the spirits who live at the top of the world, and who, according to some, live there in a hollow hill. Another kind of light in the sky that can be taken as an omen, especially of good fortune, is the sun dog. Sun dogs are fairly uncommon phenomena which are caused by sunlight being refracted by ice crystals in the upper atmosphere. They appear as brilliant spots of rainbow-colored light on either side of the sun when the sun is close to the horizon, and when there is a high, thin cloud cover. There are sometimes a pair of sun dogs, one on either side of the sun at a 22° angle from your point of view. There are some who believe that many of the ancient monuments, including Stone Henge, mark not only the position of the Sun at the Midsummer sunrise, but the positions of sun dogs as well.

Since sun dogs sometimes appear as a pair, and sometimes individually as either a left or a right, they might be taken as signs that are especially important to couples or partners. Thus, when an individual appears it may refer to just one of the partners, depending on which side of the sun it appears. Generally for a male-female partnership, the left represents the female.

In the town where Dan and I worked in the early 60s, there lived an elderly woman who shared her home with many cats. She wore colorful scarves, Gypsy-style, and a bit of eye makeup. As elderly as she was to our young eyes, there was a spark of youth about her too. She was thin and drawn, and the townspeople treated her with respect or with scorn, according to their own development; but to Dan and me she was the personification of the Crone, and for this reason, every encounter with her had profound significance.

Sometimes when one is on the path of questing for signs and omens, the most mundane situation can become an excursion into the land of Faery. Sometimes encounters with individuals can have meanings that are not apparent to others. It's all a matter of perception.

Recently, just a day or so after we received the contract from Llewellyn for *Wheel of the Year*, Dan and I were sitting in our car in the parking lot of a fast food restaurant outside of a rural town in Pennsylvania. We always liked to eat in this parking lot because next to it was a grove of willows (sacred to Hecate), and a lovely stream running through the woods that surround it. As we sat there munching our fries between the grove of willows and the golden arches, Dan heard the sound of ancient music drifting through the cold wet forest. He opened his window and we listened as we ate; then when we had finished eating we decided to find the source of the music.

We left the parking lot and drove in the appropriate direction. Soon we came to a narrow little road which we had never noticed before. As we followed the road we knew we were getting closer to the music. Suddenly we came to a bridge over the same stream we had just left, and there on the bridge was a bride on horseback. She wore a long white gown that covered the back of the horse. She was beautiful with black hair, red lips, and a crown of white baby's breath on her head. We drove slowly past her across the bridge in order to watch. On the other side of the road there was a meadow and a group of people gathered there, among them ladies in tall pointed hats and wizards in flowing robes. There were tents set up and banners flying. Alongside the bride on the bridge stood an older man in a long purple robe and a crown of gold. Just then the music changed to the rhythm of an ancient procession, and the man in the purple robe led the bride on horseback toward the meadow. As they passed right in front of us, the bride looked at us and smiled. A jester then took the reins, and the bride dismounted and entered a circle that was formed by all the people in the meadow. All was silent for a few moments, and then a cheer went up from the circle and branches of green leaves were waved. Dan and I knew that we had just witnessed a sacred marriage. Silently, we crossed the bridge back to the mundane world knowing that the Goddess had smiled upon us.

Sometimes omens are specific. For instance, the sudden appearance of a crane or a heron usually means a spirit is trying to make contact or we are to work with the written word. Other times, omens are very general; when a person that we consider to be a representative of the Lord or Lady smiles at us, it is simply to be taken as an affirmation that we are on the right path and carrying out our life's work. It has been our experience that signs and omens are like sign posts and are much more likely to appear if we are following our chosen route. If we leave that route, we will no longer see the signs for it.

Yule is the end of the old solar year and the beginning of the new one, and some of the traditions once practiced at Yule have been transferred to the New Year's Eve of the calendar year. The month of January is named for the Roman God Janus, the two-faced God who could look in two directions, both forward and backward. Traditionally, New Year's Eve is a time to look ahead to the future, to make plans and to set goals, and it is a time to look back and reflect. It is a time to review the Wheel of the Year that has just completed itself, with an emphasis on the successes and the goals achieved. It is a time to look back through many turnings of the wheel, to look at the direction our life has gone in, and to bid a fond farewell to all the paths not taken—and to do so without regret. Finally, it is an appropriate time to look back over the years and even into previous lives.

There are a number of ways to explore past lives, and one of the simplest, is to go to a psychic who specializes in past life readings. But no matter how legitimate and accurate the psychic might be, it is not the same as experiencing for oneself a past life recall. Hypnotic regression is another method, but this would involve a certain amount of input from

Fossils that are traditional amulets; two "faery loaves,"
a snake stone, two "thunder bolts" and amber.

the hypnotist. Really all that is required to directly experience a past life recall is meditation, or an altered state of consciousness and a little magick. This can be accomplished by a ritual in which everything is directed at looking into the past. Here is one way: cast a Circle according to your tradition and place a mirror in the West. On either side of the mirror place a purple or indigo candle dressed with an appropriate oil. (There are oils available for this purpose, or you can make your own by soaking the flowers of periwinkle, or "sorcerer's violet," in olive oil.) The candles might also be inscribed with the appropriate signs, such as the Rune ᚨ, which has associations with that which has come down to us from the past. Finally, the amulet that can act as a link with ages past might be worn about the neck or held in the left hand (which in some forms of palmistry is considered to have an association with the past).

One of the best natural objects for such an amulet is a fossil. There are a number of fossils that have traditionally been used as magickal amulets, and some were eagerly sought for their magickal properties. For example, Belemites, the bullet shaped fossilized shells of extinct cephalopods (related to present day squids) were called "thunder bolts," and thus associated with the Gods Zeus and Thor. Later they came to be known as "the devil's fingers." Ammonites, the beautiful, perfect spiral shells of another group of extinct cephalopods, were no doubt associated with the Goddess. In ancient Greece, they were believed to contain a soul, and if certain rituals were performed it was believed that they could predict the future. Later in Western Europe it was said that ammonites were Faeries who were turned to snakes and then to stone for their "crimes."

The chalky shells of certain sea urchins were called "faery loaves" and were carried as good luck amulets. They were also called "chalk eggs," and their chalky interiors were used as a cure for stomach upset. Their chemical composition is almost identical to the antacids sold today.

A heart-shaped species of fossilized sea urchin, called "the shepherd's crown," was also carried as an amulet of good fortune and protection.

One of the most highly prized of all fossils is the toadstone, or bufonite. This round stoney object comes from the head of an extinct group of fishes known as Pyenodonts, but was at one time believed to come from the head of a living toad. They were worn as amulets of protection, especially from poison or snake bite. A similar stone comes from the head of the crucifix catfish.

An amulet to create a link with the past need not be a fossil at all. Perhaps there is already an affinity for a particular place or historical period, and an object representative of that place or time would be appropriate.

Once the amulet has been selected, and the ritual area has been prepared, there is nothing else to do but begin. For the majority of people who recall their previous lives the one moment that is recalled is the moment of death, and this can be both painful and frightening. Thus, the best way to begin this rite is to state out loud to any helpful spirits and to your own subconscious that you wish to experience a previous life, but not the pain and the fear. Then begin to chant words like:

> *This is not a mirror*
> *But the past I gaze into.*

as you gaze steadily into the reflection of your own eyes.

Eventually the face in the mirror may not be your own; close your eyes and let the images from a previous life flood into your mind without logic and without intellectualization. When the images fade, sit quietly within the Circle for a while, reviewing what you just experienced and committing it to memory before clearing the Circle. Later, like images received through other psychic means, these pictures can be recalled and re-examined, and questions answered. A past life may not be recalled on the very first attempt, but eventually it will be remembered.

Once one begins working with past lives, it is like working with signs and omens: much synchronicity will begin to occur and supporting evidence will begin to be provided. This in itself should be accepted as an affirmation.

Finally, when working with past lives, there are two pitfalls to be avoided. The first is placing too much emphasis on who we were—surely if there ever were a continent of Atlantis, it sunk under the weight of an inordinate number of high priests and priestesses! The other pitfall is a preoccupation with karma, i.e., to accept negative situations in our lives as being deserved punishment for our actions in previous lives—this is not what Paganism is about. "To do what we will as long as it harm none" is all we need to do in order to avoid "bad karma." To be too concerned with who we were rather than who we are now—or worried about karmic debts, which interferes with the progress of our daily lives—is like driving along a highway doing the speed limit while looking out the rear windshield. The real purpose of experiencing a past life is to know, through personal experience that birth is not a beginning and death not an end, but that we are all a part of an eternal cycle of birth, death, and rebirth.

As the Sun sets on the shortest day of the year, and the sound of church bells from the small village across the river drift out on the cold, clear air to mingle with the invocations to the Old Gods and to the smoke from the Yule log. The strains of carols ancient and familiar remind us of traditions preserved for us in the thin disguise of the new religion.

One of the oldest melodies, and according to some, one of the oldest tunes still in existence is "O Tannenbaum," which comes to us from the Germanic countries where the practice of decorating a fir tree seems to have originated. Tannenbaum is usually translated as meaning "Christmas tree," but tannen is related to the Gaelic "tinne," which means "holly," and "glas-tin," which means evergreen tree. In all probability, the "glas-tin," "tinne," and "tannenbaum" originally referred to a species of evergreen oak that was sacred to the Sun God. These words share a common origin with the word "tannin," a type of acid present in the leaves and the bark of oak, and used in the ancient process of tanning leather.

The practice of bringing evergreen into the home was originally forbidden by the Church; this in itself should be proof enough that it was a Pagan practice. The idea of decorating sacred evergreen trees with fruits, nuts, and berries (which were the original decorations) was an act of Pagan magick designed to ensure the continuity of the cycles of the seasons and of the human spirit.

The German name for the Christmas tree would be something like "Kristenbaum," and so it is with certainty that the Tannenbaum, to whose glory the most ancient tune is sung:

> *Not only green when the Summer's here,*
> *But at the coldest time of year,*
> *O Tannenbaum, O Tannenbaum*
> *You give us so much pleasure!*

is the sacred oak which represents the Sun God of the Old Religion. These words reflect his two most sacred days, Midsummer and Yule.

From Wales comes the ancient melody of another much loved carol, "Deck the Halls," which was traditionally sung when the forbidden practice of bringing evergreens into the house was being performed. To most Pagans the Winter Solstice represents the death of the old solar year and the birth of the Divine Child, the new solar year, the following morning aided and celebrated by the burning of the Yule log. Though the American adaptation of this song is fairly recent (1881), the Pagan elements still remain. For instance, there can be little doubt that this song refers to the death and rebirth of the Sun God at the Winter Solstice:

> *See the blazing Yule before us*
> *Strike the harp and join the chorus*
> *Fa la la la la – la la la la*
>
> *Fast away the old year passes*
> *Hail the New Year lads and lasses*
> *Fa la la la la – la la la la*

And so, as this old folksong itself proclaims, "Toll the ancient Yuletide carol!"

The words to the old French melody "The Holly and the Ivy" compares the various features of the ancient, sacred holly tree to symbols of Jesus in an obvious attempt to replace the Gods of the Old Religion with the God of the New. But the words of the chorus still retain its former Pagan significance:

> *The holly and the ivy*
> *Now both are full well grown*
> *Of all the trees that are in the wood,*
> *The holly bears the crown.*

Clearly this refers to the Sun God in his aspect of the Holly King. The chorus goes on with the words:

> *The rising of the sun,*
> *And the running of the deer,*
> *The playing of the organ,*
> *The sweet singing of the choir.*

The reference to the running of the deer suggests the God in his aspect as the Horned God of the Hunted, the Lord of Death.

Because we Pagans can still find references to the Old Gods and the Old Religion in many of the early carols and folk tunes, there is no need for us to adapt the music played at this time of year in order to suit Pagan sentiments—for what words would be more expressive of the Pagan meaning of Yule than "O Holy Night," or "Silent Night," as we kindle our Yule fires? And as we light our candles, and await the rising of the sun and the beginning of a new cycle of life?

Wherever we go this Yuletide season we will be hearing the familiar tunes of Christmas carols. They will be as much a part of the sounds of the season as the sound of a baseball game in the Summer and the birds in the Spring. Let these songs enhance our celebration, and let us know in our Pagan hearts the ancient meaning of such words as "Joy to the World, the Lord has come, let Earth receive Her King!"

Yule is an old Anglo-Saxon word meaning "wheel." It refers to the Wheel of the Year which is completed at this time of the year. As the Celts celebrated the end of the old agricultural year and the beginning of the new one at Samhain, so did the Anglo-Saxons celebrate the end of the old solar year and its rebirth at Yule. When the two cultures intermingled, many concepts and practices were transplanted from one holiday to the other, and in some cases, overlapped both. The ancient tradition of wassailing was an early Pagan ritual performed by troops of Morris dancers, who, by imitative magick, insured an abundant apple harvest in the coming year. Considering all of the apple traditions associated with Samhain, e.g., "ducking for apples," "apple on a string," etc.; and considering that Samhain is the celebration of the final harvest, especially the apple harvest, it is almost certain that wassailing was performed at that time. But there is another connection between wassailing and Samhain which may be found in another old English Christmas carol, "The Wassailing Song," which begins:

> *Here we come a wassailing*
> *Among the leaves so green,*
> *And here we come a-wandering,*
> *So fair to be seen!*

And it goes on to say:

> *We're the daily beggars*
> *Who beg from door to door,*
> *And we are the little children*
> *That you have seen before!"*

In other words, trick or treaters. The song ends with a wish:

> *May God bless you*
> *And bring you a happy New Year!"*

As the days of December shorten into cold, dark nights, homes are slowly transformed into wonderlands of pine-scented air and twinkling lights. Silent skaters, their actions frozen in time, glide on a looking-glass lake, just as they have Yuletide after Yuletide since Dan was a child. Beyond the pond, surrounded by the snowy drifts of cotton quilt batting, the roof-tops of tiny cardboard houses glitter with "diamond-dust," just as they did beneath my grandmother's tree. Little paper Santas dangle from the delicate branches of birch placed in the old blue garnished crock on the stair landing; and in the bedroom, the fragile paper houses of Pretty Village, faded to pastels with age, adorn the mantle and the window-sills. Once the playthings of Edwardian children, they now rest, quietly nestled among sprays of Douglas fir.

Every corner of the house has been transformed to celebrate the new season. On the high mantle of the kitchen fireplace, bright red holly berries are reflected in the grey gleam of the pewter there; while in the hand-hewn wooden bowl on the table, pine cones are accented by red roseberries and a blizzard of baby's breath, In the formal parlor, sprays of holly and clean scented pine decorate the mantle, and in the corner by the front window, where it can be seen by passers-by, stands a fir tree, just as one has for generation after generation.

The first written record of a fir tree being decorated comes from Riga, Latvia, in the year 1510. The tree was adorned with paper flowers, and a round dance was performed about it—just before the merchants

An Assortment of Early Tree Ornaments

who performed this obviously Pagan ritual set it ablaze. The practice of decorating a fir tree only became popular in America after 1841, when Queen Victoria had one decorated at Windsor Castle. Prior to that, it was believed by some that the Hessian soldiers brought the practice of decorating a fir tree here during the American Revolution. The Hessians were so named because they came from an area of Germany known as the Hesse, which has long been known as a place where Witches meet—especially at the famous peak known as "The Brocken" in the Hartz Mountains. The earliest known record of a decorated evergreen in America comes from the Moravingian village in Bethlehem, in Pennsylvania in the year 1747; but this was not an actual fir tree, but instead a wooden frame covered with evergreen boughs.

Although this custom of bringing an evergreen tree into the home at Yuletide and decorating it with fruits, nuts and confections, was condemned by the early Church for being a Pagan tradition, it was, like the Old Religion itself, never completely eradicated. As late as the 1640s, the custom in Europe was still being condemned by theologians. One wrote, "Among other trifles which are set up during Christmas time instead of God's Word, is the Christmas tree, or fir tree which is put up in the home and decorated with dolls and sugar!"

It is fairly obvious that decorating a sacred evergreen with objects that resemble fruits and flowers is a magickal act designed to bring about the return of the flowers of Spring and the season of renewal and rebirth. Many of these earliest tree decorations were fruits and nuts, cakes and cookies. Later, in the Victorian Era, many ornaments were chromolithic (full color printing) on cardboard, decorated with wire tinsel. The vast majority of Victorian ornaments portrayed Santa and stylishly dressed Victorian ladies, children laden with toys, or surrounded by the flowers of Spring. As the old century turned into the new, blown glass ornaments became popular, and many of these duplicated in glass the fruits and nuts of earlier times. And among these delicate glass treasures imported from Germany by F.W. Woolworth during the early decades of this century are many that have Pagan significance.

From the fragrant boughs of fir hangs a peach that glitters with diamond dust, an orange whose paint is worn thin with age, a carrot, a cucumber, and an ear of corn. There are several bunches of grapes in the softest shades of pink and green; and walnuts, their gold paint in various stages of wear. Flowers and flower baskets hang among the branches, and so do a variety of pine cones, pale blue frosted with white and the softest green brushed with gold. One pine cone ornament has a red-capped elf emerging from the top of the cone. This suggests an old folk tale told to me once and only vaguely remembered.

Many, many years ago a man and a woman lived in a cottage near a wild forest. The forest supplied much of the couple's needs, but the man still had to work hard to earn money to buy the things they needed that could not be found in the forest. But one day, the man became sick and not able to do as much work as he needed to do. In order to help her husband, each day after she finished her own chores of baking and cooking, washing and cleaning, she would go into the forest to gather pine cones which she would take to the village and sell as Yuletide decorations. Each day as the woman gathered pine cones, she was being watched without her knowledge. Finally, one day the little man who had been watching her introduced himself to her. "I am the Pine Cone Faery," he said to her, "Why are you picking up pine cones?" "I'm picking them to sell them so that I can help my husband who is very sick," she said.

"Well that's alright then," said the elf, "but be warned. Do not pick up any pine cones from under a certain tree." And he showed her which one.

The woman promised never to pick the pine cones from under that special tree, but soon she had picked all of the best pine cones. She had gone as deep into the forest as she dared, and all she could find was a little handful of small and broken ones. The pine cones under the special tree were big and plump, and there were many of them. She knew she could sell them for a lot of money, but she had promised the Pine Cone Faery; and so she put her meager handful of cones into her apron and walked home. On her way she encountered the elf again.

A Pine Cone Elf Ornament

"How is your husband?" he asked, and, "How is your pine cone gathering?" Although he already knew the answer to this question because he had been watching her.

"Not very well, I'm afraid," she told him, "and I'm having a very hard time finding enough pine cones to sell."

"That's too bad," said the elf, and he walked away and vanished into the forest.

But that evening, when the woman returned home and emptied her apron onto the kitchen table, much to her amazement and great joy, she discovered that there were many more than she had thought, that they were all big and plump, and that they all turned to silver! Naturally, the woman was able to sell them for a great deal of money, her husband soon recovered, and they lived happily ever after.

Pine cones were symbols of the Faeries of the wild pine forest of the Germanic countries, and perhaps it is for this reason that the first molded glass tree ornament ever made, in the storybook village of Lauscha, nestled in a little valley among pine forested slopes, was in the shape of a pine cone.

The pine cone and the acorn are both symbols of fertility and the cycles of rebirth. As the saying goes, "A forest of a thousand trees is contained in a single acorn." Among the branches of our tree at Yuletide hang at least three ornaments that represent clusters of oak leaves with acorns. One is pearly white with red acorns, another has red acorns on the palest green and silver leaves, and another is a deep metallic blue. There are also an assortment of acorns, some tiny and shiny silver and green, some studded and some ribbed. But of all the ornaments representing the vegetable kingdom, the greatest number are of berries. While not depicting any particular type of berry, these early examples of the glassblower's art show an extraordinary variety of shape and color. There are deep indigo blue ones, mouthwatering raspberry red ones, shining silver and amber gold ones.

Among the fruits and flowers, nuts and berries suspended from the needled branches, there are perched a variety of birds. Delicately blown glass creatures with pastel plumage and spun glass tails display their beauty in silence. A veritable wild kingdom of animals can be found among the antique ornaments of the turn-of-the-century, and at one point trees were decorated with shoals of fish made of pressed cardboard. These Dresden ornaments, named for the town in which they were made, were extremely realistic and had the accuracy of a field guide to marine life.

Aside from the blown glass birds and animals, there is also an entire orchestra of blown glass instruments: violins and harps, drums, horns and whistles, and most popular of all, little glass bells. Inside of many of the glass bells hang a tiny glass bead on a wire which enables the bell to ring with the clearest note. As anyone who has seen the film, "It's a Wonderful Life," has heard, when you hear a bell ring, it means that an angel has got his wings. This may be true for the spirits of the new religion, but for followers of the Old Religion, the ringing of a clear, sweet bell purifies the air and is an invitation to friendly spirits.

The glass blower's art of tree ornaments, which began with the single glass bubble coated inside with silver nitrate and outside with colored lacquer, eventually turned full circle after WWII, when the most popular ornaments once again became the simple glass balls. In bright metallic reds, greens, blues, gold and silver, these metallic spheres of glass catch and reflect the light in all directions. Even these simplest of tree ornaments have a history rooted deep in the magickal past.

During the eighteenth century, a popular garden ornament (which is still popular today) is a simple pedestal supporting a blown glass ball, coated on the inside with silver nitrate and on the outside with colored lacquer. As garden centerpieces, these spheres of glass reflect the entire garden and the entire sky. These garden ornaments were called "witch balls" and are a form of mirror magick. These spheres have been used for centuries as protection against the "evil eye." They work simply by reflecting evil magick and bad intentions back at the sender. Small one inch balls worn on a chain around the neck are excellent amulets of protection, although it might look a bit strange if worn other than at Yuletide.

As tree ornaments at the time of the Winter Solstice, these shiny glass balls catch the light of the new born Sun and send it back as a magickal means of enhancing the Sun's energy.

This idea was put to full use when the simple glass ball was given a geometric indentation that served to catch and reflect light, whether it is the clear white light of the Winter Sun reborn, or the soft, warm light of a candle's glow.

There are two more types of traditional tree ornaments that deserve mention as having Pagan significance. One is the thin metallic strips of tinsel that, in the city where I was born, and in the suburbs where I grew up, was called "icicles." (But here in the country, where we live now, it is called "rain.") Rain, or rather an imitation of it, is one of the most basic and ancient of all forms of fertility magick.

The other type of ornament is the candy cane, and it is a matter of written record that the earliest trees were decorated with sugar confections. I have no idea of the origin of the peppermint stick, nor how it got a hook on the end (this may have been added as a means of hanging it on the tree, or it may have been designed that way to resemble a shepherd's crook); all I know is that as I gazed at our own tree, while writing this chapter, I was suddenly struck with the visual similarity between the red and white spiral stripes of the candy cane and the Maypole entwined with red and white ribbons. The ribbons of the Maypole, as mentioned previously, may have originated with the cult of Attis, in which a fir tree was wrapped in a white woolen shroud and sprinkled with the blood of his priests. It was in honor of this God that the first fir tree, not of historical record but of ancient myth, was decorated. Where the blood of Attis fell, violets sprang up, and the great Goddess Cybele who loved him gathered up the violets and adorned a fir tree with them in his memory.

Finally, there are three ways of finishing off the traditional tree. For the new religion, an angel is popular, but for others there are finials of blown glass, or the star. The star does have a connection with the mythology of Christianity, but as it is often a five-pointed star, it is also especially significant to Pagans because this star represents a unity of all the elements, plus spirit; sometimes this star is enclosed in a circle, symbolizing the eternal cycle of birth, death, and rebirth.

Since the practice of hanging representative objects on a fir tree at the time of the Winter Solstice is an ancient and magickal one, and since the magick must have been very powerful for it to have been preserved for almost two thousand years, then the collection, selection or creation of all ritual objects should be done with utmost care. Once the tree has been selected, cut, and if desired, consecrated (suggestions for this are given in *Wheel of the Year*), then it should be set up in a place of honor and hung with ornaments in a ritual of joy and celebration—either as part o f the Yule Sabbat rites, or as a separate celebration unto itself, days or weeks prior to the Solstice. It might be appropriate that at least some of the ornaments be representative of certain types of magick. If this is the case, then the ornaments might be enchanted as they are hung. For instance, if a simple silver ball is hung as a protective charm using the principle of mirror magick, the utterance of words such as the following will add power to the spell:

> *Evil be gane*
> *To whence ye came.*

For abundance, hanging a fruit or an ornament representing a fruit will be enhanced with words like:

> *Fruit on the tree*
> *A harvest they'll be.*

And for power, an acorn or similar ornament might be enchanted by words like:

> *Sacred tree*
> *Empower me.*

Just as there seems to be no limit as to the imaginations of the glass blowers and other creators of the Yuletide ornaments, there is no limit to the kinds of magick that can be wished for as the sacred tree is being

MAKING A YULE LOG

METHOD #1
A HALF LOG

METHOD #2
A SLIGHTLY
FLATTENED LOG

METHOD #3
SUPPORTS
NAILED TO LOG

HOLES DRILLED
FOR CANDLES

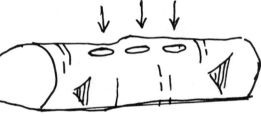

THE **YULE LOG**
ADORNED & READY
FOR THE SABBAT

adorned. When the tree is decorated and the ornaments have all been hung, crown the tree with a finial or a star, and light the lights. If it is possible, dance around the tree and sing songs in its praise—O Tannenbaum is not inappropriate. But if this is not possible, then just sit back and gaze at this most ancient and magickal of spectacles and rejoice, remembering that the season is the reason!

One of the most delightful traditions of the Yuletide season is the practice of gift giving. Adherents to the new religion will be quick to tell us that this originated with the Three Wise Men, or Magi, bringing gifts of gold, frankincense and myrrh to the manger in Bethlehem. But in fact, the practice was centuries old when the story of the Nativity was put to paper. In Rome, where the end of the old year was celebrated in a week long festival known as the Saturnalia, in honor of Saturn, the God of Death, gifts were exchanged as tokens of love among friends and family members.

Perhaps one of the oldest of all Pagan Yuletide traditions is the burning of the Yule log. At this, the coldest and darkest time of the year, the burning of the Yule log, expressed in the simplest magickal terms what was needed most: warmth and light. The power of the Yule log gave its strength to the new born Sun when another solar year was born.

Today not everyone has a fireplace in which to burn the Yule log, but the ancient ritual can still be performed.

In recent years, small logs, particularly of birch, have been especially prepared and decorated, and called Yule logs. To prepare such a log, obtain a length of natural log with the bark left on. The log will then need to be split so that it can rest on the flat side, or flattened just enough on one side to keep it from rolling. A third method is to nail two flat strips of wood to the base. Once the log is steady and secure, drill two or three 3/4 inch holes in the top of the log to receive candles. In cities, such logs may be available from a florist.

Then, just prior to the Sabbat Rites, add candles to the log, red or white ones, that have been anointed with the most sacred oils, and adorn it with fresh sacred greens, holly and fir, pine and yew. Then, at the appropriate point in the Sabbat Rites, light the candles and chant:

> *May the Yule log burn.*
> *May all good enter here.*
> *May there be wheat for bread,*
> *And vats full of wine.*

A major part of the Yule log tradition is that the ashes of the log are kept throughout the year as an amulet of protection and fertility, and that an unburned portion of the Yule log be kept and used to kindle the Yule log the following year. Of course, there will be no ashes from this log. Instead, the log itself might be kept for year after year, gathering unto itself a great deal of magickal power; and the stumps of the candles may be kept as amulets throughout the year and used to light the new candles on the following Yule.

One final tradition that had been transplanted from Yule to New Year's is worth discussion. Every year on New Year's Eve, tens of thousands of people flock to Times Square in New York City, while millions of others gather at parties or around TV sets to await one particular second in time. That one instant, decreed by man, serves to mark the end of one solar year and the beginning of the new. And when that instant arrives, it is greeted with shouting and screaming and the blasting of horns and the banging of drums. In the suburbs, neighbors greet one another with noisemakers in their backyards; and in the quiet of the country, the stillness of the midnight air is shattered by shouts and gunshots. And no one really seems to know why. But in a little village in Germany, where so many of our Yuletide traditions come from, on Christmas Eve the young, unmarried men of the village bundle themselves in wheat straw and then tie about their middles huge bells and cymbals. They are led about the village by a young girl (who embodies the Maiden aspect of the Goddess) in a procession of deafening noise. Although this ritual is performed on Christmas Eve in the now Christian village, it is clearly and admittedly an ancient Pagan custom that once belonged to the Winter Solstice; and although the practitioners today claim to be frightening away demons or the devil, all they are really frightening away are the darkness and the decay of Winter in order to make way for a new life.

The Altar at Yule, with a tree adorned with ornaments in the background and the Yule Log ready to be burned.

To our Pagan ancestors, the Winter Solstice was an entire night, the darkest one of the year, which was followed by a day that dawned just a little earlier. Today we can know the exact moment of the Winter Solstice, that precise moment when the days stop growing shorter and begin to grow longer. A moment decreed by Nature, not by men. And when the exact time is known, it can be worked into the Yule Sabbat, and celebrated in the ways of our ancient ancestors. What more traditional way to bid a fond farewell to the Year Wheel that has just ended, and to greet the year about to be born, than with cheers of joy, the ringing of bells, the rattling of tambourines and the blowing of horns?

When the animals have all been fed, and are warm and safe in their shelter, we gather by the evening fire to gaze into its flames and reflect on the day that is done. Outside, in silence, the snow falls, and beneath its frozen crust the Mother sleeps, and awaits Her lover.

CONCLUSION

It is a fairly safe guess that most of us were raised in a Judeo-Christian tradition, and that the seasonal celebrations of our parents and grandparents were some of the most wonderful times of our childhood. As we grew up we questioned the religious beliefs of our parents, and eventually many of us found our way back, to the Old Gods and the Old Religion.

One of the most painful parts of this spiritual quest was having to give up those wonderful family traditions that gave us so much joy in our childhood.

But it isn't so. Some of the most wonderful traditions practiced by our parents and grandparents are purely Pagan in origin. So go ahead and celebrate the customs of your childhood. Send Valentines, dye Eostre's eggs, bring a fir tree into your house and decorate it with ornaments that came down in the family, and know in your Pagan heart that what you do is a traditional way of honoring the Old Pagan Gods. And when someone says to you, "I thought you were a Pagan. Why do you have a Christmas tree in your house?" You can look them straight in the face and say, "Because it's a Pagan tradition—why do you?"

STAY IN TOUCH

On the following pages you will find listed, with their current prices, some of the books and tapes now available on related subjects. Your book dealer stocks most of these, and will stock new titles in the Llewellyn series as they become available. We urge your patronage.

However, to obtain our full catalog, to keep informed of new titles as they are released and to benefit from informative articles and helpful news, you are invited to write for our bi-monthly news magazine/catalog. A sample copy is free, and it will continue coming to you at no cost as long as you are an active mail customer. Or you may keep it coming for a full year with a donation of just $5.00 in U.S.A. and Canada ($20.00 overseas, first class mail). Many bookstores also have *The Llewellyn New Times* available to their customers. Ask for it.

Stay in touch! In *The Llewellyn New Times'* pages you will find news and reviews of new books, tapes and services, announcements of meetings and seminars, articles helpful to our readers, news of authors, advertising of products and services, special money-making opportunities, and much more.

The Llewellyn New Times
P.O. Box 64383-Dept. 090, St. Paul, MN 55164-0383, U.S.A.

• • •

TO ORDER BOOKS AND TAPES

If your book dealer does not have the books and tapes described on the following pages readily available, you may order them directly from the publisher by sending full price in U.S. funds, plus $1.50 for postage and handling for orders *under* $10.00; $3.00 for orders *over* $10.00. There are no postage and handling charges for orders over $50. UPS Delivery: We ship UPS whenever possible. Delivery guaranteed. Provide your street address as UPS does not deliver to P.O. Boxes. UPS to Canada requires a $50 minimum order. Allow 4-6 weeks for delivery. Orders outside the U.S.A. and Canada: Airmail—add retail price of book; add $5 for each non-book item (tapes, etc.); add $1 per item for surface mail.

FOR GROUP STUDY AND PURCHASE

Because there is a great deal of interest in group discussion and study of the subject matter of this book, we feel that we should encourage the adoption and use of this particular book by such groups by offering a special "quantity" price to group leaders or "agents."

Our Special Quantity Price for a minimum order of five copies of *Ancient Ways* is $38.85 cash-with-order. This price includes postage and handling within the United States. Minnesota residents must add 6% sales tax. For additional quantities, please order in multiples of five. For Canadian and foreign orders, add postage and handling charges as above. Credit card (VISA, Master Card, American Express) orders are accepted. Charge card orders only may be phoned free ($15.00 minimum order) within the U.S.A. or Canada by dialing 1-800-THE-MOON. Customer service calls dial 1-612-291-1970. Mail Orders to:

LLEWELLYN PUBLICATIONS
P.O. Box 64383-Dept. 090 / St. Paul, MN 55164-0383, U.S.A.

WHEEL OF THE YEAR: Living the Magickal Life
by Pauline Campanelli

If like most Pagans you feel elated from the celebrations of the Sabbats and hunger for that feeling during the long weeks between Sabbats, then *Wheel of the Year* can help you to put the joy of celebration and the fulfillment of magic into your everyday life.

The wealth of seasonal rituals and charms contained in *Wheel of the Year* are all easily performed with materials readily available, and are simple and concise enough that the practitioner can easily adapt them to work within the framework of his or her Pagan tradition. Learn how to perform fire magic in November, the best time to make magic wand and why, the ancient magical secrets of objects found on a beach, and the secret Pagan symbolism of Christmas tree ornaments.

Whether you are a newcomer to the Craft or found your way back many years ago, *Wheel of the Year* will be an invaluable reference book in your practical magical library. It is filled with magic and ritual for everyday life and will enhance any system of Pagan Ritual.

0–87542–091–5, 192 pgs., 7 x 10, illustrated   **$9.95**

THE LLEWELLYN ANNUALS

Llewellyn's MOON SIGN BOOK: Approximately 400 pages of valuable information on gardening, fishing, weather, stock market forecasts, personal horoscopes, good planting dates, and general instructions for finding the best date to do just about anything! Article by prominent forecasters and writers in the fields of gardening, astrology, politics, economics and cycles. This special almanac, different from any other, has been published annually since 1906. It's fun, informative and has been a great help to millions in their daily planning.   **State year $4.95**

Llewellyn's SUN SIGN BOOK: Your personal horoscope for the entire year! All 12 signs are included in one handy book. Also included are forecasts, special feature articles, and an action guide for each sign. Monthly horoscopes are written by Gloria Star, author of *Optimum Child*, for your personal Sun Sign and there are articles on a variety of subjects written by well-known astrologers from around the country. Much more than just a horoscope guide! Entertaining and fun the year around.   **State year $4.95**

Llewellyn's DAILY PLANETARY GUIDE and ASTROLOGER'S DATEBOOK: Includes all of the major daily aspects plus their exact times in Eastern and Pacific time zones, lunar phases, signs and voids plus their times, planetary motion, a monthly ephemeris, sunrise and sunset tables, special articles on the planets, signs, aspects, a business guide, planetary hours, rulerships, and much more. Large 5 1/4 x 8 format for more writing space, spiral bound to lay flat, address and phone pages, time zone conversion chart and blank horoscope chart.   **State year $6.95**

Llewellyn's ASTROLOGICAL CALENDAR: Large wall calendar of 48 pages. Beautiful full color cover and color inside. Includes special feature articles by famous astrologers, introductory information on astrology. Lunar Gardening Guide, celestial phenomena, a blank horoscope chart for your own chart data, and monthly date pages which include aspects, lunar information, planetary motion, ephemeris, personal forecasts, lucky dates, planting and fishing dates, and more. 10 x 13 size. Set in Central time, with conversion table for other time zones worldwide.   **State year $9.95**

THE MAGIC IN FOOD
by Scott Cunningham

Now, with the guidance of this popular magical writer, you can take control of your life through your diet. In *The Magic in Food*, you'll learn the secrets of food magic, the mystical properties of everyday, as well as exotic, dishes, and how to call upon the powers of food to enhance every area of your life.

Included are numerous magical diets, each designed to create a specific change within its reader; increased health and happiness, deeper spirituality, enhanced sexual satisfaction, protection, psychic awareness, success, love, prosperity—all are possible with the proper combination of nutritional choices.

Scott Cunningham has had a life-long interest in magic and, believing that all aspects of nature and daily life are suffused with magic, even the mundane act of preparing and consuming a meal can be done in magical ways. He relates foods to the planets, elements and energies, and discusses their lore and magical uses. The book is filled with recipes, generously illustrated with drawings and color photos guaranteed to set your mouth watering.
0-87542-130-X, 364 pgs., softcover, illus.   **$14.95**

CUNNINGHAM'S ENCYCLOPEDIA OF MAGICAL HERBS
by Scott Cunningham

This is an expansion on the material presented in his first Llewellyn book, Magical Herbalism. This is not just another herbal for medicinal uses of herbs—this is the most comprehensive source of herbal data for magical uses ever printed! Almost every one of the over 400 herbs are illustrated, making this a great source for herb identification. For each herb you will also find: magical properties, planetary rulerships, genders, associated deities, folk and Latin names and much more. to make this book even easier to use you will also find a folk name cross reference, and all of the herbs are fully indexed. There is also a large annotated bibliography, and a list of mail order suppliers so you can find the books and herbs you need.

Like all of Scott's books, this one does not require you to use complicated rituals or expensive magical paraphernalia. Instead, it shares with you the intrinsic powers of the herbs. Thus, you will be able to discover which herbs, by their very nature, can be used for luck, love, success, money, divination, astral projection, safety, psychic self–defense and much more. Besides being interesting and educational it is also fun, and fully illustrated with unusual woodcuts from old herbals. This book has rapidly become the classic in its field. It enhances books such as 777 and is a must for all Wiccans.

0–87542–122–9, 352 pgs., 6 x 9, illus., softcover   **$12.95**

YEAR OF MOONS, SEASON OF TREES
by Pattalee Glass-Koentop

This book explores the Druidic sacred trees native to the British tradition of Witchcraft, providing the history, interpretation, symbolism and ritual of these ancient beliefs in modern-day language, accessible to all. Veneration of trees as gods, or as the dwelling places of gods, is a common thread in cultures all around the world.

The tree symbol is the basic form upon which knowledge has been illustrated throughout the ages: witness the tree of life, the tree alphabet, the Ogham form of writing, lunar calendars, and so forth. In *Year of Moons, Season of Trees*, the author provides the how-to for rituals celebrating Nature through its Moons, its Seasons and Months of Trees Here is the history, the lore of each tree, the rituals of Temple Workings, songs and chants, even recipes for foods that complete these celebrations. Also included are Ogham correspondences charts, and descriptive lists of solar and lunar trees. It is a valuable sourcebook of material and inspiration.

0-87542-269-1   **$14.95**

CHARMS, SPELLS AND FORMULAS
by Ray Malbrough

Hoodoo—a word many have heard, but few have understood. Hoodoo magick is a blend of European techniques and the magick brought to the New World by slaves from Africa. Hoodoo is a *folk magick* that can be learned and easily mastered by anyone.

In this book, Ray Malbrough reveals to you the secrets of Hoodoo magick. By using the simple materials available in Nature, you can bring about the necessary changes to greatly benefit your life and that of your friends. You are given detailed instructions for making and using the *gris-gris* (charm) bags only casually or mysteriously mentioned by other writers. Malbrough not only shows how to make gris-gris bahs for health, money, luck, love and protection from evil and harm, etc., but he also explains how these charms work.

He also takes you into the world of *doll magick*; using dolls in rituals to gain love, success, or prosperity. Complete instructions are given for making the dolls and setting up the ritual.

Hoodoo magick can be as enjoyable as it is practical, and in this fascinating book you can learn how to be a *practitioner*, working your spells and charms for yourself or for others. Learn the methods which have been used successfully by Hoodoo practitioners for nearly 200 years, along with many practical tips for dealing with your clients.

0-87542-501-1, 192 pgs., 5 1/4 x 8, illus., softcover   **$6.95**

THE SACRED CAULDRON
by Tadhg MacCrossan

Here is a comprehensive course in the history and development of Celtic religious lore, the secrets taught by the Druids, and a guide to the modern performance of the rites and ceremonies, as practiced by members of the "Druidactos," a spiritual organization devoted to the revival of this ancient way of life.

The Sacred Cauldron evolved out of MacCrossan's extensive research in comparative mythology and Indo-European linguistics, etymology and archaeology. He has gone beyond the stereotypical image of standing stones and white-robed priests to piece together the truth about Druidism.

The reader will find detailed interpretations of the words, phrases and titles that are indigenous to this ancient religion. Here also are step-by-step instructions for ceremonial rites for modern-day practice.

0-87542-103-2, 304 pgs., soft-cover, illus.   **$10.95**

CELTIC MAGIC
by D. J. Conway

Many people, not all of Irish descent, have a great interest in the ancient Celts and the Celtic pantheon, and *Celtic Magic* is the map they need for exploring this ancient and fascinating magical culture.

Celtic Magic is for the reader who is either a beginner or intermediate in the field of magic, providing an extensive "how-to" of practical spell-working. There are many books on the market dealing with the Celts and their beliefs, but none guide the reader to a practical application of magical knowledge for use in everyday life. There is also an in-depth discussion of Celtic deities and the Celtic way of life and worship, so that an intermediate practitioner can expand upon the spellwork to build a series of magical rituals.

Presented in an easy-to-understand format, *Celtic Magic* is for anyone searching for new spells that can be worked immediately, without elaborate or rare materials, and with minimal time and preparation.

0-87542-136-9, 240 pgs., mass market, illus.   **$3.95**